THE COMPANION GUIDE TO

*The country
round Paris*

GW00360972

THE COMPANION GUIDES

General Editor: Vincent Cronin

It is the aim of these guides to provide a companion, in the person of the author, who knows intimately the places and people of whom he writes, and is able to communicate this knowledge and affection to his readers. It is hoped that the text and pictures will aid them in their preparations and in their travels, and will help them remember on their return.

LONDON · OUTER LONDON · EAST ANGLIA
NORTHUMBRIA · THE WEST HIGHLANDS OF SCOTLAND
PARIS · THE SOUTH OF FRANCE · THE COUNTRY ROUND PARIS
NORMANDY · THE LOIRE
FLORENCE · VENICE · ROME · NEW YORK
MAINLAND GREECE · THE GREEK ISLANDS · JUGOSLAVIA · TURKEY
MADRID AND CENTRAL SPAIN · IRELAND

In preparation

OXFORD AND CAMBRIDGE
UNION OF SOVIET SOCIALIST REPUBLICS

THE COMPANION GUIDE TO

The Country Round Paris

IAN DUNLOP

COMPANION GUIDES

First published in Great Britain 1979 as
The Companion Guide to the Ile de France
Revised paperback edition 1986

Reissued 1996
Companion Guides, Woodbridge

ISBN   1 900639 00 9

Companion Guides is an imprint of Boydell & Brewer Ltd
PO Box 9, Woodbridge, Suffolk IP12 3DF, UK
and of Boydell & Brewer Inc.
PO Box 41026, Rochester, NY 14604-4126, USA

British Library Cataloguing-in-Publication Data
Dunlop, Ian,
The companion guide to the country
around Paris.
1. Ile-de-France (France) – Description and
travel – Guide-books
I. Title II. Dunlop, Ian, 1925–. Companion
guide to the Ile-de-France
914.4'3404838   DC611.I27

Printed in Great Britain by
Robert Hartnoll (1985) Ltd, Bodmin, Cornwall

To
DEIRDRE
with all my love

Acknowledgements

I would like to express my debt of gratitude to the late marquis de Contades for all his help and hospitality, and to his daughter the comtesse Michel d'Ornano; I would also like to thank Philip Hawkes, whose knowledge and love of the Ile de France have always been at my disposal, and his wife Patricia for her unfailing hospitality; Monsieur Georges Poisson, Conservateur en Chef du Musée de l'Ile de France at the Château de Sceaux, and to the staff of his splendid *service de documentation*, where nearly all the material for this book was sought; Monsieur Bertrand Monnet, Architecte en Chef des Monuments Historiques, for all his help; Mr Geoffrey Hitchcock of the British Council for useful introductions; Madame Simonet for her unfailing hospitality at Compiègne; and Mrs Yvonne Smith for the same at Le Vésinet.

I would like to thank the duc de Brissac, the duc de Luynes, the marquis de Ganay, the marquis de Breteuil, the comte Étienne de Bertier-Sauvigny and the princesse Thérèse de Caraman-Chimay for their help and encouragement, and the princesse Maria-Pia d'Orléans-Bragance, comtesse de Nicolay, for her charming hospitality at Le Lude.

I would like to thank Miss Jane Erith for typing the manuscript, and the Reverend Robert Prance who acted as chauffeur-secretary on one tour. Finally I would like to thank my wife Deirdre, to whom this book is dedicated, for being the ideal companion to guide round the Ile de France.

Contents

✢

List of Illustrations

❧

Maps and Plans

❧

KEY TO THE SYMBOLS USED IN THE MAPS

Château

Church

Introduction

❧

'The Ile de France has no real regional unity,' wrote its topographer, Marc Bloch; 'it does not offer any precise boundaries which the historian has to treat seriously.' He cautiously entitles his own book *The Country round Paris*. I have therefore assumed considerable liberty in determining the limits of this book.

One possible, and very common, approach to the problem is to say a little about as many subjects as possible. In the *Guide Michelin* the Petit Trianon rates one hundred and fifty words and its gardens ten. The suggested time allowed for a visit is a quarter of an hour. In my opinion the Petit Trianon is one of the most beautiful buildings in France; the gardens played an important part in preparing the unpopularity of Marie-Antoinette and the downfall of the monarchy. I feel obliged to deal with them at far greater length.

My own solution to the problem is to devote considerable space to the really important buildings. They provide the 'set pieces'. With a vast building like Versailles I consider it far more important to understand its social significance than to attempt a room-by-room description. What was Louis XIV trying to create? Why did Louis XV modify it in the way he did? How far did the buildings themselves affect the course of history? These are the questions which we need to ask if we are to understand the place.

It is more important to me to see the little princesse Louise running as hard as she could through room after room in order to get to her elder sister's apartment in time for coffee with her father, Louis XV, than to know exactly who carved the panelling in each of the rooms. At Compiègne I would rather show you what it was like to be a member of one of Napoleon III's house parties than to give you the pedigrees of the furniture.

I have also a passionate desire to know what things really looked like when they were first built. So often we only see a building as it was restored in the nineteenth century. This is particularly true of Fontainebleau. It takes a great deal of patient unravelling to see it as it was. A ruin sometimes has this advantage over a restoration:

what you do see is probably genuine. To reconstruct Montceaux from the crumbling blocks of masonry which survive is a fascinating occupation.

With the great churches we are more concerned with the vision of Christianity which the builders of the Gothic age were trying to express – the dare-devil quest for height which raised the vault of Beauvais forty-seven metres above floor level; the passionate pursuit of light which glazed the entire walls of the Sainte Chapelle, and the obsession with colour which turned Chartres Cathedral into an Aladdin's cave.

At a humbler level the parish churches were often inspired by the same *folie de grandeur*. How could a tiny village like Nesles-la-Vallée presume to imitate the style of Notre Dame?

There are hundreds of interesting churches in the Ile de France and they are becoming increasingly difficult to visit. Shortage of clergy and an alarming increase in the amount of pilfering has caused the authorities to keep many buildings locked. The key is usually at the *Mairie*, but I came across one church where the key was kept at the local *charcuterie*. *Charcuteries* are usually closed on Mondays and it was a Monday which I had selected for visiting this church.

I hope that what I have to say about some of these smaller churches will help my readers to know what to look for in others. They are often very beautiful; and I have tried to analyse their beauty. It often lies in their proportions. The very term 'Gothic' represents a misunderstanding of the Middle Ages. The artists of the Renaissance seem to have imagined that they had rediscovered the word 'proportion'. They merely betray their ignorance. The architects of the thirteenth century were deeply concerned with the theory of proportion and fascinated by geometry. Otto von Simson produced a most convincing theory that the deliberate use of mathematics determines the proportions of Chartres Cathedral.

There is another sort of beauty about which it is not so easy to write – the simple charm of the countryside. The Michelin maps put a green line alongside a road which is particularly attractive, and this is a useful guide, especially when one is looking for an idyllic spot for a picnic. A bottle of wine, a French loaf and a slice of pâté are perfect complements to the surrounding scenery. But there is a proper time for certain landscapes: the Vaux de Cernay, for example, are never so beautiful as when the leaves are down and the naked woods embrown the slopes; then we can see between their branches how the great builders of the past adorned the beauties of nature with the refinements of art. The land to the north-east of Paris, the Vexin Français, is liberally provided with fruit trees and should be visited in spring. Brie is rose-growing country, and Provins or Grisy-Suisnes are at their best in high summer. But for the great forests October is the ordained month. It is the moment also for the gardens of Versailles. For it was in October that the last scene was enacted; there is a beauty not unmixed with sadness which is wholly appropriate.

CHAPTER ONE

Sceaux: the Ile de France Museum

❧

There could be no better introduction to the Ile de France than a visit to the **Château de Sceaux**. It can be reached by the Métro from Bourg la Reine and the approach is impressive.

The château, a pastiche of the Louis XIII style built in 1856 for the duc de Trévise, is quite unworthy of its surroundings; if it were the *mairie* of some provincial town one would not bestow a second glance upon it. But it contains today the collection known as the **Musée de l'Ile de France** and its attic storey houses an excellent *service de documentation* which has provided most of the material for this book.

In the first room on the ground floor is a huge map – the *Carte des Chasses de Louis XV* – which reveals at a glance the main formative influence on the landscape of this part of France: the passion of its ruling House for hunting. A vast proportion of the area is afforested, and every forest is criss-crossed with rides and alleys for the convenience of the huntsmen.

One can see also the distinctive impact of André le Nôtre upon the French scene. Le Nôtre was one of the most remarkable characters of the seventeenth century. At Vaux-le-Vicomte, at Versailles, Trianon, Marly, St Cloud, Meudon, Chantilly and countless other princely domains he left his unmistakable mark upon thousands of acres of land, laying out noble avenues and long perspectives, their contours gradated into massive terraces and Gargantuan flights of steps and their parterres adorned with cascades and fountains, canals and lakes whose waters reflected the marble statues from a whole workshop of sculptors. What 'Capability' Brown did for the landscape of England in the eighteenth century, Le Nôtre did, in a very different style, for France in the seventeenth.

After the maps is a room devoted to the Château of Sceaux and its owners, with an excellent model of the old house that was built by Colbert, but showing it as it was in the days of his son – for it was he who added the great Orangerie, two thirds of which survive today. The original house, as we can see from Robert Denimal's model, was not architecturally distinguished.

But if the château had a certain becoming modesty about it, at least the park was magnificent. It must be remembered that considerable extensions and elaborations, including the Grand Canal, were made by Colbert's son, the marquis de Seignelay. But Le Nôtre's work has survived in broad outline, together with the Pavillon de l'Aurore, designed by Perrault, and the entrance pavilions with their two groups of statuary by Coysevox. These are worth a second look. Violence in the animal kingdom was always an acceptable theme to set before the eyes of that great dynasty of Nimrods, the Bourbons, but here there is a symbolism as well. The dog and the unicorn stand for fidelity and loyalty – the two virtues which Colbert claimed. Louis XIV would not have missed the allegory.

In the same room as Denimal's model are portraits of the principal owners of Sceaux, including a fine canvas by de Troy of the duchesse du Maine. For in 1699 the extravagance of the marquis de Seignelay obliged him to sell his estate which was bought by the duc du Maine, son of Louis XIV and Madame de Montespan. The duc du Maine had been 'made legitimate' by Louis XIV and it was here at Sceaux that his wife, the granddaughter of the great Condé, organized her shadow court with its own Order of Knighthood, the Knights of the Honey-Bee. Her court was patronized by many of the great literary figures of the age including Chaulieu, Fontenelles and Saint-Aulaire. Later Voltaire wrote his *Zadig* and *Micromégas* here, reading aloud in the evening what he had written in the course of the day, and here he organized the duchess's private theatre.

Another portrait by Van Loo shows the last proprietor of Sceaux, the duc de Penthièvre, who lived in an atmosphere of piety and abundance at Rambouillet. He was a predictably benevolent landlord, turning a blind eye to the cows which were put in to graze by neighbouring farmers and granting to the general public the freedom of the park, some of which he turned into a *jardin anglais*. He died in 1793, respected even by the Revolutionaries.

During the Revolution Sceaux was purchased for a ridiculously small sum by a native of St Malo named Lecomte. He decided to pull down the château, which was in urgent need of costly repair, and he also cut down many of the trees in the park. It was his son-in-law, the duc de Trévise, who undertook the restitution, replanting on the same lines as those of Le Nôtre. One has only to visit the park – and it is worth a long walk – to acknowledge his success. There is something truly magnificent and essentially French about the great wall of poplars that encloses the canal. They should be seen in mid-April when they first come into leaf.

Dahlia time is another great month at Sceaux – the only time when one is allowed to visit the **Pavillon du Hanovre**, a building brought here from Paris, where the architect Chevotet had built it on the Boulevard des Italiens for the Maréchal de Richelieu. Richelieu might be said to have organized the immoralities of Louis XV and was assiduous in supplying him with mistresses. It was at this pavilion that Louis first met Jeanne Bécu, later to become famous as Madame du Barry.

The rest of the museum is devoted mostly to the pictorial record of an Ile de France which has long since vanished. There is another superb model by Denimal of the two châteaux of Meudon which co-existed side by side for nearly a century. An inspection of the model is the indispensable prerequisite to an exploration of the site.

Many of the paintings are poignant reminders of a lovely country-side at the very gates of Paris, a landscape of which Queen Victoria wrote: 'we returned [to St Cloud] by the banks of the Seine, which are very picturesque and remind one of Richmond. The rows of poplars and houses with their coloured shutters are so pretty and gay.'

Along with the vanished beauties of the countryside go the many lovely buildings which once adorned it. There is a magnificent canvas by Hubert Robert of the gardens at Méréville. There is an exquisite watercolour of the elegant, bow-fronted mansion at Montmorency built in 1704 by the rich financier Crozat. But perhaps the most interesting of all is the wide panorama by Gravenbroeck of the château belonging to Lenormand d'Étioles at Evry on the fringe of the Forest of Sénart. Lenormand d'Étioles had the dubious distinction of being husband to Madame de Pompadour. Evry is now one of the most completely thought-out new towns of the Ile de France.

Together with this evocation of the landscape and architecture, the paintings of the museum depict the social life, chiefly of the nineteenth century, at all levels. From Guillaume Lepaulle comes a hunting scene from the Chantilly Forest, *le bat l'eau* at the Étang de la Reine Blanche. On the staircase are scenes from bourgeois life of *la belle époque* – the famous Bal des Canotiers at Bougival and glimpses of bathing parties where all are almost fully dressed. A painting by Jean Béraud shows ladies in bloomers indulging in the craze for cycling in the Bois de Boulogne.

Finally there are collections of household articles which range from bottles manufactured at St Denis in all sorts of bizarre shapes including the busts of famous personages, to the delicate faïence de

Sceaux – a manufacture founded by the duchesse du Maine – of which the museum houses an important collection. Nothing could bear more striking witness to the *douceur de vivre* of the upper classes in the eighteenth century than the provision of an objet d'art for every contingency of life – such as the elaborate *fontaine d'appartement*, to provide the refreshment of running water, or the *veilleuse* or nightlight – both in the most exquisite porcelain.

The museum's *Service de documentation* was largely the creation of the Conservateur, Monsieur Georges Poisson, one of the greatest authorities on the Ile de France. It is largely thanks to the courtesy and co-operation of M. Poisson and his staff that the intricate research necessary for this book became not only a possibility but a pleasure.

CHAPTER TWO

Versailles: the Palace

❧

'When you arrive at Versailles,' wrote Voltaire, 'from the courtyard
side you see a wretched, top-heavy building, with a façade seven
windows long, surrounded by everything which the imagination
could conceive in the way of bad taste. When you see it from the
garden side, you see an immense palace whose defects are more than
compensated by its beauties.'

Voltaire underlines the essential duality of Versailles. Nobody
seeing for the first time a picture of the garden front alongside one
of the entrance court could ever infer that they were two sides of the
same building.

Only a careful unravelling of its history can enable us to make
sense of Versailles. It is a tangled skein that takes up a century and a
half of French history. If we add to this the fact that the palace
has some ten hectares (twenty-five acres) of roof, we may begin
to appreciate that the size and complexity of it all pose the most
formidable challenge to the visitor. Even those well acquainted
with the palace in its prime were up against the same problem.
'One might compare the palace of Versailles,' wrote one of Louis
XVI's pages, 'to a vast labyrinth. One needed a long familiarity to
find one's way about.'

The visitor today requires the same. A previous study of the history
of the château and a leisurely approach to its seemingly endless
rooms, pictures, statues, fountains and outbuildings will repay the
trouble. Today we do not without adjustment see eye to eye with the
France of the *Grand Siècle*. As Lytton Strachey wrote: 'their small,
bright world is apt to seem uninteresting and out of date unless we
spend some patient sympathy in the discovery of the real charm
and the real beauty that it contains'.

Above all we must consider the fabric of the palace in close
connection with its human context. It is a two-way process. The
buildings are the direct expression of the personalities of those
who created them; but in their turn the buildings exercised a creative
influence over those who inhabited them.

23

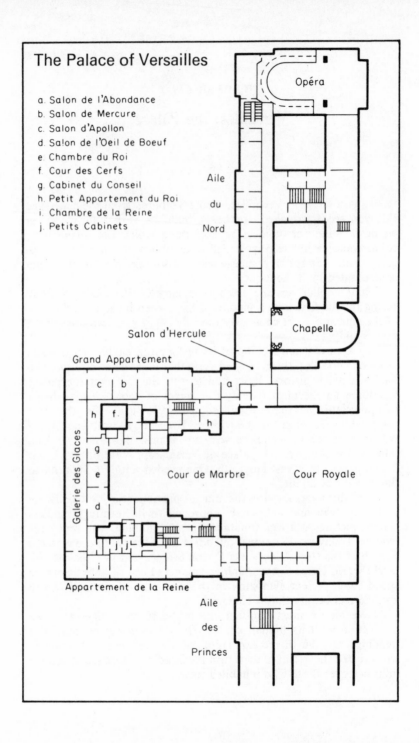

The Palace of Versailles

a. Salon de l'Abondance
b. Salon de Mercure
c. Salon d'Apollon
d. Salon de l'Oeil de Boeuf
e. Chambre du Roi
f. Cour des Cerfs
g. Cabinet du Conseil
h. Petit Appartement du Roi
i. Chambre de la Reine
j. Petits Cabinets

Opéra

Aile

du

Nord

Chapelle

Salon d'Hercule

Grand Appartement

Galerie des Glaces

Cour de Marbre

Cour Royale

Appartement de la Reine

Aile

des

Princes

For the life of the Court, those who experienced it must be allowed to speak for themselves. It is interesting to notice how their keynote changes with each successive phase They begin with a flourish and a fanfare; they settle down to the sheer grinding boredom of it all: '*La vie de la Cour*,' wrote La Bruyère, '*est un jeu sérieux, mélancholique, qui applique.*' And then, suddenly, towards the end, the whole scene seems to come into sharper focus. A landscape is never so vivid as in the last hour before the sunset fades.

Supreme among the memorialists is the duc de Saint-Simon, whose thirty-seven volumes represent an achievement proportionate to the palace which forms the backdrop to the drama which he describes. 'Throughout the endless succession of his pages,' writes Lytton Strachey, 'the enormous panorama unrolls itself, magnificent, palpitating, alive.' That is the impression we must somehow recapture when visiting Versailles.

* * *

The first thing which needs explanation is the choice of site. Nobody, setting out to build a palace the size of Versailles, could possibly have chosen to put it where it is. We need Saint-Simon to remind us that it was originally 'the most dreary and barren of places, with no view, no water and no woods'.

There was, however, something about this forlorn wilderness which made its appeal to the young Louis XIII. He was a passionate hunter, and his first house, begun here in 1624, was a simple hunting lodge where he could sleep, sometimes fully dressed, while indulging in his favourite pastime. In 1632 this original *château de cartes* was enlarged to form three sides of a quadrangle, which remains the basic structure of the Cour de Marbre today.

It was not until 1661 that Louis XIV showed any particular interest in Versailles. His formative years had seen the humiliations of the Fronde, which probably accounted for his determination not to reside in Paris.

But in 1661 all that was over. It was a momentous year for Louis. In March Mazarin had died at Vincennes; his general advice to his royal godson could be condensed into the word: 'Govern!'

It was the moment of Louis' true coming of age. 'Only then,' he wrote in his memoirs, 'did it seem to me that I was King; born to be King.'

The story of his clash with Fouquet belongs to another chapter, under Vaux-le-Vicomte. What is relevant to Versailles was the inspiration afforded to Louis by that over-sumptuous ensemble, together with the availability of its creators – that great triumvirate of definite articles: Le Vau, Le Brun and Le Nôtre.

One further circumstance must be added. In July Louis had fallen in love with Louise de la Vallière, 'the violet', as Mme de Sévigné puts it, 'which hid in the grass and blushed alike to be a mistress, a mother and a duchess'.

The official seat of the Court was Saint Germain, and the privacy and proximity of Versailles were obvious advantages to a lover. 'The King used to go there once or twice a week,' wrote Saint-Simon, 'with a very small entourage, to spend part of the day with Mlle de la Vallière, and he devised a coat with a special kind of embroidery which he bestowed upon some dozen noblemen whom he allowed to escort him during these little private rides at Versailles.' 'This sort of distinction,' wrote Mlle de Montpensier, 'intrigued the whole Court.'

Louis was not slow to exploit this human vanity. By multiplying the occasions for which invitation could be eagerly sought and judiciously granted, he lured the aristocracy of France to 'eat out of his hand'. Every detail of the royal routine offered some opportunity to single out or to ignore; to reward or to humiliate. To be constantly at Versailles became the prerequisite for any sort of success: to be absent was to ensure oblivion. Saint-Simon recognized the creation of Versailles as 'just one more of his political stratagems'. Louis very soon found that the house was not large enough to serve this purpose.

There is no better way of appreciating the extent of his creation than by comparing two paintings now in the **Museum of Versailles**. The first, by Patel, was done between 1664 and 1668; the second by P. D. Martin in the early days of Louis XV.

Patel has filled his canvas with perfect precision and faultless perspective, and, by the skilful use of the shadow cast by a cloud, has brought a vivid sense of reality to the scene. In the centre is the château – a bright array of brick and stone and slate and gilded lead which, Sir Christopher Wren noted, 'makes it look like a rich livery'. All the leaden ornament on the roof was picked out in gold leaf which glistened in the sun.

Behind the château the gardens are already beginning to take recognizable shape. To the right, the Parterre du Nord begins its gentle slope towards what is today the Bassin de Neptune. To the left the Orangerie, framed between the twin ramps of the Hundred Steps, carries the Parterre des Fleurs upon a solid platform of masonry, while in the centre the main perspective is traced '*à perte de vue*' with the canal, beginning to take on its cruciform shape, already large enough to carry a number of fully rigged ships. In front of the château, from the wide hemicycle of the Place d'Armes, the three avenues fan out towards Paris, St Cloud and Sceaux.

We look now at Martin's picture. It is the perfect portrait of a palace. His accuracy is scrupulous but his detail never obtrusive. He shows to its full advantage the long, regular, ever-widening procession of the forecourts. The quadrangle of Patel's château is now the inner sanctuary – the Cour de Marbre. It has been joined on to its office blocks which have been enlarged and ennobled by twin colonnades facing the Avenue de Paris. The wings thus formed flank the Cour Royale which is enclosed by a wrought-iron screen, ornate and gilded.

Behind the vast complex of slate and gilded lead which formed the roofscape to Versailles, the artist has allowed a glimpse of the long, uninterrupted outline of balustrade and urns suggestive of the more princely architecture of the garden front. This was the 'immense palace' referred to by Voltaire.

To understand the garden front we need to compare the façades as we see them today with another, anonymous painting in the Museum of Versailles, done in about 1675. It shows the west façade as Le Vau first enlarged it in 1668. In the centre, between two boldly projecting pavilions, is the original west front of Louis XIII's château, but faced with stone and dignified by an Ionic order. Behind the two pavilions run two wings containing to the north (left of the picture) the Grand Appartement and to the south the Queen's rooms.

This phase was known as the Château Neuf, or, more appropriately, as the Enveloppe, for it enveloped the old château on three sides. But the architecture of Le Vau, however admirable in itself, made little attempt to come to terms with that of Louis XIII, and the junctions were awkward and ungainly.

In 1678 Louis was at the height of his career. The Peace of Nimeguen had just secured for him the territory of Franche Comté and no power in Europe seemed able to check his ambitions. But above all the *Grand Siècle* was now a reality. 'It was a time worthy of the notice of the ages to come,' wrote Voltaire; 'the days when the heroes of Corneille and Racine, the characters of Molière, the symphonies of Lully, quite new to the nation, the voices of Bossuet and Bourdaloue could be heard by Louis XIV . . . by a Condé, a Turenne, a Colbert, or by this crowd of outstanding men who

27

appeared in all fields.' Versailles was to become the monument to the *Grand Siècle*.

In 1678 also, François Dorbay, who had succeeded Le Vau as the architect in charge, died. Louis confided the task of carrying out the final enlargement to Jules-Hardouin Mansart, a young man of thirty-two, nephew of the architect François Mansart.

Mansart was required to make Versailles the greatest royal house in Europe – the permanent seat of the Government and the Court of France. It was to be Whitehall as well as Buckingham Palace.

On the garden side this entailed the construction of two enormous wings – the Aisle des Princes, running south to the extremity of the Orangerie, and the Aisle du Nord which was to end in an opera house. These two wings gave the façade a total length of 670 metres. The finished palace contained 2143 windows, 1252 chimneys and 67 staircases.

So far as style was concerned, the most important alterations of Mansart are the introduction of round-arched windows through-out the first floor and the filling in of the deep recess in the centre of Le Vau's west front so as to present a united façade articulated only by colonnades.

The visit to the **state apartments** begins with the **Chapel**, where the pure, cream-coloured stone and the delicate play of light on the carvings create a cool and refreshing atmosphere. Robert de Cotte, who designed the chapel, made full use of the element of light. First, he chose for his material a beautiful white stone known as *Banc Royal*; then he inverted the relative importance of the nave and tribunes – for the royal closet had to be at first-floor level. The result is a subdued lighting to the nave; but in the apse, where the arcading curves into a graceful ambulatory, the windows provide a dramatic illumination of the altar. Gilding, conspicuously absent from most of the chapel, is used to focus attention on the sanctuary and to conduct the eye thence, by way of the organ case, to the brilliant profusion of the painted ceiling – a happy example of the collaboration of Antoine Coypel and Charles La Fosse. The chapel was not finished until 1710.

Between the chapel and the Grand Appartement is the **Salon d'Hercule**. This room was also designed by Robert de Cotte but its essential ornament was a vast canvas by Veronese, *Le Repas chez Simon le Pharisien*, which has only recently been returned from the Louvre. It was to harmonize with this that François Lemoine, the son of a humble postilion who was to become *Premier*

Peintre du Roi, painted his enormous ceiling. It took him three years, from 1733 to 1736, after which he committed suicide.

The **Grand Appartement**, which extends along the north range of the central block, consists of a suite of rooms beginning with the **Salon de l'Abondance** – which also connected with the King's rooms – and ending with the **Salon d'Apollon**, which was the throne room. Three nights a week Louis gave a reception in these rooms for the whole Court. It was called a *Jour d'Appartement* and consisted of four hours of gambling, dancing, music and refreshments. The latter were provided in the appropriately named Salon de l'Abondance. *'On donne de très excellent vin à ceux qui le souhaitent,'* wrote the Abbé Bourdelot.

These rooms today are sparsely furnished, which is as it should be, for supper tables or card tables were placed as required and removed afterwards when the space was needed for dancing. But the **Salon de Mercure**, the last but one in the suite, is difficult to visualize in its former magnificence. Only what might be called the architecture of the room, together with the ceiling, painted by J.-B. de Champaigne, survive. For, although it was very seldom used as such, this was the state bedroom without which no suite of reception rooms would have been complete. Louis slept in it for a few weeks in 1701 when his own room was being redecorated and here, for nine days after his death, he lay in state.

We must therefore refurnish this room in our imagination with a great four-poster surmounted by an impressive domed canopy, fringed and tasselled and proudly plumed with ostrich feathers. The hook from which this canopy was suspended can still be seen on the ceiling. We must insulate the bed from the room by means of a solid silver balustrade and provide a silver table, silver chandelier and eight silver candelabra to match.

We must always remember, when looking at the heavy gilding and brawn-like slabs of marble which decorate so much of Versailles, that this decor was intended to be seen in the becoming light of candles. 'Just imagine the brilliance,' wrote the Abbé Bourdelot, 'of a hundred thousand candles in this huge suite of apartments.'

We need to take note also of the sumptuous hangings which have long since vanished from the walls. Where these were not of marble they were hung with what was called a *meuble* which formed the background to the magnificent pictures in Louis' collection. Each room had a *meuble d'hiver* – usually a rich and sombre patterned velvet – and a *meuble d'été* which was often of an almost unbelievable richness, being thickly but exquisitely embroidered with gold and silver thread. The capitals of pilasters were accomplished by this method, the mouldings and volutes standing out as much as fifteen centimetres – 'so that one mistook for sculpture what was pure embroidery'.

The apotheosis of *Le Roi Soleil* was the magnificent **Galerie des Glaces**, lit by seventeen of the twenty-three first-floor windows. To do honour to this monument to the greatness of France even the classical Orders were set aside; in place of the Doric, Ionic or Corinthian, Le Brun designed a special *Ordre Français* which incorporated the *fleur de lys*, the sun and two cocks set against the palms of Victory.

A whole team of artists, working under the integrating directions of Le Brun, took seven years to decorate this enormous room. On 15 November 1684 – the very day for which completion was promised – the Court returned from Fontainebleau to find the Galerie des Glaces in all its glory.

It is difficult today, standing in this noble apartment, to imagine the astonishment and admiration with which it must have been seen for the first time.

Against the stately background of the marble pilasters and the tall windows – each reflected in its corresponding mirror – and the ceiling with its riotous profusion of allegorical figures – each reflecting some facet of the glory of Louis – we must see white and gold brocade curtains and two enormous Savonnerie carpets; we must line the walls with tables and *guéridons* and fill the window recesses with massive flower tubs all of solid silver and of a workmanship so exquisite that the value of the metal formed but a tenth part of their worth. 'This sort of royal beauty,' exclaimed Madame de Sévigné, 'is unique in the world.' Seventeen great crystal chandeliers and forty-one silver candelabra lent an indescribable lustre to the scene.

Every day Louis went from his bedroom into the gallery and passed right down the imposing enfilade of the Grand Appartement to attend Mass. Every room along his passage was a profusion of coloured marbles, opulent tapestries, silver furniture and golden decorations. The doors of the Salon d'Hercule were thrown open and the King passed into the vestibule of the chapel.

This state of magnificence, however, did not last long. In 1689 nearly all the silver furniture was melted down to help pay for the War of the Austrian Succession. In 1743 Louis XV had the entire *meuble brodé* melted down also – a process which realized nearly 52,000 *livres*.

At the turn of the century a new atmosphere began to be felt at Versailles. Its origin was a girl of twelve, Marie-Adelaide de Savoie, who came in 1697 to marry Louis' grandson, the duc de Bourgogne. Her impact upon Versailles was immediate: as Saint-Simon puts it, *'elle l'animait tout entière'*. She was the source of a great rejuvenation in the heart of the King which found its expression in the extensive redecorations to the palace carried out in 1701. To his architects Louis gave the significant directive: *'il faut de l'enfance répandue partout'*. This was to be the keynote of the new style which was to develop into the light and fanciful decorations associated with the name of Louis XV.

At the same time, Louis decided to reconstruct the main rooms of his personal apartment, creating what we see today as the **Salon de l'Oeil de Boeuf**, which was the chief ante-room to the **King's Bedroom**, which now took its place in the centre of the façade of the Cour de Marbre. This room was the hub around which the ceremonial life of the Court revolved.

The two ceremonies of the *lever*, when Louis got up, and the *coucher*, when he went to bed, were the principal occasions. Merely to be present was a matter of vital prestige to the courtier; to hold the shirt or the candle was the height of distinction. To Louis etiquette was no mockery, no hollow façade behind which a king might hide his human frailty. As Voltaire stated, the French regarded their king 'as a sort of Divinity'. As such he exacted, and was accorded, a deference not far removed from worship. Versailles was the architectural expression of this quasi-religious cult. But Louis' successors paid less and less attention to etiquette, and some of the shrewder observers saw in this one of the cracks which led to the downfall of the monarchy. 'Strip the Prince of the glory with which he is surrounded,' wrote the comte d'Hézècques, 'and he will be no more in the eyes of the populus than an ordinary man.'

It is doubtful if Louis XIV was ever seen thus naked. His successor, however, was almost the exact opposite. 'To separate Louis de Bourbon from the King of France,' wrote Madame Campan, 'was what this Monarch found most *piquant* in his royal existence.' His alterations to Versailles exactly express this duality: his whole delight was in the creation of little intimate apartments. Visits to the **Petits Cabinets** and **Petits Appartements** are indispensable to an understanding of the Versailles of the eighteenth century.

High up under the roofs of the palace, around the little courtyard known as the Cour des Cerfs, Louis XV began, as early as 1727, to construct a network of cabinets, linked by narrow galleries and little winding stairs. Here were tiny libraries of the neatest invention and the most elegant design; a bathroom with a bedroom next door in which Louis could relax after his ablutions; a workshop with a lathe and a roof garden with trellis screens and an aviary.

In the privacy of the Petits Cabinets Louis XV shed that awkwardness and aloofness which was so noticeable on state occasions; 'at supper in the Cabinets,' wrote the duc de Luynes, 'he is, so to speak, like an ordinary individual.' An *ordinary individual*: the phrase was to recur with disastrous consequences in the story of Marie-Antoinette.

The architect of the new reign was Ange-Jacques Gabriel, but the two carvers Verberkt and Rousseau must share the credit with the designer. So must Étienne Martin. The panelling was usually not gilded but painted in delicate colours and finished with a special process known as *vernis Martin*, which gave the walls the gloss and freshness of porcelain. It often needed as many as sixteen coats to achieve the desired result.

The Petits Cabinets were later redecorated for Madame du Barry and gilding was re-introduced to suit her taste. Perhaps the most successful room in this suite, known as the **Galerie des Petits Cabinets**, was the one lit by the dormer windows overlooking the Cour de Marbre. These provided a feature of which Gabriel made the happiest use, creating thereby a series of panelled recesses, which are still to be seen.

It was in these rooms that Louis held his famous, not to say notorious, supper parties. Invitation could be obtained virtually only through Madame de Pompadour, and the list of guests was brought to Louis on his return from hunting. Those who hoped to be asked presented themselves at the door of the **Cabinet du Conseil**; Louis marked off the names of those to be invited which were then read aloud by the usher, and one by one the guests made their way up to the Cabinets. One can imagine the thrill of climbing the little oval staircase and finding oneself in this inmost sanctuary of the Court. 'The dining room was delightful,' wrote the duc de Croy, 'the supper enjoyable, without restraint. The King was easy and gay, but always with a certain grandeur which one could not overlook; he did not appear in the least shy, but very much at home, talking very well.' The duc de Croy was relieved to find that, contrary to Court gossip, there was no debauchery and that he could partake of these suppers '*sans rien faire de mal*'.

On summer evenings the King and his guests would go up on to the roof and walk round the palace behind the balustrade. It is

Aerial view of Versailles from the west. In the foreground is the Parterre de Latone.

The Opera House at Versailles: auditorium looking towards the Royal Box

Versailles: Louis XV's study
with the desk made by Riesner

The chapel at Versailles, seen
from the Royal Tribune

the most fascinating walk in the whole of Versailles. Louis had the mind of an architect and understood enough about the building to know which chimney connected with which room. 'He has been known several times to converse with Madame de Chalais,' wrote the duc de Luynes, 'by a window which opens on to the roof, and with Madame de Tallard by the chimney.'

If the Petits Cabinets give us an insight into the taste of the epoch, the **Petit Appartement du Roi** shows us its style in all its gilded glory. In 1738 Louis decided that he could no longer sleep in Louis XIV's state bedroom. His official reason was the cold, to which we may add his reluctance to wake the servants whose job it was to light the fire. '*Il faut laisser dormir ces pauvres gens,*' he said to Luynes; '*je les en empêche assez souvent.*' Perhaps he was also influenced by the easier communication which the new room offered with those of his current mistress, Madame de Mailly.

Designed by Gabriel, executed by Verberkt and furnished throughout with an exquisite luxury, this room offered a perfect example of *le style Louis XV*. Unfortunately it was partly dismantled during the Revolution and the furniture dispersed, but it has recently been rehabilitated. Paintings by Nattier of Louis' daughters replace the original overdoors; a bed not unlike the original *lit à la duchesse* has been placed in the alcove and a beautiful Savonnerie carpet laid on the floor. To these we should add in our imagination a balustrade enclosing the alcove and two pillars in the form of palm trees whose gilded foliage enclosed the upper half of the recess.

The next room, the **Cabinet de la Pendule**, served no particular purpose other than connecting Louis' bedroom with the rest of the suite and housing the remarkable clock from which it gets its name. In its present form the room dates from 1760. The clock, designed by Passement, executed by Dauthiau and ornamented by Caffieri, shows not only the hour, but the day, the month, the year and phase of the moon. It is surmounted by a crystal globe in which the planets perform their revolutions according to the system of Copernicus. Louis XVI used to stay up until midnight on New Year's Eve in order to see the complete change recorded on his clock.

Next in the suite is the **Cabinet Intérieur** or **Cabinet Intime**. Once again it is a perfect example of the style and a triumph for Verberkt. It was in this room that Louis did most of his work, and it is here, appropriately enough, that his magnificent desk used to stand. Thanks to the co-operation of the authorities of the Louvre, it now stands here again. It took nine years to make. Ordered in 1760 from Oeben, it was completed after his death by his widow's second husband Riesner. Every drawer in it locks by means of a single mechanism except for the little ones which contain the ink-pots, which could be refilled by the groom of the chambers without the King having to unlock the whole. A copy of this desk was made for Sir Richard Wallace and is now in the Wallace Collection.

The Cabinet Intime is for ever associated with the most moving occasion of Louis' private life – the funeral of Madame de Pompadour. It was arranged that the cortège should leave Versailles at six in the evening; etiquette forbade the presence of the King. Alone with his valet de chambre, Champlost, Louis had shut himself into the Cabinet Intime and was standing on the balcony which overlooks the Cour Royale. When he turned to re-enter the room, two large tears ran down either cheek. '*Voilà les seuls devoirs que j'ai pu lui rendre*,' was all that he could say.

Immediately below this balcony is the door which formed the private entry to the King's apartments. It was on his way out from here, on 5 January 1757, that Louis was stabbed by Damiens. Although the wound was a slight one, Louis was convinced that the knife was poisoned and behaved as if he were dying. It was his huntsman, Lasmartes, who assessed the situation correctly: 'that's nothing, Sire,' he told the King; 'in four days' time we'll take a stag.'

A little anecdote by Mme Campan shows how inimical Versailles was to family life. Every morning Louis XV would go down to Mme Adelaide's rooms on the ground floor, often bringing coffee which he had made himself. Adelaide pulled a bell rope which alerted her sister Victoire, who in turn rang to summon her next sister Sophie, who passed the message on to the fourth sister Louise. Poor little Louise was slightly deformed and very short in the leg. 'The apartments of Mesdames were enormous. Mme Louise lived in the remotest of them. In order to attend the daily reunion the poor princess, running as fast as she could, crossed a great number of rooms and in spite of her efforts often had only time to kiss her father before he went off hunting.'

In 1752 new rooms were decorated for Adelaide in the Petits Appartements. Her **Music Room** is one of the finest examples of the style to which Louis XV gave his name; but the panels in the alcove were added later, in 1767. The four elaborate 'drops', two representing musical instruments and the others reflecting the princess's interest in gardening and fishing, are the last recorded work of the great carver Verberkt. Their design was by Gabriel.

To pass from this room to the **Library of Louis XVI** is to pass from one style to the next and to see each in its perfection. It is somehow typical of Versailles that the new style was the creation of two of the most distinguished exponents of the old. The library is the last work of Gabriel in the château and also the last of the carver Antoine Rousseau.

The ornament is restrained and exceedingly subtle. The rounded corners of the room are relieved by drops representing the great diversity of subject matter in the library shelves – globe, telescope, Roman sword, shepherd's hat, books (which vary from the Henriade to the works of Bossuet) and the masks of Comedy and Tragedy, all joined together by a network of flowers and ribbons. The centre of each bookcase is surmounted by a gilded bas relief, on one side Apollo leaning on his lyre and on the other France receiving homage from the Arts. The greatness of France in the world of art and letters was a fitting symbolism for Versailles, and Louis peopled his library with Sèvres statuettes of the great authors of his country.

Here, surrounded by the images of a glorious past, Louis loved to sit at a little desk drawn up into the window recess so that he could look out on the people who came and went about their business in the courtyard of his palace. Behind him the vast mahogany table, made of a single piece of wood, was littered with books and papers. It was his favourite room and it is still one of the few at Versailles which have that 'lived in' appearance which distinguishes a house from a museum. It was a fact which Arthur Young noted in 1787. 'In viewing the King's apartment, which he had not left a quarter of an hour, with those slight traits of disorder that showed he *lived* in it, it was amusing to see the blackguard figures that were walking uncontrolled about the palace, even in his bedchamber; men whose rags betrayed them to be in the last stage of poverty. One loves the master of the house who would not be hurt or offended at seeing his apartment thus occupied if he returned suddenly. This is certainly a feature of that *good temper* which appears to me so visible everywhere in France [this was two years before the Revolution!]. I desired to see the Queen's apartment, but I could not. Is Her Majesty in? No. Why then not see it as well as the King's? *Ma foi, Monsieur, c'est une autre chose.*'

The **Queen's Rooms**, on the south side of the Cour de Marbre, consisted also of state apartments and Petits Cabinets. These rooms were in her turn occupied by Marie-Antoinette and her ladies, their towering head-dresses and their unwieldy trains imposing upon them a stately deportment and an odd, distinctive gait by which a lady of the Court could always be identified. 'It was a great art,' wrote the marquise de la Tour du Pin, 'to be able to walk in this vast apartment without catching the train of the lady who preceded you. You had to avoid ever raising the foot, but to let it slide along the parquet flooring, which was always highly polished.'

Marie-Antoinette, although opposed by nature and by upbringing to solemnity and etiquette, was by no means devoid of natural majesty, and she stood out in clear relief against the already brilliant background of the ladies of the Court 'as a great oak in a forest dominates the trees around it'.

The **Queen's Bedroom** was the centre of all the ceremonial on her side of the palace. The actual decorations are those ordered for Marie-Leczinska in 1729 when she gave birth to a dauphin. They were not completed until 1736. This was the first state room to be redecorated in the new Louis XV style. It has recently been restored to its original splendour as Marie-Antoinette last saw it.

The walls are hung today with an exact reproduction of the last *meuble d'été* ordered for Marie-Antoinette from the Desfarges silk looms at Lyons, together with the sumptuous hangings of the *lit à ta duchesse* and the carpet, made in 1730 for Marie-Leczinska.

The four stools are reminders of a special point of etiquette. Duchesses were accorded the *droit du tabouret* – the right to sit on one of these stools in the royal presence. Everyone else had to stand. Marie-Leczinska was very careful about this sort of distinction.

The worst ordeal occasioned by the etiquette of the Court was the obligation laid upon the Queen to have her children in public. When Marie-Antoinette had her first child screens were erected round the bed to keep off the 'crowds of sight-seers who rushed into the room'. They even climbed on the furniture to get a better view of the proceedings; 'one could fancy oneself in a public place' wrote Madame Campan. It was on this occasion that Louis XVI smashed open one of the windows 'with a force that only his love of the Queen could have given him', for the Queen was in danger of suffocation, and the princesse de Lamballe had fainted.

Unfortunately, though most understandably, Marie-Antoinette tried to get away from the solemnity and protocol of the Court and to lead her own private existence. '*Je ne suis plus la Reine,*' she exclaimed on arriving chez Mme de Polignac; '*je suis moi.*' If she could not escape to Trianon, at least she could retire to her Petits Cabinets, where only her narrow circle of personal friends had access to her.

Her redecoration of these rooms started in 1779 with the library.

This did not arise from any inclination towards reading; 'apart from a few novels,' wrote Besenval, 'she never opens a book.' Perhaps on this account many of the volumes were dummies and the bookbinder Martial provided a selection of decorative backs to ornament the shelves.

The **Méridienne**, a little octagonal room with a recess for a day bed, was mostly decorated with mirrors, for it was here that the Queen had her interminable conferences with her dressmaker Rose Bertin. An album was kept with samples of the materials of all her costumes and was brought to her each morning. She marked with a pin the choices for the day, which were then brought up from the Garderobe. The room was designed by the Queen's architect Mique and executed by the brothers Rousseau, sons of Antoine Rousseau. The delicate patterns carved on the panels have all the precision of the bronze *appliqués* on the mirrors; they incorporate peacocks and flowers, hearts pierced with arrows and above all the dolphin, in honour of the birth, on 22 October 1781, of an heir to the throne. The event caused an outbreak of rejoicing which restored for a time the waning popularity of the Queen.

In 1783 the largest of the rooms, the **Cabinet Intérieur,** was re-decorated and changed its name to **Cabinet Doré**. The decorations were in the very latest style, with winged sphynxes, displayed eagles and smoking braziers which could almost pass as *Empire*. Here stood the Queen's harp and harpsichord, used when she sang with Grétry and Mme Vigée-Lebrun. There is a picture of her at Versailles by Gautier-Dagoly playing the harp in her bedroom. None of the original furniture has been recovered, but a very fine harp by Naderman has replaced the authentic instrument, and appropriate furniture, some from the Queen's apartment at the Tuileries and some from the comtesse d'Artois' rooms at Versailles, has been arranged with a happy effect.

Although the constructions of the eighteenth century were most typically those of small and intimate apartments, the architects of the epoch were capable also of handling large-scale compositions of the utmost magnificence, as Gabriel was to demonstrate.

The marriage of Louis XVI and Marie-Antoinette was the occasion of the last major addition to the palace of Versailles – the **Salle de Spectacle** or **Opéra**. It was not, by eighteenth-century standards, an extravagantly conceived plan, for the architecture is entirely of wood painted to resemble a marble called Serancolin. The colour scheme is one of the most successful at Versailles. The marbling is achieved in a warm salmon pink against a background of grey-green known as *verd-verd*, both of an infinitely subtle variety of tone and lavishly enriched with gilding. Contrasting with this is the cold, bright cobalt of the silken hangings and the more sombre blue of the patterned velvet upholstery.

The auditorium, in the form of a truncated ellipse, is encircled by a colonnade which breaks into a graceful apse above the royal box. Each bay of the colonnade is backed by a mirror; and each mirror reflects, and thus completes, a half chandelier which hangs against its surface. The rest of the house is lit by fourteen great chandeliers, each of them one and a half metres high and each containing ninety-six crystal pendants. In the apse is an even larger one, two and a half metres high with more than three hundred pendants. The duc de Croy noted that these chandeliers were left illuminated throughout the performance; 'thus lighting up from below a superb ceiling, they produced the most admirable effect'.

Painted by du Rameau and representing *Apollo preparing crowns for those illustrious in the arts*, the ceiling reflects the dominant colour scheme of pink and blue, which is continued in the smaller ceilings in the bays of the colonnade. By Gabriel's express instructions, du Rameau was charged 'to decide on all the tones and mixtures of colours in order to create an all-embracing harmony'. In this he has most wonderfully succeeded.

The stage was fully equipped with all the elaborate machinery required for theatrical productions at that date, but it could also be made to join up with the auditorium and thereby form a single unit. The scene could be set to reflect the amphitheatre, the floor of the pit jacked up level with the stage, and the whole opera house transformed into one enormous ballroom or an immense banqueting hall.

In October 1789, the Gardes du Corps borrowed it to give a dinner. This was reported as a counter-revolutionary orgy in which the tricolour cockade had been trampled underfoot and the white cockade donned defiantly. The incident prepared the way for the attack on the palace by the mob on the night of 5 October.

Although no single building could have symbolized the *Ancien Régime* more completely than Versailles, the Revolution did surprisingly little damage to its fabric. The dispersal of all the furniture was indeed an irreparable loss, but otherwise the effacing of most of the *fleurs de lys* and other insignia of royalty was all that the building had to suffer. At the Restoration, Louis XVIII even contemplated returning here and built the Pavillon Dufour to match the Aisle Gabriel at the entrance to the Cour Royale.

Lamartine paints a moving picture of him revisiting the scenes of his gay and gilded youth and 'measuring with a wistful eye the distance which separated his old age from his cradle'. Supported on the arms of his servants he would mount the stairs which led to his old apartments at the end of the Aisle des Princes, in which he had caused such articles of furniture as were still in the Garde Meuble to be replaced 'to give him a momentary illusion of the old days'. Leaving his servants at the door, he would sit there, in his crimson velvet chair, alone with his memories.

It was Louis-Philippe who first took a practical view of Versailles and turned it into a museum dedicated '*à toutes les gloires de la France*'. To make room for his galleries hundreds of the most beautiful eighteenth-century interiors were swept away. One of his more pointless mutilations was the levelling out of the Cour de Marbre with the Cour Royale, from which it had previously been separated by five steps – an alteration which ruined the proportions of Le Vau's façades without serving any very obvious purpose. It has now been restored to its original appearance. But, regrettable though his taste in some instances may have been, the 'Bourgeois King' deserves the indulgence of posterity; he devoted some twenty-four millions of his Civil List to his museum of Versailles and therby saved it from becoming a barracks; a destiny which, for noble edifice, can only be regarded as a fate worse than death.

CHAPTER THREE

Versailles: the Gardens, Park and Town

❧

The Gardens and Park of Versailles still extend over 800 hectares (2000 acres) of ground, but before the Revolution the total area was well over three times as much. The whole of the Grand Design included the vast stables, capable of housing two thousand four hundred horses and six hundred carriages; it included three other châteaux, two at Trianon and one at Clagny, built for Mme de Montespan and replaced today by the Lycée Hoche; it included the Ménagerie which disappeared after the Revolution.

The vast, elaborate lay-out of Le Nôtre survived more or less unchanged until the days of Louis XVI. In 1775 the trees were in such poor condition that they were all felled, but fortunately for Versailles, Louis XVI was a traditionalist. It was decided that the replantation should follow the main lines of the original design.

This meant that all the elaborate arrangement of fountains, colonnades, statues and urns could be retained. The main theme of the statuary was taken from Louis XIV's device of the Sun. It began in the Grotte de Thétis, which occupied the area where today visitors obtain their tickets and purchase postcards (the Grotto was abolished when Mansart made his final extension of the Aisle du Nord). Three great groups of statues represent Apollo and his horses being refreshed in the palace of Thétis after completing their day's course across the sky. The group of Apollo and his nymphs is by Girardon and Regnaudin; those of the horses by Marsy and Guérin. In 1776 they were placed in a grotto designed by Hubert Robert in the bosquet to the north of the **Bassin de Latone.**

This stands just below the terrace of the **Parterre d'Eau** before the château, where the ground begins to fall away. Latona was the mother of Apollo and the mistress of Jupiter. One day, while fleeing the wrath of Juno, Jupiter's wife, she was prevented from drinking by the peasants of Lycea who threw stones and clods of earth into the water. She appealed to her lover, who avenged the insult by turning the offending peasants into frogs. As the mother of Apollo, Latona was bound to have her place of honour in the gardens of

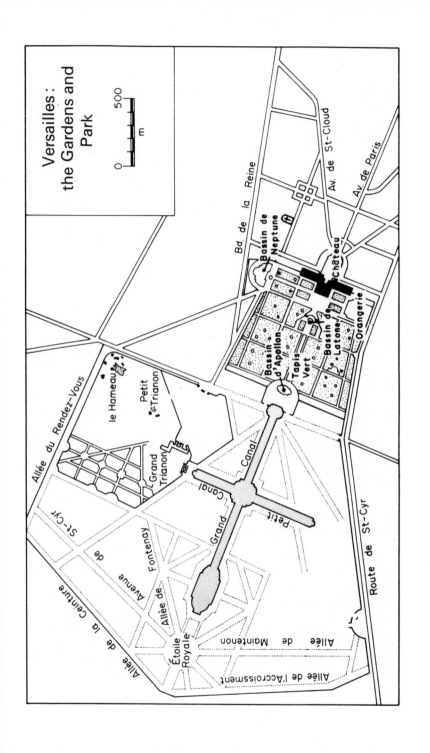

Versailles:
the Gardens and
Park

0   500
m

Bd. de la Reine

Bassin de
Neptune

Château

Av. de St-Cloud

Av. de Paris

Orangerie

Bassin de
Latone

Tapis
Vert

Bassin
d'Apollon

Allée du Rendez-Vous

le Hameau

Petit
Trianon

Grand
Trianon

St-Cyr

de

Avenue

Fontenay

Allée de

Étoile
Royale

Grand Canal

Grand Canal

Petit Canal

Allée de Maintenon

Allée de la Ceinture

Allée de l'Accroissement

Route de St-Cyr

THE COUNTRY ROUND PARIS

Versailles; but to more shrewd observers was there not a lesson here in the fate of those who dared throw mud at the mistress of a king?

From here the **Tapis Vert**, lined with urns and statues, continues the gentle descent down to the level of the Canal where the **Bassin d'Apollon**, executed by Tuby in 1671 from the design of Le Brun, forms the last important group.

It should be remembered that all these leaden figures were originally gilded and had their gilding renewed every year.

The **Canal** is the principal *pièce d'eau* of the park and designed to set the scale for the whole lay-out. From east to west it measures 1560 metres, but it is cruciform in shape and has a total perimeter of 5670 metres. On the occasions of the great illuminations of the park, such as that organized for the marriage of Louis XVI and Marie-Antoinette, this entire perimeter was lined with coloured lights with a huge *château d'eau* brilliantly illuminated at its extremity.

The Canal was equipped with a whole fleet of ships and on summer evenings the Court would embark upon its waters *'pour goûter la fraîcheur du soir'*. One of the barques was reserved for Lully and his orchestra, and a number of gondolas had been presented by the Senate of Venice. The gondoliers lived in houses to the north of the Bassin d'Apollon which still retain their name of **Petite Venise**.

The right arm of the Canal leads to the north where a little village called Trianon had to be swept away to make room for the ever-expanding gardens.

In the autumn of 1669 the love affair between Louis and Madame de Montespan was at its height. He wanted to build a pavilion somewhere rather remote in the gardens where they could be alone together. He chose the site of the former hamlet of Trianon and constructed there a charming little château, half Chinese, half Doric in style and decorated inside and out with tiles of Delft porcelain. This building, which stood for only eighteen years, was known as the Trianon de Porcelaine.

It was the architectural focus of a flower garden of the most fantastic nature. The navy was charged with supplying it in winter with flowers from warmer climates, so that in December or January Louis could walk his guests round borders stuffed with daffodils and hyacinths. *'Je vous prie,'* wrote Colbert to the Commander of the Galleys at Marseilles, *'d'acheter toutes les jonquils et tubéreuses que vous pourrez trouver.'* To deal with these colossal orders and to be able to plant them out at a moment's notice, the head gardener at Trianon, Le Bouteux, maintained the almost unbelievable figure of one million nine hundred thousand flower pots.

But everything which Louis built had to become larger and grander. When Madame de Montespan fell from favour the Trianon de Porcelaine had served its turn. In 1687 it was pulled down and replaced by the present building which is properly known as the **Trianon de Marbre** – though it has come to be called the **Grand Trianon** to distinguish it from the much later Petit Trianon.

It was designed by Mansart, but by this time Mansart was receiving help from his son-in-law Robert de Cotte – a rather more gifted architect. It was he who created the beautiful **Péristyle** which links the left wing – where the Dauphin had his establishment – to the royal apartments on the right wing, while giving direct access from the cour d'honneur to the gardens.

Externally the Trianon de Marbre is almost as Louis XIV left it – except for the urns and trophies which used to adorn the balustrade and alleviated the monotony of the skyline which we see today.

Like Versailles and Marly, Trianon played its part in Louis' policy towards the Court. Invitations were issued or withheld in order to keep the nobility assiduous in their efforts to remain in the royal favour. The invaluable Saint-Simon reveals how the niceties of etiquette were manipulated to his own discomfort. When a lady was invited to Marly, her husband accompanied her without need for a personal application, but this was not so if the invitation was for Trianon. By consistently asking the duchesse de Saint-Simon to Trianon – the greater honour – and by refusing her application for Marly, Louis was able to convey in no uncertain terms his displeasure with the Duke.

Trianon has recently been the subject of the most lavish restoration. Silk hangings have been re-spun, carpets re-woven, pictures replaced and furniture recovered from museums and private collections to present a suite of apartments of a richness and *éclat* which gives more idea of a royal or imperial palace than any other building in France. Basically it shows the architecture of Louis XIV's Trianon with much of the furnishings of Napoleon, to a certain extent modified by Louis-Philippe.

The rooms to the south of the Péristyle were originally those of the Grand Dauphin. His **Bedroom** is largely unchanged except for the furniture. The bed is that used at the Tuileries by Napoleon and later by Louis XVIII, who died in it. It was brought here in 1837 by Louis-Philippe with the rest of the furniture.

It would be difficult to guess that the room next to it was once the chapel. It looks perfectly fitted for its later function of being the

Ante Room. Only the ears of corn and bunches of grapes, symbols of the Eucharist, in the frieze bear witness to its former use.

Another room, the first one opening out of the Péristyle on the King's side, was also equipped as a chapel under Louis XV, who wished to be able to hear Mass without leaving his apartment. It is known as the **Salon Rond**, and is one of the finest examples of architectural design in the building. In fact this whole suite of apartments along the west side of the château provides a superb series of late seventeenth-century interior decorations with rich cornices and beautifully modelled overdoors such as even Versailles itself does not possess.

On the east side of the north block were the private rooms of Louis XIV, but his memory here has been entirely effaced by that of Napoleon. The **Chambre de l'Empereur** has regained its authentic furnishings, with the commode and bureau ordered from Baudoin; and the hangings of lilac and silver silk, originally woven for Joséphine's rooms at the Tuileries and brought here by Napoleon, have been faithfully re-woven to the original design.

The **Gallery,** more than any other apartment, retains its original appearance. This is largely due to its wonderful set of paintings – twenty-one by Cotelle and one by Martin – of the gardens of Versailles as Louis XIV knew them. They are among the most precious documents in the archives of Versailles. The curtains and upholstery reproduce the original red of the *Grand Siècle*; but the furniture, and the lovely crystal chandeliers, date from Napoleon.

It was Napoleon's second wife, Marie-Louise, the niece of Marie-Antoinette, who particularly liked Trianon, and the Imperial Court began to have more and more receptions in this palace: no matter that the ladies had to travel the twenty-nine kilometres from Paris *en grande toilette.*

Louis XV showed little interest in Trianon until the advent of Mme de Pompadour in 1745. The secret of her hold upon the King lay partly in the fact that he was easily bored. She quickly saw that to retain his affections she must keep him interested. One of his interests was architecture: he was never so happy as when seated at a table with Gabriel and the marquise with the designs for a new building spread before them. He was also interested in pigeons, chickens and gardening.

These interests, fostered by the delicate hand of the favourite, expressed themselves first in the creation, to the north of Trianon, of the New Menagerie.

The New Menagerie was a somewhat grandiose name for what was little more than a farmyard. The hen coops, pigeon houses, cow houses and sheep pens were surrounded by a little garden whose architectural focus was a pavilion in the form of an Irish cross – one of Gabriel's most charming inventions. It is now known as the **Pavillon Français**.

A rotunda with a frieze of farmyard scenes supported by eight Corinthian columns opens by four tall windows on to the gardens; and between the windows four small doors lead each into a tiny closet which forms, on the outside, one of the limbs of the cross. The rich relief of the building and the sculptural effects on the skyline are typical of the period; there is nothing to suggest the new style which Gabriel was to create, twelve years later, in the Petit Trianon, within a hundred metres of this pavilion.

By 1749 this exquisite little rotunda was completed. The following year the King appointed Claude Richard – a man described by Linnaeus as 'the ablest gardener in Europe' – to be in sole charge of a botanical garden to the north of the New Menagerie. By 1761 a huge area had been laid out with greenhouses and flower beds, and scientific experiments were being carried out that were the centre of interest to the botanical world of Europe. Mme de Pompadour saw an opportunity for a further building venture, which was to be known as the **Petit Trianon**. In 1763 the foundations were laid, and by the end of the next year the shell of masonry had been completed. It was a design which, by the simplicity of its conception, the purity of its line and the delicacy of its ornament, was at once the first and finest example of the classical revival which is usually labelled Louis XVI.

Simplicity is the keynote of the Petit Trianon, but simplicity is nearly always deceptive. It cannot be achieved without a perfect command of technique. In designing his façades, Gabriel appreciated nicely the variety of texture possible in the fine, honey-coloured stone. A rusticated lower storey, fluted pilasters and a delicately chiselled entablature set off the contrasting smoothness of the undecorated wall surfaces. A subtle use has been made of a drop in the ground level to obtain two façades of two storeys and two of three. The north and west fronts have their basements masked by a terrace and *perron*, whereby the rooms may be approached directly from the gardens; the more imposing height of the entrance front is balanced by the low outbuildings which enclose the forecourt. The original orientation being towards the Pavillon Français, the west front was accorded the richest treatment; only towards the east, where the windows overlooked the botanical gardens, has

Gabriel omitted any ornament.

The King's interest in botany is reflected in the interior decorations. The beautiful lilies in their circular wreaths which decorate the panels of the **Salon de Musique**, the swags and drops over the arched mirrors, the bunches of roses in the **Cabinet du Roi** – later the **Chambre de la Reine** – are carved with an accuracy and precision which had to pass the scrutiny of a botanist king.

The Petit Trianon was designed for privacy. Even the presence of servants placed an unwelcome restraint upon the intimate circle of the King, and in the **dining room** tables were designed after the manner of the already famous *table volante* at Choisy-le-Roi. By means of a mechanism 'far superior to that of Choisy for its simplicity' the tables could disappear through the floor to the kitchens to be cleared and reloaded with the second course. They were the invention of Loriot and were exhibited in Paris in 1769, but for some reason they were never installed at Trianon.

One of the first acts of Louis XVI on ascending the throne was to present the Petit Trianon to Marie-Antoinette. At first the public was pleased at the news. It was a refreshing novelty to have a King whose only mistress was the Queen. More shrewd and always well informed through her Minister Mercy, the Empress Maria-Theresa foresaw the possible danger and wrote to express her hope that 'the King's charming first present may not provide occasion for too large expenditure, let alone for dissipation'.

There was little scope in the actual buildings for expenditure, for they were already perfect. The tiny **Boudoir** behind the Queen's Bedroom was the only new addition. It was in the **gardens** that Marie-Antoinette was to realize her mother's worst fears and earn herself the name of '*Madame Déficit*'.

In 1776 the duc de Croy made his first visit to Trianon since the death of Louis XV. 'I thought I must be mad or dreaming,' he wrote; 'never have two acres of land so completely changed their form nor cost so much money.' The ground to the north-east had been cast into a miniature range of hills, and a lake had been dug, fed by a cascade which gushed from the mouth of a mysterious grotto. Next to the grotto stood the **Belvédère,** designed by Mique and remarkable for the exquisite ornament of the carvings without and the delicacy of the painted arabesques within.

East of the lake, through green meadows and loosely planted groves, wandered a river, now forming a little backwater towards the château, now dividing its stream to leave an island planted with lilac and laburnum from which rose the twelve stately columns of

Mique's **Temple de l'Amour,** carrying their stone cupola over Bouchardon's statue of Love. A rich variety of trees, many of them species recently acclimatized at Trianon, formed the background to this artificial paradise. Only the trickle of water and the song of nightingales could be heard. 'One could fancy oneself,' wrote the prince de Ligne, 'three hundred miles from Court' and the truth of his statement is the measure of Marie-Antoinette's success.

'I have already let you know my wishes with regard to Trianon,' wrote Marie-Antoinette to the duc de Fronsac; 'I have no Court there; I live as a private individual.' The Queen's attempt to live as an ordinary person was certain to embitter all parties: the Court, who expected that noble birth and high position should be sufficient claim on the attentions of the Queen; and the people, who, while they protested at any undue extravagance, looked to see the dignified tradition of their monarchy worthily upheld.

Marie-Antoinette, however, lived as if she were the mistress of some country house in England. When she entered the Salon at Trianon the ladies did not rise from the piano or their embroidery frames, and gentlemen did not interrupt their billiards. To further this impression of a country-house life she had constructed a model village, the **Hameau.** Round the borders of a small lake were disposed a number of rustic houses such as might have formed a tiny rural village – or the background of a painting by Greuze. A farm with a monumental gateway, several thatched cottages and a mill worked by a rivulet fed from the lake. 'The pleasure of wandering about all the buildings of the Hameau, of watching cows milked and of fishing in the lake,' wrote Madame Campan, 'enchanted the Queen.'

One of the houses in the Hameau was set apart for her personal use – **la Maison de la Reine.** It was really two buildings, joined by a wooden gallery. The exterior was painted to represent an artificial state of dilapidation. The galleries were lined with flower pots of blue and white porcelain bearing the Queen's monogram. But all this picturesque and rustic beauty was merely external. The interior had all the gilded elegance and sophistication of the rooms at the château.

It was in this garden on 5 October 1789 that the news reached Marie-Antoinette that the mob was marching on Versailles. The messenger found her seated in the grotto. 'This grotto,' wrote the comte d'Hézècques, 'was so dark that the eyes, dazzled before, needed a certain time to be able to discern objects clearly.' For years Marie-Antoinette had played her little game of make-believe in this lovely garden. Now the game was up. Carriages were in waiting to take her to safety, but she refused them proudly. '*Puisqu'il y a du danger,*' she said, '*ma place est auprès du Roi.*' When, the next day, she faced the mob alone on the balcony of the King's bedroom, she showed herself, as never before, the Queen. But the days of Versailles as a royal palace were over. On 6 October the royal family was escorted ignominiously to Paris. As they were bundled into the great *Berline*, Louis turned to the marquis de la Tour du Pin. '*Vous restez le maître ici,*' he said; '*tâchez de me sauver mon pauvre Versailles.*'

* * *

On the east side of the château are a number of large buildings which were originally connected with it. The **Grand Commun** was built by Mansart in 1682 to house most of the kitchens and some 1500 of the palace staff. Three hundred and eighty-six of these were required for the *Office de la Bouche*, whose business was to provide meals for those who were granted the privilege of *bouche à la Cour*. The Commun also provided apartments for such high officers as Le Nôtre.

Most of the ministries were situated to the south of this, in the rue de l'Indépendance Américaine. The old **Ministère de la Marine et des Affaires Etrangères** is now the municipal library, but the lovely suite of rooms designed by Berthier in the mid-eighteenth century is open to the public. Behind these is the old **Couvent des Récollets**, now a barracks. Over the door are the figures of angels swinging censers. There used to be a monstrance between them which was destroyed in the Revolution. During the Terror this became the principal gaol of the town and its church was used for the tribunal. A royalist named Jullian recorded his experiences in this prison. Boredom was the chief enemy, and he sought to relieve it by playing chess. But his chess set had first to be purged by the republicans; the gaoler broke off the crowns from the King and Queen.

Beyond the Place d'Armes, Mansart built the stables. Although they are both the same size, the block to the north, which was used for saddle horses, is called the **Grandes Écuries**, and that to the south, which was used for coach horses and vehicles, the **Petites Écuries**.

At the back of the Grandes Écuries was the École des Pages, where the sons of the high nobility could receive a somewhat Etonian education. The boys usually went at thirteen and stayed for three or four years. In the early morning and at night they were on duty at the palace. For this they donned their liveries, which were provided 'with a truly royal magnificence'. They consisted of white knee breeches worn over white silk stockings; a waistcoat of cloth of gold and a cerise velvet coat with wide embroideries down all the seams, with facings and collar of blue velvet.

The young comte Hilarion de Beaufort joined the household of the comte de Provence (later Louis XVIII) in January 1776. He describes how his headmaster, the *Gouverneur des Pages*, conducted him to the palace for his official presentation; 'proud as a young peacock in my embroidered coats, I was convinced I was already a personage at Court'. His disillusionment was immediate: *Monsieur* received him in silence – 'scarcely deigning an indifferent glance at my small person, he gave me only the courtesy of a barely perceptible nod'.

In contrast with his younger brother, Louis XVI took a delight in the pages and not infrequently joined in their youthful pranks. Between the Queen's apartment and the King's was a passage (the same down which Marie-Antoinette was to flee from the mob on the night of 5 October 1789) which the King often used. It was lined with upholstered benches on which a number of the palace servants slept, providing an irresistible temptation to bored but spirited young gentlemen – their open mouths inviting a syringe full of water or their closed lips the delicate application of a moustache by means of a burnt cork. In these and other practical jokes they received encouragement from their sovereign, and when the victim awoke, blinking and spluttering, 'the King, laughing heartily, would flee from the scene of battle with as much speed as his young army'.

The proper function of the pages was largely ornamental and entailed long hours of standing about at the *lever* and the *coucher*. In *Monsieur*'s apartment they stood by a marble-topped commode: 'I knew every vein in it,' wrote Hilarion, 'for I had much idle leisure in which to study it.' They waited while the Usher threw open the doors to the Grand Service with a courteous 'Pray enter, Gentlemen'; they waited while the marquis d'Avaray slipped on His Royal Highness's shirt – sometimes affording the pages a glimpse of His Royal Highness's posterior 'plump and white' while he tucked in the shirt tails; they waited while His Royal Highness donned his Court coat of embroidered satin or velvet; they waited while the barber enveloped His Royal Highness in a huge wrapper of muslin and lace to protect his clothing while his hair was powdered and curled; they waited while his face was gently wiped with a soft cloth in case any specks of powder had trespassed upon it. 'Now came the great task for which the two pages had been waiting. Just imagine: it was no less than to step forward and each remove a slipper from the Prince's feet. We carried them back, with as much respect and solemnity as possible, to the commode by which we had been standing.'

* * *

It must be remembered that Versailles is a town as well as a palace. South of the Avenue de Paris, where the site of the original village is preserved in the name rue du Vieux Versailles, all is shabby and ill-maintained. But the narrow streets, with their leprous stucco façades, open in accordance with a master plan into the large square in which stands the **Cathédrale St Louis.**

The Cathedral was not begun until 1742, and was the work of Mansart's grandson. He has based his design on his grandfather's church of Notre Dame, which it answers in the symmetry of the town plan; but he has grouped his columns together and given more height and movement to his façades, which are distinctly baroque in flavour. Inside, his design is more pedestrian and loses much through being executed in a most displeasing mud-coloured stone.

The other half of the town, to the north of the Avenue de Paris, is much smarter. The **Place Hoche** is a fine square, or rather octagon, and the **Boulevard de la Reine** a pleasant street. About half-way along it, on the south side, is the little **Musée Lambinet**. It is worth visiting for two reasons: its architecture and its contents. It is a delightful example of a town house such as was lived in by a fairly wealthy building contractor in the mid-eighteenth century – J. B. Porchon, its builder, was *Entrepreneur des Bâtiments du Roi.* He doubtless knew where first-rate craftsmen were to be found, and the decoration of the house is exquisite. One is immediately struck, however, by the smallness of the rooms. This was no house for large receptions, but rather for charming and intimate *causeries.*

The collection is miscellaneous to say the least. Some of the pictures are fascinating documents on the history of Versailles, such as the view of the Trianon de Porcelaine, an ambitious but unfinished aerial view of the palace and its gardens, and a set of ivory buttons, each painted with a different scene at Versailles in miniature.

Upstairs we pass from the two salons – charming memorials of the Age of Enlightenment – to a room consecrated to Marat and the Revolution, including an extremely bad but none the less moving depiction of the farewell of Louis XVI to his family. There is a room on the top floor devoted to Mme de Maintenon, and another with an interesting painting by Robert Tournières entitled *Le Déjeuner au jambon*, showing Lalande, music in hand, entertaining Couperin and others to what appears to be an extremely frugal repast.

Near the Lambinet Museum is the **Parish Church of Notre Dame**, built by Mansart in 1684. One can only suppose that Mansart was too preoccupied with other matters at this time to give it much attention, for it is a somewhat pedestrian achievement. The façade of Notre Dame has a certain grandeur, but the twin belfries seem just to stand on the platform upheld by the Doric order of the ground floor and not to relate properly to their supports. The circular chapel at the east end is a nineteenth-century addition.

A little beyond the grille that marks the boundary between Versailles and Viroflay an avenue leads left to the **Pavillon de Musique de Madame**. In 1952 I had the good fortune to live here while I was teaching at the Lycée Hoche and writing my first book, which was about Versailles.

I had a room on the top floor, added when the wings were added in 1825, to the right of the front door. But when the proprietor, Madame Meunier, discovered that I was writing a book about the palace she insisted that the octagonal salon should be my study. It is a delightful room, a real gem of the Louis XVI style, all flounced about with floral swags and animated *amorini* supporting Wedgwood plaques with the initial M for *Madame*.

'*Madame*' was Joséphine-Louise de Savoie, comtesse de Provence. She was the wife of Louis XVI's younger brother, who later, after she was dead, succeeded as Louis XVIII.

The Pavillon de Musique was her Petit Trianon, built by the architect Chalgrin in 1781. Originally it consisted of only the middle portion – a central rotunda set in a Greek cross. It had four sizeable rooms, of which the octagonal salon was always the largest, and four tiny cabinets or staircase wells in between. The central rotunda or Salon de Musique is a triumph of mural painting. One appears to be in an open Ionic temple, such as the Temple of Love at the Petit Trianon; between its fluted columns one looks out into the Salon, which in turn looks out on to a miniature *jardin français* with trim lime avenues, a row of statues and a *tapis vert*.

I shall always remember with gratitude and delight the happy hours I spent in this room.

CHAPTER FOUR

Les Hauts de Seine: Meudon to Bougival

✦

A number of excursions can be made from Paris to places which used to be in the country but are now enveloped within the city outskirts. The high wooded hills on the left bank of the Seine, with their sweet air and panoramic views, offered the most attractive sites to builders; and the Hauts de Seine once boasted an almost uninterrupted succession of palaces – Meudon, Bellevue, St Cloud, Rueil, Malmaison, Marly and St Germain. Of these only Malmaison and St Germain survive, but the parks of Meudon and St Cloud are worth visiting, both for their intrinsic beauty and for their historical associations.

Meudon is a magnificent site where the natural contours have been emphasized by massive embankments and steep-cut terraces. At the end of the main avenue used to stand a château, built in 1520, beneath which the **Orangery**, now used for exhibitions, was hollowed out. At right angles to its terrace there is an observatory which incorporates the central pavilion and the whole ground floor of a second château built on the site of the Grotto designed by Primaticcio for the Cardinal of Lorraine in 1552. This juxtaposition of two palatial houses was the result of the purchase of the estate in 1679 from Louvois' widow by the Grand Dauphin, Louis XIV's eldest son.

He was a man devoid of any qualities to justify the title 'Great'. 'As for his character,' wrote Saint-Simon, 'he had none. He was without enlightenment or knowledge of any kind and radically incapable of acquiring any; very idle, without imagination or productiveness; without taste, without discernment, neither seeing the weariness he caused others, nor that he was a ball moving willy-nilly at the impulsion of others.' This unfortunate victim of the Duke's merciless but penetrating perception lived 'absorbed in his fat and his ignorance' at Meudon, where he was capable, the duchesse d'Orléans claimed, of spending the whole day reclining on a sofa tapping his feet with a cane.

The steadily increasing prospect of such an easily manipulated puppet succeeding to the throne drew ambitious men in ever-larger throngs to Meudon; and in 1706 another mansion, the Château Neuf, was built on the terrace above the Grotto to accommodate them. The architect was Mansart; but he was getting old by now – this was his last work; and Louis was impoverished by war. The Château Neuf was not the most distinguished of their buildings. But in the slight arching of the window heads and the curves which the pediments borrow from their lines, the light touch of the eighteenth century is none the less apparent.

Hardly was the building completed when the Grand Dauphin died of smallpox. Louis was beside himself with anguish. Saint-Simon records malevolently how Madame de Maintenon sat alongside him 'and attempted to cry'.

In June 1789, a few days after the summoning of the States General which heralded the Revolution, Meudon was once again the scene of a Dauphin's death, but this time it was the passing not of a middle-aged nonentity but of a pretty little boy of eight whose advent into the world had made all France delirious with joy. An inexorable fate decreed that at the very moment when Louis XVI and Marie-Antoinette were called upon to face the gravest crisis that had ever confronted the monarchy of France they had to face in their domestic life the most heart-rending of all tragedies. Within six years they had drunk the cup of bitterness to the dregs. Two years afterwards Meudon also succumbed to the times. Converted into a munitions factory, the Vieux Château was burnt to the ground.

In 1811 the Château Neuf became the residence of Napoleon's son, the King of Rome. The Emperor had the idea of installing here a 'School for Kings' – mostly of his own family – but it came to nothing. In 1870 the Prussians established a battery here for the bombardment of Paris. In January the following year it was burnt out together with St Cloud.

For those who wish to delve further into its history and resurrect its vanished glories, Meudon offers a small **Museum** at 11 rue des Pierres, recently re-established, thanks to the energy of M. Georges Poisson. We can study here the former châteaux and also the Château de Bellevue, built nearby in 1784 by Gabriel for Madame de Pompadour. Its last occupants were Madame Adelaide and Madame Victoire, unmarried daughters of Louis XV. The château was demolished in 1823. The museum houses souvenirs of the architects Philibert de l'Orme, Mansart and Gabriel, and of course Le Nôtre. Rabelais, who was once curé here, the ubiquitous Rousseau, Redouté – the celebrated painter of roses – and Wagner – who wrote his

Flying Dutchman here – are also represented. The house itself, a charming and well-preserved piece of seventeenth-century architecture, was that inhabited by Armande Béjart, wife of Molière.

On the other side of the valley is the **Villa des Brillants** where Rodin lived, and in the grounds is an annexe to the **Musée Rodin** of Paris. It contains casts of some of the sculptor's most famous works: *Le Penseur,* who mounts guard over his grave; *les Bourgeois de Calais*; *le Baiser* and the model for *la Porte de l'Enfer.*

Meudon is also intimately connected with the development of aeronautics. As early as 1793 the first military aerostation in the world was set up in the Orangerie. The idea of using balloons for military observation became a reality, and in the following year the Compagnie d'Aerostiers was formed. Napoleon, however, dissolved it, and it was not until 1878 that the idea was seriously taken up again, by Capitaine Charles Renard. On the site of his aerostation at Meudon there is today a **Musée de l'Air,** founded in 1919 and the first museum of its kind in the world. There is a fascinating variety of models, many of them originals, and some unique.

They range from the Biot Massia of 1879 – the earliest known working model of a machine designed to make a bird out of a man – to the Potez 53, built in 1933, which is beginning to look like the Spitfire. One of the earliest flying machines to have an engine is the bat-like Vuia of 1906, described as capable of achieving '*des bonds de quelques mètres*'. Three years later the Levavaseur Antoinette was the first to attain an altitude of 1000 metres. It clings to the idea of an airship in its boat-like construction to which the engine is just screwed on. The copying of birds also died hard, for in the German Etrich of 1913 the swept-back wings and fanned-out tail unmistakably recall the silhouette of the kite.

At **Sèvres,** the next station but one along the line from Meudon, the old buildings of the **porcelain manufacture,** where Louis XV and Louis XVI were frequent visitors, can still be seen and, behind the main building, the charming **Pavillon de Lully** where that great musician had his country house. Across the road is the new **Manufacture de Sèvres** which houses a predictably magnificent collection of ceramics.

Stretching away to the north and west of Sèvres lies the **park of St Cloud.** There is not much to attract us here today except the evocation of historical events and the opportunity to walk in this finely wooded park in an area which is becoming increasingly over-developed. The most important feature in the park is the **Grande Cascade,** designed by Le Pautre with additions by Mansart.

Three great ramps, separated by the twin arches of a grotto, descend steeply, following the natural slope of the ground; down these ramps a succession of vases, basins and troughs each receive the water from the one above and toss it up again in a new fountain. This, together with the **Jet de la Grande Gerbe**, which projects a column of water forty metres into the air, are the only significant remains of the waterworks contrived here by Francini during the reign of Louis XIV, when St Cloud was the country residence of the King's brother, the duc d'Orléans.

Near the top of the cascade is a level space marked out with yew trees trimmed to sharply pointed cones. This was the **site of the château**, which was destroyed during the Franco-Prussian war.

Among the persons of distinction entertained at St Cloud during its last period of glory was Queen Victoria, accompanied by Prince Albert and their two eldest children. She was the first reigning English sovereign to visit France since 1431. Her own rooms, mostly decorated with white and gold panelling and ceilings painted to resemble skies, enjoyed the outlook towards Paris 'the view of which is splendid', while her sitting room and drawing room – 'quite lovely' – overlooked the gardens with their cascades and fountains. 'These regular old gardens,' she noted, 'are beautiful and very gay.' On the furniture she is less informative, contenting herself with the remark that it was all 'so charming and so well stuffed, that by lying a little while on the sofa you are completely rested'.

Architecturally the St Cloud that Queen Victoria knew was very much the same as J.-H. Mansart had built it in 1675. It was his third royal commission. At Versailles there is a vast bird's eye of the St Cloud palace, painted by Allegrain with the marvellous exactitude of those seventeenth-century artists who succeeded in visualizing from the air what could only be seen from the ground. It tells us all we need to know about St Cloud.

It was here, on 9 November – the ever-famous 18 Brumaire – 1799, that Napoleon accomplished his *coup d'état*, and established the Consulate. It was here also in July 1830 that Charles X brashly issued the Four Ordinances of St Cloud. Five days later he was forced to abdicate.

Rueil was once the site of a famous château which belonged to Cardinal Richelieu, whose gardens and fountains excited the admiration of their age. But the château has disappeared together with almost every vestige of its gardens.

It might be expected that the church of the parish in which the Cardinal lived would show some signs of his presence; and in fact the west façade of **St Pierre and St Paul**, stuck on to the end of an older building, is by the architect Lemercier, who did so much work for Richelieu. It is dated 1635. The church itself, apart from the transepts which belong to the Geometric period, was built in 1584. It was largely due to Antonio I of Portugal that it was built at all. He was living in exile here after his defeat by the Spaniards in 1580.

It is a remarkable example of the translation of the thirteenth-century formula of construction into a Renaissance idiom. Looking up the nave towards the sanctuary one cannot help being struck by the happy blend of quadripartite vaulting and Ionic pilasters. There is an austere dignity about the tall, round arches of the chancel which sets off to great advantage the rich but sombre lighting of the apse. For, thanks to the coloured glass, the otherwise rather colourless grey stone glows with a mysterious golden light. Once again here the marriage of fluted pilasters and ribbed vaulting is entirely successful.

Turning round at the chancel, the visitor has a surprise in store. Over the entrance doors is one of the finest organ cases in the country. It is more like a gigantic coffer, upon which its huge, ornate entablature lies like a heavy lid. It makes no attempt to adjust its architecture to the grouping of the organ pipes. It is the work of a sixteenth-century Florentine named Baccio d'Agnolo, and was presented to the church in 1863 by Napoleon III.

It was, of course, on account of the proximity of Rueil to Malmaison that Louis Napoleon interested himself in the church, which received considerable repairs at the same time. It was he who inserted the enormous marble memorial to Queen Hortense, his mother, to match the one placed in 1825 in memory of Joséphine.

The church at Rueil was destined, accidentally, to play an important, even a decisive role in the religious life of France. One Sunday, about the year 1800, Napoleon was out in the gardens at Malmaison. 'I was taking a solitary walk there,' he told his friend Thibeaudau, 'when all of a sudden the sound of the Rueil church bells struck my ear. I felt very moved, so great is the influence of our early habits and our education. I thought "what an impression these bells must make on simple, credulous people!" Let your philosophers and your ideologists answer that. The people must have religion.' The following year Napoleon opened negotiations with the Holy See and in due course the Catholic hierarchy was re-established in France.

Malmaison is not a distinguished house architecturally, but its setting is still evocative of gracious living. The gardens are beautifully kept up, and are particularly attractive in tulip time – and again when the roses are in their full glory. For Malmaison was the creation of Joséphine Bonaparte, and Joséphine took her roses seriously. She availed herself of the services of the botanist Ventenat and the rose specialist André du Pont to create a collection of some two hundred and fifty varieties. Redouté, who was also on the staff of Malmaison, has immortalized their efforts in his charming watercolours which form an important part of the decoration of the château today.

It is in fact as a garden – in the wider sense of *jardin anglais* – that we should think of Malmaison. The house was not so much a place to love and live in as a rendezvous from which one could reach the park. The tent-like forms of some of the rooms enhance this *al fresco* feeling. There used to be another, real, tent, covering the bridge which spanned the moat from Napoleon's *cabinet particulier* and connected it with the garden. Here he would often have his writing table placed so that he could enjoy the fresh air which was so necessary to his constitution and his temper. 'When I am in the open air,' he used to say, 'I feel my thoughts take on a new altitude and a new breadth.' It was at Malmaison that Napoleon did most of his thinking. The famous portrait of him by Isabey, in one of the upper rooms of the château, is fortunately documented, for Isabey wrote a journal. 'From morning until evening I watched him walking in the park alone, lost in thought, his hands clasped behind his back . . . he liked my portrait and congratulated me on being able to work without having to ask my model to sit.'

It was here at Malmaison that Napoleon also probably passed the pleasantest moments of his life. 'Nowhere, except perhaps upon the field of battle,' wrote his secretary, Bourienne, 'have I seen Bonaparte more happy than in his gardens at Malmaison.'

These gardens are easily evoked thanks to the painstaking watercolours of Auguste Garnerey, now in the collection of the château. Every variety of scene possible is contrived within their narrow confines – now opening on to the wide vistas of the Hauts de Seine towards Bougival and Marly – now closely embowered by the trees, with temples, grottoes and cascades appearing at each new winding of the way.

Because of the emphasis on its gardens, Malmaison was essentially a *maison d'été*. The rooms are cool and refreshing, and the tall windows, opening on to the shaded walks and alleys, give infinite promise of 'a summer of roses and wine'.

We must not be disappointed, then, to find the house itself a little undistinguished. From the outset, Joséphine had placed her affairs in the hands of two contractors, Percier and Fontaine, who were to play, thanks to her patronage, an important role in the creation of the style *Empire*. But they were never allowed to do anything more than patchwork here. 'We note with regret,' they complained, 'that we are losing the chance of doing something we could be truly proud of, namely, building a residence worthy of the great man whom we serve. We are obliged to restore a badly planned, tumble-down house and make it habitable – a house which had only been built for someone very ordinary.'

But in spite of its name, Malmaison is not a bad house. There is a certain homely charm about its unpretentious façades, upon which the tall, narrow windows confer a note of dignity. Notice also the grouping of the windows on the entrance front: the subtle variation in the spacing nicely saves the whole ensemble from dullness.

The rearrangement of the interior was chiefly a matter of creating more spacious reception rooms. In March of 1800 an order was given 'that the dining room be enlarged and that all the small rooms which precede the bedroom be done away with'. Malmaison was being adapted to larger-scale entertainment such as would be required of the wife of a First Consul.

A few months later came Napoleon's command 'to transform his bedroom on the ground floor into a Council Chamber and to make a library in the adjoining pavilion'. The dining room, council chamber and library are the most important rooms on the ground floor.

The **Dining Room** is a pretty room to which Percier and Fontaine have given a new rhythm by means of the tall, rounded arcade which runs right round the walls and frames the doors and window embrasures; but the rhythm is unfortunately marred by the restless movement of the prancing 'Pompeian' figures painted by Lafitte on each of the panels. The main interest of this room at present is the exhibition of what remains of the great *Surtout de Table* in enamel – 26 pieces only, out of the 1075 originally offered to Napoleon by the City of Paris at his coronation. It is shown in Casanova's painting at Versailles of the banquet at the Tuileries after the wedding of Napoleon and Marie-Louise.

The **Salle du Conseil**, in the form of a tent, was reconstituted in 1972 after the original designs. It is most effective – partly through the originality of its conception and partly through the strong contrasts made possible by the use of black paint. The table in the centre of the room corresponds with that in the designs of Percier and Fontaine, but the chairs are from St Cloud.

The **Library** presented the builders with a problem. A chimney flue from the kitchens below climbed up the wall and could by no means be dispensed with nor repositioned. The only alternative was to conceal it – and this was effected with great ingenuity by Jacob Desmalters, who was to contribute so much to the furnishings and decor of the Empire.

He divided the room into three sections by two Doric screens, in the form of an arch upheld by twin columns on each side. One of these screens, by the skilful use of mirrors, encases the offending flue while appearing, to all but the sharpest eyes, to be open like the others. Napoleon, although he admitted that it would have been difficult to have done better 'with such unpromising premises', complained that the room reminded him of a church vestry. Not many churches have vestries which can stand the comparison.

In 1933, two octogenarians, Monsieur and Madame Jaffé, celebrated their diamond wedding by purchasing Napoleon's collection of books and presenting it to the library at Malmaison.

At the other end of the house are **Joséphine's Apartments**. They are mostly devoted to a collection of furniture and objets d'art which evoke the elegant style of living of the châtelaine of Malmaison, rather than resurrect the original appearance of her rooms. Everything speaks of a minute attention to detail, and it is often in the smallest bibelots that the greatest charm is to be found. Consider, for instance, the *nécessaire de toilette* which stands in her bathroom. This was her travelling dressing-table. Everything is of the most exquisite workmanship; everything beautifully thought out; every need provided for.

It is only in the **Bedroom** that we see anything like the original decor. In 1867, fifty-three years after the death of Joséphine, the Empress Eugénie had this room restored, using a watercolour by Loelliot and the recollections of Queen Hortense to guide her. The hangings are not the original purple cashmere, but the embroideries have been transferred to the new, red cloth. The chairs, from the Tuileries, were said to resemble the originals closely. Only the bed, which was returned in 1868 by the grandson of Eugène de Beauharnais, can be confidently claimed not only as part of the original furniture, but as the actual bed on which Joséphine died on 29 May 1814.

Napoleon was in exile at Elba at the time. Just over a year later, on 26 June, shortly after Waterloo, he revisited Malmaison. The gardens were in the full luxuriance of summer. He must have known that it was the last time he was to see them. Every view, every winding path and every delicate embellishment of architecture recalled the happy days of the Consulate and spoke of Joséphine. 'I keep seeing her,' he told Hortense, 'appearing at the end of one of these walks and picking one of the roses of which she was so fond. She was the most graceful woman I have ever seen.'

In the grounds there is a small **carriage museum** which contains the famous carriage the Opal, which carried Joséphine from the Tuileries to Malmaison when she was finally repudiated by her husband.

Near the carriage museum is the **Pavillon Osiris**, which contains the Napoleonic collection of M. Daniel Iffla, whose pseudonym was Osiris. The collection shows, especially in such articles as snuff boxes, the extraordinary extent to which Napoleon had become a popular institution. It was Osiris who saved Malmaison. In the anti-monarchist, anti-imperialist mood of the late nineteenth century no one cared for this imperial museum and it passed once again into private hands. In 1896, almost by accident, M. Iffla heard of its plight and bought it. In 1904 he generously presented it to the State.

Adjoining the domain of Malmaison is the **Château de Bois Préau**, which forms an adjunct to the museum and houses many interesting souvenirs of Napoleon, the King of Rome and Murat which do not particularly belong to Malmaison.

In 1809 when the owner of the estate, Mlle Julien, died Napoleon wrote to Joséphine from Schönbrunn: 'the house of the old maid is not worth more than 120,000 francs; they will never get more for it'. Joséphine nevertheless paid 200,000 and used the little château to house her doctor, some of her staff and any guests who could not be lodged at Malmaison.

In 1920 the house and grounds were bought by Edward Tuck and his wife Julia. Tuck was American Consul in Paris in 1865 and learned to love France. Returning to America he went into business and amassed a vast fortune. He came back to Paris and soon acquired a great reputation as a collector and a benefactor.

Among the many moving souvenirs of the Emperor is his clock made by Pignenet which stood on his desk at Longwood in St Helena. Its hands still mark the hour of his death.

Continuing along the N13 from Malmaison we come to **Bougival**, which used to be a great centre for oarsmen. At the Hôtel La Grenouillière was held the famous 'Bal des Canotiers, which was patronized by Corot, Sisley and Pissarro and formed the subject of Renoir's painting *Déjeuner des Canotiers à Bougival*.

The **Church of Notre Dame**, founded by Louis VII in the mid-twelfth century, retains its fine Romanesque tower and spire. To this tower the thirteenth century added a nave with aisles, but in so doing suppressed some of the buttresses and thus endangered the fabric with the result that the church had to be heavily restored in the 1870s. Two remarkable twelfth-century capitals have survived at the entrance to the choir. There is a sumptuous seventeenth-century altar with twisted columns and, in the sacristy, a painting of the Last Judgement attributed to Jordaens.

Bougival was the site of the 'Machine de Marly', one of the most successful of Louis XIV's attempts to bring water to the 1400 fountains of Versailles. It was built in 1681 by Arnold de Ville and Rennequin Sualem, both of Liège. Fourteen gigantic water wheels, each eleven metres in diameter, communicated their movement to 221 pumps, which worked in relays up the hillside, thus raising the water to a height of 162 metres above the Seine. It was capable of producing 5000 cubic metres of water in twenty-four hours. The water came out into the Marly Aqueduct, whence it flowed to Marly, Versailles or Trianon as required. It was replaced by a second machine in 1812 which used the water wheels while suppressing the pumps. This in turn was abolished as recently as 1967.

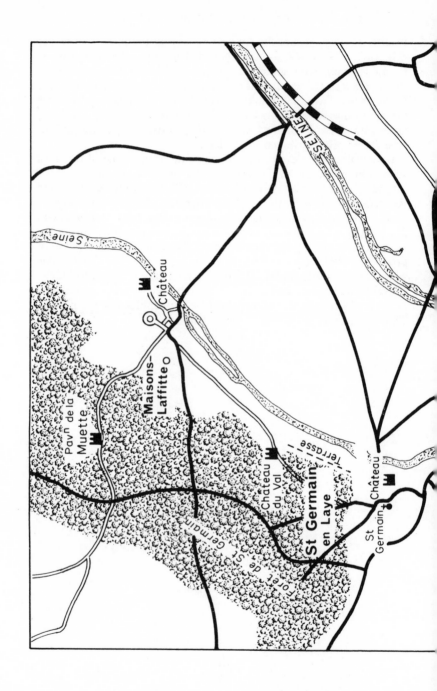

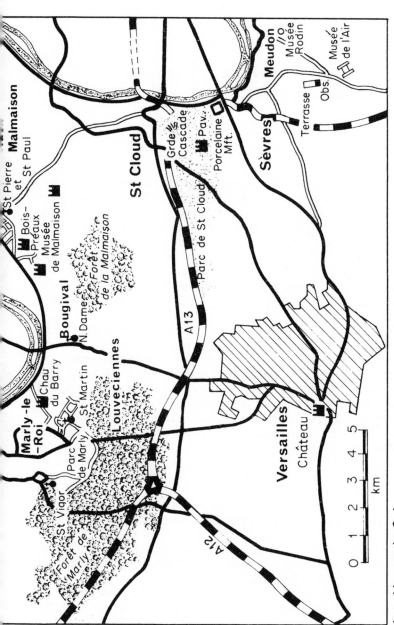

Les Hauts de Seine

CHAPTER FIVE

Les Hauts de Seine:
Louveciennes to Maisons-Laffitte

❧

The **Church of St Martin** at **Louveciennes** dates from the thirteenth
century, though much restored. It is peculiar in that the nave arcades
do not correspond with one another, having three arches on one side
and two on the other. Since there is only a wooden ceiling this did
not pose any insuperable problems of vaulting. The church is chiefly
of interest for two pictures; one is a Crucifixion by Charles Lafosse,
who painted the ceiling of the Salon d'Apollon at Versailles and the
dome of Les Invalides. He also worked at Montagu House in London. The other is the only religious work of Mme Vigée le Brun, a
'portrait' of Ste Geneviève done in 1821.

At the end of the rue de la Machine is the **Pavillon de Mme du
Barry**. In 1769 Louis XV offered the château to his mistress, who
immediately commissioned a young and largely unknown artist
C. N. Ledoux. It was one of the first buildings of the new Greek
revival. The Ionic portico screens a large apse with a bacchanalian
frieze above the door which announces the purpose of the building.
It was essentially a banqueting house; and on 2 September 1771
the countess gave a magnificent dinner here for Louis XV.

Mme du Barry's last lover was the duc de Brissac, who was set
upon by the mob and cut to pieces in front of the Orangerie at
Versailles on his way to prison in Paris. His head was brought
to Louveciennes and hurled into du Barry's sitting room. This
frightful episode was witnessed by André Chénier. Brissac's skull
was later found in the garden and buried by the side of the road
to Prunay.

In December 1793, Mme du Barry, denounced by her Negro page,
Zamore, was sent to the guillotine and died imploring the executioner
for one more minute's grace.

The Pavillon du Barry was originally in the grounds of the
Château of Louveciennes, a house built in about the year 1700 for
Arnold de Ville. His portrait proclaims him as '*Inventeur de la Machine*

Bosquets de Trianon

Petit Trianon: the entrance façade

St Cloud in the seventeenth century: from a painting by Allegrain

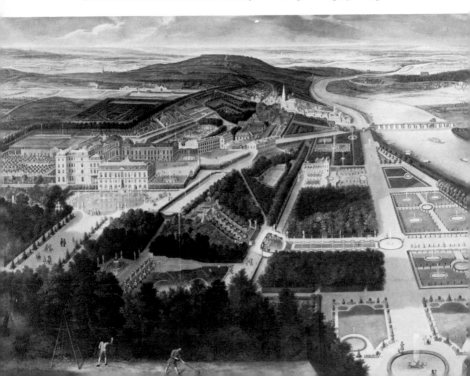

de Marly'. His assistant, Rennequin Sualem, made a more exclusive claim. His epitaph in the church of Bougival asserts that he was 'the only inventor of the Machine de Marly'.

Although there is no building of any importance left, it is still worth a visit to **Marly**. The site of the gardens is unencumbered; the beautiful trees remain, with here and there a statue or the vestiges of some ornamental *pièce d'eau* to stimulate our imagination. The sense of seclusion – a wonderful get-away-from-it-all feeling – still pervades.

And this was the essential quality of Marly. In 1679 when the final enlargements were being made that were to transform Versailles from a royal pleasure ground into the permanent seat of the Government and the Court, Louis realized that he must have somewhere to which he could escape – as he used to escape *to* Versailles when it was still the colourful little *maison de chasse* of Patel's painting. He found at Marly the site for which he was looking. Mansart, Le Brun and Le Nôtre were commissioned to create a royal retreat whither the King might retire with a select number of guests from the crowds that thronged Versailles. In due course the highest hopes of assiduous courtiers were summed up in the customary application for invitation 'Sire, Marly?'

Two nights before a visit to Marly the ladies who attended the King's dinner were more numerous than usual and got up in their most extravagant fashion. They endeavoured to attract the favourable attention of the King in the hope that they would be selected for the forthcoming voyage. This custom was known as '*se présenter pour Marly*'.

The old road from Saint Germain to Versailles, today the N184, climbs up to the Abreuvoir, which received the waters from the garden in a pond for watering horses. The road bends left along the Côte du Coeur Volant until it reaches the Grille Royale which was the main entrance to Marly.

Turning in at these gates, the carriages crossed a circular space flanked by quadrant arcades and began cautiously the steep descent of the Allée Royale. From this moment the château was visible, framed between neat outbuildings and nestling comfortably amid the luxuriant foliage of its surrounding woodland.

The impression created was one of extreme richness. The balustrade, with its figures and vases, was brilliantly gilded, as were the frames of the windows; the bass reliefs which decorated the pediment and the panels above the windows were picked out in gold against a royal blue; the tall pilasters were of red marble, *rouge de Languedoc,*

and the whole rested upon a base of green marble, *vert antique* –
or so it seemed at a distance. In fact all the architectural details were
painted in *trompe l'oeil* upon a flat façade. It was a palace in fresco.

Opposite the chapel and Salle des Gardes, which were the first
buildings reached by the Allée Royale, were two similar pavilions
joined by a wall on which was painted Jacques Rousseau's famous
Perspective. The effect was that of an open peristyle, similar to that
of the Grand Trianon; between its stately rows of columns appeared
two long colonnaded wings and a distant prospect of classical
landscape.

Every detail of the lay-out of Marly as it was in 1714 can be known
from three large folios of drawings in the National Archives. They
suggest a cosiness and an intimacy which it is difficult to recapture
when visiting the site today; the numerous little closed-in bowers
and arbours helped to create that flattering sense of intimacy and
exclusiveness which lent its savour to an invitation to Marly.

The natural formation is that of a steep re-entrant in the shape of
a long horseshoe opening towards the river Seine to the north.
The disposition of the buildings was made to conform with the
natural lie of the land, the King's house, or Pavillon du Soleil,
occupying the focal point of the whole lay-out, and twelve smaller
pavilions for his guests linked by a trellis pergola, lining either arm
of the horseshoe. The low ground in the centre, between the two
lines of pavilions, was cast into terraces and a series of monumental
lakes contrived, following the line of the main axis.

The Pavillon du Soleil was a square block with four identical
façades, each of two storeys contained within a single Corinthian
order and crowned with pediment, balustrade and trophies – not
unlike the west front of Chatsworth.

The high wooded hills gave Marly a pleasing sense of privacy,
and with it intimacy. Here, more than anywhere else, the royal
family was *at home*. Racine, one of the first to be invited here,
remarked: 'It seems to me that the Court here is quite different
from what it is at Versailles'.

At meals much of the formality was dropped. Louis was even
known to discard his royal dignity and throw bread pellets at
the ladies, who had permission to return his fire. His example was
quickly followed. The princesses smoked pipes, composed obscene
verses and indulged in horseplay.

Marly and the Vieux Château at Meudon were the only two royal
palaces to fall victims to the Revolution. Marly was first used as a
barracks, then as a cotton mill. Finally the owner pulled it down to

realize the value of the materials.

The **Church of St Vigor and St Étienne de Marly** is one of J.-H. Mansart's more pedestrian achievements but its contents are interesting. The pulpit, where Bourdaloue was wont to preach, is still there and opposite to it hangs a good Renaissance painting of the Entombment. The high altar comes from one of the earlier chapels at Versailles. There is a picture of Ste Françoise Romaine after Mignard who has given the saint the features of Madame de Maintenon. In the chapelle du Calvaire, behind the sacristy, the cross is mounted on the back of the seat in which Louis XIV sat when he attended Divine service here.

Of all the places in which the French monarchy has made its habitation, the site of **Saint Germain** is without doubt the most beautiful. Backed by an immense stretch of forest and overlooking from a considerable altitude one of the long meanders of the Seine, it commanded a free air and a fine view.

Its name derives from the foundation, in 1020, by Robert the Pious of a convent dedicated to St Germain. In 1124 Louis VI built the first castle on the site. Some of the present foundations may be his, but the earliest actual building which survives is the **Sainte Chapelle**. This recalls the ownership of St Louis. It was built to his orders by the same architect who rebuilt St Denis and not, as has often been asserted, by Pierre de Montreuil. It is one of the real gems of medieval art and it is tragic that it has lost its stained glass. In its structure Gothic architecture has achieved its ultimate aim. There is no longer any question of inserting windows, however big, into the wall space: the whole rectangle between the buttresses is glazed.

But the great glory of St Louis' chapel was the rose window at the west end. This was not only blocked in by François I to make a Salle des Fêtes in the room behind, it was also plastered over. It was not until 1874 that an architect, Eugène Millar, discovered the tracery beneath the plaster and restored the balance, if not the luminosity, of the original design.

It is unfortunate that the Sainte Chapelle should be used as an exhibition space for a number of old fonts, altars and sarcophagi, which are doubtless interesting but which encumber its beautiful lines and volumes.

The next castle to rise upon the site was built by Charles V, but nothing is known of its appearance except the outline of its foundations which still exist. François I did here what he had done at Blois; he superimposed a Renaissance palace upon a medieval foundation, for of the former château he retained only the *donjon* and the chapel. His alterations were begun in 1539 under Pierre de Chambiges; but du Cerceau has something significant to say about the real authorship. The King, he says, 'took such an interest that one could well say that he was the architect'.

The building was one of considerable originality and interest. The use of the *chemin de ronde*, for instance, at ground-floor level instead of in its usual place beneath the parapet, not only provides the convenience of a passageway, but offers a solid base, or podium, from which the façades can rise.

There is great dignity in the tall arches which form the dominant feature of the design, but the brick ornaments to the windows are inadequate. It has to be said also that the corner pavilions do not succeed. They are built merely a little higher than the rest of the façade. The architect has been timid and tentative where he should have been bold. The *donjon* has a full extra storey of height; the pavilions should have had the same.

Unlike François' other houses – Blois, Chambord, Villers-Cotterets – Saint Germain has a flat **roof** which offered the most delightful walk to the inmates of the house. 'This terrace,' noted du Cerceau, 'is, I think, the first of its sort in Europe and a thing worthy to be seen and considered.'

On fine Sundays in the summer the roof may still be visited, and from it there is an incomparable view. It is reached by spiral staircases whose corkscrew vaulting represents a masterpiece of the art of the bricklayer. From the top the narrow walk, hedged between balustrades and tall stone vases, overlooks an immense sweep of the countryside. To the east it is much the same as the view painted by Corot and Bonnington, extending from the wooded slopes of Argenteuil and Louveciennes – to whose skyline Louis XIV added the gigantic balustrade of the Aqueduc de Marly – to Paris, set between the hills of Montmartre and Mont Valérien, and, on a clear day, to the distant towers of St Denis – '*ce doigt silencieux levé vers le ciel*' – last resting place of the kings of France.

In 1557 Henri II invited Philibert de l'Orme to design a new château on the very edge of the escarpment. From his father's building one had to mount on to the rooftops in order to get the view: his own was to enjoy the magnificent panorama directly from its windows and terraces. Philibert de l'Orme's work was not finished by the time of Henri's death, and the Wars of Religion postponed its completion. It was resumed in 1594 for Henri IV by du Cerceau and Jean de Fourcy.

Seen from the old château it formed a complex of low buildings centred on a courtyard which took the shape of a quatrefoil circumscribed within a square. Seen from the river it dominated the colline du Pecq and clothed its slopes with masonry. Two long galleries, each supporting a single storey above, united the small central block to end pavilions which were capped with domes. The westernmost of these is the sole survivor of the Château Neuf, now housing a restaurant known as the **Pavillon Henri IV**. It was originally a chapel and it was here, on 5 September 1638, that Louis XIV was baptized.

Beneath the château, the rest of the slope was cut back into two perpendicular faces, which were contained by walls adorned with arcades and pilasters. Each of these faces was traversed by two enormous ramps. The upper stage of these survives, though it has lost its architectural decor. The lower was cut away to make the present road from le Pecq.

Along these terraces, cut into the hillside from time to time, were the famous grottos. It is unfortunate that none of these extraordinary contrivances has reached us intact from the France of the Renaissance. Their essential feature was the moving figures and changing scenery. Among the many at Saint Germain two were particularly remarkable. One was the Grotte de la Demoiselle qui joue des Orgues. The lady's fingers were activated by water so that she played her organ, producing a music (claims a document of 1644) 'hardly inferior to the best of concerts'.

The other, the Grotte des Flambeaux, required torchlight to penetrate its cavernous recesses. It illuminated a scene like a stage set. This presented at first the sun rising over a calm sea in which marine monsters were swimming. But as the spectator watched, ominous clouds overspread the sky, the sea was lashed to a fury and a terrific thunderstorm broke upon them.

For some years the two châteaux continued side by side. During the Fronde, one night in January 1649, the young Louis XIV and his family escaped from Paris and arrived at Saint Germain. They found the Vieux Château almost unfurnished. Beds were somehow produced for the King and his mother, but the others, even the duchesse d'Orléans, had to sleep on straw. Mlle de Montpensier tells how she and her sister sang themselves to sleep, dossed down on the floor of a room in the Château Neuf 'beautifully painted and gilded, but with hardly any fire and no windows, which is not pleasant in January'. It may have been this humiliating experience which caused Louis to dislike Paris and to make his seat at Saint Germain.

For nearly forty years Saint Germain remained the seat of the Court. The most important creation of this period, which happily survives, is the work of Le Nôtre, who created the great **terrace** – a triumphal road from Saint Germain to the Château du Val – and in 1664 planted five and a half million trees.

But thirteen kilometres away to the south, in the unimpressive Val de Galie, another palace was steadily extending its façades and avenues until it became large enough to receive the whole Court. Saint Germain was already too small for this purpose, and courtiers found themselves lodged '*étrangement à l'étroit*'. In 1682 it was abandoned for the greater glories of Versailles.

Saint Germain remained, however, a royal palace. In 1689 James II of England and his Queen came here to spend their exile.

In the nineteenth century Napoleon III established in the Vieux Château what is now the **Musée des Antiquités Nationales**. It is a magnificent exhibition of the remains left by prehistoric man and of the Gallo-Roman and Merovingian periods, up to Charlemagne. The setting up of this exhibition however destroyed what little was left of the château's original interior decoration.

The **Parish Church of Saint Germain**, built in the form of a Greek temple, was completed in 1829. It is a dark and heavy building, the darkness and heaviness of which is underscored by the lurid modern glass in the ambulatories. But there is something majestic about the shallow crescent of Ionic columns standing shoulder to shoulder in the apse behind the high altar. Opposite to them, over the main doors, is a fine organ case of the early eighteenth century, much restored. In the first bay on the right can be seen a monument to James II of England, marking the spot where his heart is buried. It was thrown out during the Revolution and replaced after the Restoration. The pulpit, said to have been intended for the royal chapel at Versailles, was presented by Louis XIV in 1681.

Until a few years ago the space between the château and the parish church was occupied by the railway station. It was the first in France. On 26 August 1837 the first train completed its journey from Paris to Saint Germain in half an hour.

Much of the **town** of St Germain is old, shabby and undistinguished – and therefore rather attractive. At the north of the town is the **rue d'Alsace**. Standing in the middle of the road between numbers 10 and 11, one would be on the site of the entrance to the Hôtel de Noailles, of which these two houses were the two wings. This was one of the most sumptuous of the private palaces of Saint Germain, built in 1701 by Jules-Hardouin Mansart. Nearer the town centre, at 23 rue du vieil Abreuvoir, is the **Hôtel de Maintenon,** with its tiny window panes and its intricate, elegant wrought-iron balconies. There is a whole world of decaying grandeur about its façade.

Deep in the forest, just off the Conflans – St Honorine road, is **La Muette,** one of Louis XV's many hunting lodges, built in 1776 by Gabriel to replace the ruins of a former lodge of François I.

Continuing along the minor road eastwards from La Muette we come to **Maisons-Laffitte,** an expensive area of villas and verdure, the houses so closely embowered by the trees as to be scarcely visible in summer. But the stately alleys, now intersecting at right angles, now radiating out from some *rond-point*, betray the fact that this residential area has been superimposed upon the lay-out of a noble mansion.

The residential area recalls the name Laffitte, for in 1818 Jacques Laffitte, '*roi des banquiers et banquier des rois*', purchased the domain. Twenty-five years later he made over the Great Park for housing development and pulled down the stables, which almost rivalled those of Chantilly, in order to re-use their materials. The name of Laffitte is thus attached irrevocably to the devastation of Maisons.

In 1900 the last inhabitant of the château, a painter called Tilman Gromme, died. His heirs now offered the château and its gardens to private speculators, who would certainly have completed the work of destruction. But the State intervened and Maisons was saved. That is to say, the shell of architecture was saved. It needs a well-informed imagination to summon up the splendour of the château built in 1643 by René de Longueil, first marquis de Maisons.

The Longueil family enjoyed the best of both worlds. Originally *noblesse d'épée*, it had been represented since the early fifteenth century by a long line of opulent lawyers. These were men with trained minds and cultivated tastes who stood apart from the bickerings of the feudal aristocracy and fished quietly in the troubled waters of the State.

Under Louis XIII, René de Longueil amassed a considerable fortune and sufficiently enlarged his paternal estates to be able to undertake a vast construction. As Superintendent of Finance, Longueil was a predecessor of Fouquet. Maisons stands at the beginning of the sequence which leads by way of Vaux-le-Vicomte to Versailles.

His portrait shows a man with the plump face of the *bon viveur* – of one accustomed to take his pleasures seriously. And yet there is a certain cynical astuteness about his eyes which hints at the secret of his success. He entrusted the building of Maisons to François Mansart. Mansart was a perfectionist, always ready to pull down what he had just built in order to make some improvement. At Maisons he produced a piece of architecture which has been admired throughout the ages. Blondel, the great eighteenth-century architect and critic, considered it to be '*une merveille de notre architecture française*' and admired the 'scholarly way in which he has managed to combine together the three Greek orders'. Maisons remains today essentially a building for the connoisseur.

But today we are not seeing the **Château of Maisons** as it was meant to be seen. It is apt now to appear dull and formal, lacking only a clock in the central pediment to make it an admirable Town Hall. Whereas originally it was set in a maze of parterres at the end of a vast perspective formed by the stable block on the left and an identical building on the right, the château today rises starkly out of the enormous, depressing cavity of its dry moat. The façades also have suffered – as so often – from nineteenth-century plate glass. Only on the south side can we still see a few windows which retain the original glazing bars. If we replace these in the mind's eye, we can picture a rather more pleasing set of façades.

The main entrance is by means of a central **vestibule** which was once enclosed by two magnificent wrought-iron grilles, now in the Louvre. It is a noble piece of architecture to which the sculptor Sarrazin has added the distinction of his bas reliefs over the doors and the eagles at the four corners. The eagle, with its 'long eye', forms a play on the name Longueil. The 'M.B.' of the initials refer to Madeleine de Boulenc, wife of René de Longueil, who claimed to be of the same family as Anne Boleyn.

The vestibule gave access to the main apartments of the château. To the left on the ground floor were those of the master of the house – known as **l'Appartement des Captifs** from the carved overmantel to the main bedroom. This is the work of Gilles Guérin and shows Louis XIII between two crouching prisoners of war. The tall four-poster bed hung with crimson velvet, detailed in the inventory, has long since disappeared and the room provides exhibition space for two Beauvais tapestries of the late seventeenth century which came from Marie-Antoinette's rooms in the Tuileries.

To the right of the vestibule is the Grand Staircase and beyond that the rooms – known as **l'Appartement de la Renommée** – of the marquise de Maisons. It was, however, largely remodelled and redecorated just before the Revolution by Louis XVI's youngest brother, the comte d'Artois, who purchased the house in 1777.

He turned the marchioness's bedroom into his summer dining room. His architect Bélanger, already deeply taken by the classical revival, used as his sculptor Lhuillier, fresh from a study of Herculaneum and Pompeii. They produced together an extremely rich ensemble, proportioned to a Corinthian order, with a fine fireplace, delicate overdoors and niches containing statues of the four months of summer. Owing to the financial straits of the comte d'Artois the stone statues were never executed, but the plaster casts put up instead. They are still there.

The **main staircase**, which connects the ground floor with the state apartments, is one of the greatest achievements of Mansart. He appears to have had a particular appreciation for the naked stone, for the staircase is devoid of colour and almost devoid of ornament until the upper levels of the first floor. Here are groups of winged boys in the fullest relief and the most natural postures, dangling their legs over the cornice as they display the emblems of Science and Art, War and Peace, Music and Singing, Love and Marriage.

The staircase opens into the sumptuous **Salle des Fêtes**, a theatrical conception opening by a proscenium-like arch into the **Salon d'Hercule**, thus magnificently framing its ornate fireplace.

The salon provides the overture to the **King's Apartment**. The King of France enjoyed, by very ancient custom, the right to sleep at the seigneurial house of Maisons and René de Longueil was determined that he should not regret availing himself of that right. Louis XIV claimed this *droit de gîte* in 1671 when his second son, the duc d'Anjou, died at Saint Germain. The King's bedroom was originally known, from its cupola ceiling, as la Chambre à l'Italienne. It was adjoined by another room, circular in plan, with an exquisite inlay floor and lined with mirrors to compensate for its most inadequate fenestration. It was also crowned with a cupola ceiling. These internal domes virtually deprived Maisons of any second storey, which meant that the dormer windows were often merely ornamental.

It also meant that the house, though very large, offered relatively little accommodation. It did not even suffice for Longueil's daughter, Marie-Renée, who had to be lodged in the stable block. It may have been in a sumptuous apartment, for the stables were larger than the château.

One of the few mansard rooms was that occupied by Voltaire who installed himself here in 1723 to write *Marianne*. He nearly died of smallpox but was saved by the Cardinal de Rohan's doctor Gervais who made him drink two hundred pints of lemonade. Eight years later his host, the third marquis de Maisons, died in his arms of the same disease, as the result of the culpable neglect of his physicians. It was one of the heaviest blows Voltaire was to suffer. '*J'ai perdu mon ami, mon soutien, mon père,*' he wrote: an odd title to bestow on a layman some six years his junior.

The château survived the Revolution and was bought by Maréchal Lannes, duc de Montebello, whose widow sold it in 1818 to Laffitte. Laffitte was a liberal and the house soon became the centre of opposition to the newly restored monarchy. By an irony of fate it was in the former residence of the comte d'Artois that the final downfall of Charles X and the Bourbon dynasty was planned.

CHAPTER SIX

The Chevreuse Valley

❧

It would be a good sequel to a visit to Versailles to make one's way further south-west to **Port Royal**. To pass from one to the other is to see both sides of seventeenth-century France. In the one is the apotheosis of worldly power: in the other a deep sense that 'here we have no abiding City'. For, perhaps appropriately, Port Royal has been demolished.

But there was something here which even Louis XIV could not destroy – the atmosphere of peace and privacy which owes much to the natural formation of the ground. There had been an abbey here since the early thirteenth century, built by Robert de Luzarches, but like so many it fell on evil days. In 1603 there were only twelve nuns and their abbess – Angélique Arnauld – a girl of eleven who had been appointed for family reasons. Her sister, aged five, was already Abbess of St Cyr.

Even the most corrupt and indefensible system of appointment, however, may produce felicitous results. Those who had appointed Angélique had unknowingly picked a winner. She developed a real vocation; and at the age of sixteen set about reforming her nunnery. For some years the community was transferred to Paris, during which time a number of men, mostly connected with the Arnauld family, made use of the buildings. When the nuns returned, these men, known as the Solitaires, moved to the farm of Les Granges. Some of the greatest names of the century in literature and art were among them, notably Pascal, Racine and Philippe de Champaigne, whose painting of the Last Supper, now at the Louvre, was once the retable to the abbey church.

Unfortunately the nuns, caught up in the Jansenist movement, became involved in a sixty-year struggle with the Jesuits. Finally in 1710 Louis XIV, under the influence of Madame de Maintenon, who was ruled by the Jesuits, gave orders for the eviction of the nuns and the demolition of the conventual buildings. His orders were that the church should be 'razed to the ground'. By a happy chance, some sixty years previously, they had raised the floor level by a few feet to counteract the damp. In 1844, when the duc de Luynes had the foundations dug up, he found the original floor and the bases of the pillars intact. The tombstones were torn up and for over a century formed the pavement to the nearby church of Magny-les-Hameaux, where they still may be seen ranged round the walls.

The dovecot is the only portion of the conventual buildings of Port Royal to survive intact, but the **Château des Granges**, built in the 1650s to serve as the school run by the Solitaires, has been restored and is now a museum containing among other relics of the Jansenists a model of the abbey as it was and some fine portraits by Philippe de Champaigne.

Besides the learned and the pious, Port Royal attracted some of the upper members of the aristocracy. Two duchesses built their own establishments at its gates – the duchesse de Longueville, sister of the Grand Condé, and the duchesse de Luynes, a niece of the Chancellor Séguier. The latter had had the choice, not untypical of her age, between becoming a nun and becoming a duchess. She chose the second alternative, but one suspects that her little Château of Vaumurier, which she built at Port Royal, bore more resemblance to a convent than to a ducal house.

She was the mother of Charles-Honoré, duc de Chevreuse. Not only was he also deeply religious, but he was endowed, in Saint-Simon's words, with 'plenty of wit . . . with a taste for concentration and an aptitude for work and for all forms of Science'. Through his grandfather's marriage with Marie de Rohan the dukedom of Luynes and Chevreuse had been united and ever since the titles have been borne alternately by father and son. Through this marriage also the **Château de Dampierre**, some five or six kilometres to the south of Port Royal, passed into the possession of the Luynes. In the 1680s this Charles-Honoré pulled down the old Renaissance château and commissioned Mansart and Le Nôtre to design an ensemble more in keeping with the Age of Versailles.

The outcome of their collaboration is one of the most delightful domains in France. The most obvious viewpoint from which to admire it is from the green slope opposite the entrance gates. From the altitude thus gained one can look down into the complex of courtyards and gardens and be conscious of the ground plan as well as the façades. The house has a dignity imposed by its size and a charm derived from its simplicity. For Mansart, while giving it all the grandeur and poise of one of his palaces, has decorated the fronts in the homely local tradition, picking out the string courses and architraves in brick so as to form a grid-like pattern of warm red across the honey-coloured stone of the façades.

An interesting feature of the entrance front is the preservation of the moat and the incorporation of turrets in an otherwise purely classical façade. The tower, in France, was the hallmark of the aristocracy and a status symbol which was abandoned with reluctance.

The distinctive contribution of Le Nôtre is in the satisfying contrast between the trim formality of the gardens, with their tidy paths and regimented waters, against the massed foliage of the richly wooded slopes behind.

If the exterior of Dampierre is still very much as Charles-Honoré left it, the interior reflects, for the most part, the taste of his grandson and successor, Charles-Philippe, duc de Luynes. He was the author of seventeen volumes of Memoirs in which he gives a chronicle of the reign of Louis XV that is as informative, though not nearly so readable, as that provided by Saint-Simon of the Grand Monarque. Together with his wife and his brother, the Cardinal de Luynes, he belonged to the inner circle of friends of Queen Marie-Leczinska, and it was doubtless to provide a setting worthy of her not infrequent visits that the state rooms were redecorated in the white and gold style to which Louis XV has lent his name.

The two communicating salons which occupy the centre of the ground floor afford a perfect example of the style, which is matched by contemporary furniture in a remarkable state of preservation. In the **First Salon** is a portrait of the Cardinal by Van Loo. He was a man of genuine, if simple, piety and of an endearing absence of mind. Van Loo shows us a countenance which is innocent alike of guile and perspicacity.

In the **Queen's Bedroom** which follows, the balustrade has gone – not inappropriately – to serve as an altar rail to the chapel, and there is no bed. But the decoration of the walls and the beautiful overdoors by Boucher remain much as that unhappy Queen must have known them.

The Luynes family was well-liked in the neighbourhood and its members survived the Revolution. After the fall of Robespierre they were allowed to return to Dampierre; since they had not emigrated their huge estates were never confiscated, and remain in the family's possession today.

In the nineteenth century Dampierre experienced a Renaissance. Honoré, duc de Luynes, born in 1802, was one of 'that race of rare men who realized . . . that to be a *grand seigneur* could only mean to be a great citizen'. He achieved a considerable reputation as artist, scientist and antiquarian; and it was he who was entrusted with the classification of the new Egyptian and Greek acquisitions in the Louvre. Inspired by Berthier's *Traité de la Chimie*, he set up a laboratory at Dampierre and began a *Cabinet d'Histoire Naturelle* of the fauna of the Chevreuse Valley.

Dampierre became thus not only his home – '*sa résidence de prédilection*' – but his workshop, and between 1840 and 1843 the house was thoroughly restored by the architect Félix Duban. The one regrettable result of this was the substitution of windows with large panes and narrow glazing bars for the small panes and thick glazing bars of the original windows, such as can still be seen in the office buildings. This has, as so often, upset the balance of the façade.

The adaptation to nineteenth-century use involved certain radical internal rearrangements. Of these the most important was the creation of the vast **Salle de la Minerve** occupying the space immediately above the two salons of the ground floor. It was a bold conception: a high vaulted space in the centre with a narthex at either end crossed by a gallery supported on caryatides. Each of the two side walls was treated as a huge semicircle destined for the great murals ordered from Ingres – *l'Age d'Or* and *l'Age de Fer*. Of these the first was the only one to come anywhere near completion, for Ingres appears to have behaved shabbily towards his noble patron. He obtained the condition that no one should enter the room until he had finished. He then set up his own studio and went on with work for other clients in the Duke's time. When this was discovered he was dismissed and posterity was deprived of what might have been his masterpiece.

Honoré de Luynes was a man comparable in some ways to his great contemporary the duc d'Aumâle. Both were collectors of note and both cut distinguished figures in the world of art and letters. Both also attained to that greatness of character which has been refined by suffering. It was when giving personal assistance to the wounded after the battle of Mentana in October 1867 that Honoré de Luynes caught the illness of which he died. At Dampierre his stricken widow found a retreat in every way qualified to house her grief. The long tradition of piety and charity which centred upon the chapel upheld and comforted her. The château became 'the splendid monument in which she cherished the beloved memory of a husband to whom his widow wished to remain faithful even beyond the tomb. Nothing was changed so that the memory of their father could be kept alive for the children.' Nothing has been changed since.

The valley of **Vaux de Cernay**, south-west of Dampierre, is the most attractive part of this whole area, reminiscent, in its frequent rocky outcrops, of the Forest of Fontainebleau. From the ruins of the abbey the stream follows the contour beneath the wooded slopes until it opens out into a lake created by the monks as a vivarium for fish and waterfowl. From the lake the land falls away steeply, forming a series of cascades down to the Bouillons de Cernay. From here, or from the Moulin des Rochers, there is a delightful walk up to the abbey gates.

Founded in 1118, the **Abbey of Vaux de Cernay** was taken over twenty years later by the Cistercians, who left their unmistakable mark upon its architecture. Ruined on two occasions during the wars of the Middle Ages, it was restored in the sixteenth century when the beautiful Renaissance cloisters were built. Ruined again in the Revolution, it became the property of a vandal called General Christophe, who entertained his friends from time to time by blowing up a portion of the ruins. Later in the nineteenth century it passed into the hands of the Rothschild family, who carefully restored the remains – especially the long double nave of the Monks' Building which is considered the most beautiful in France. It is much to be deplored that the company which owns the abbey at present denies all access to it.

Just to the south of Cernay is the little valley of the Celle in which is the pretty village of **Celle-les-Bordes**. Here is a handsome brick and stone **Gentilhommière** dating from 1610 and belonging to the duc de Brissac. It is chiefly famous for having housed the duchesse d'Uzès, who took it over in 1878 when her husband was killed in a shooting accident. From then almost until her death in 1933 she pursued her passionate enthusiasm for the chase – expressed only too forcibly in the interior decoration of the château, which bristles with no less than 2400 sets of antlers, all taken by her pack, the Équipe de Bonnelles.

The duchesse Anne, as she liked to be called, was a woman of many parts; something of a poet, something of an artist and capable of playing the harmonium for Mass in the little church. She became a local legend to the extent of providing the subject matter for a series of postcards of the 1920s showing the ceremony of St Hubert in the forecourt of the château.

'*Si j'étais Michelin,*' said a small boy after a visit to **Breteuil**, '*je donnerais cinq étoiles au château.*' Michelin, however, fails to mention it. And yet here, in easy reach of Paris, in one of the most beautiful valleys of the Ile de France, is a delightful château set in a beautiful park, with owners dedicated to making a visit to Breteuil an interesting and enjoyable experience for all. It lies north-east of la Celle-les-Bordes, just off the main Chevreuse-Rambouillet road.

The house itself is typical of those built just after the Wars of Religion. The materials are humble and permit no flourish of Italian architecture. They derive their dignity and beauty from the interplay of colours – brick and stone and slate – and from a careful grouping of the blocks, each of different size, each with its own independent roof.

There was considerable alteration and rebuilding in the late nineteenth century, but the original style was respected and it still has the overall appearance of an early-seventeenth-century house. The latest addition was the swift and sudden rebuilding of the single-storey projection on the east side of the courtyard, known as 'Chester Cottage'. The explanation of this name is that King George V decided to send the Prince of Wales – later Edward VIII – to spend four months with the marquis de Breteuil in order to improve his French. He travelled incognito, using the name the Earl of Chester, and when at Breteuil was lodged in this pavilion.

Henri, the eighth marquis, was a close friend of Edward VII and it was here at Breteuil that he organized the meeting between Edward and Gambetta which led to the founding of the *Entente Cordiale*. The event has been reconstructed in a group of wax figures. By this rather original means the present owners have sought to recreate certain scenes in history in which their illustrious family has played a part.

In the **Library** can be seen the figure of Louis XVIII, in the very chair in which he sat, in consultation with Charles, the fifth marquis and the duc de Decazes – an ancestor of the present marquise – who were both members of his government.

More important still is the group showing Louis-Auguste, baron de Breteuil – a cousin of the fourth marquis – presenting the Treaty of Teschen to Louis XVI and Marie-Antoinette. Louis-Auguste was one of the greatest diplomats of his age and this treaty was one of his triumphs. It is commemorated also here by the famous table presented to him by Maria-Theresa on this occasion – 'a chiselled gilt bronze table, the top of which is inlaid with a mosaic of 128 gems and hardstones' made by Johann Christian Neuber at Dresden.

The baron de Breteuil was the man in whom Louis XVI probably placed his fullest confidence. In 1790, when the monarchy was already seriously compromised by the Revolution, Louis gave him authority to do whatever he saw fit at any Court in Europe.

'*J'approuve tout ce que vous ferez pour arriver au but que je me propose.*' The document is exhibited today in the château.

By 1964 the family fortunes had declined and the château had declined with them. It was on the verge of total ruin. It was made over to Henri-François, the present marquis, on his attaining his majority. For years he had felt a passionate love for his family home and could envisage no future without it. In 1967 he married Séverine, a daughter of the duc de Decazes, who quickly identified herself with his love for Breteuil. Their resurrection of the fabric has been described as a miracle. Their love for the building is equalled only by their enthusiasm for the park, which provides an almost natural bird sanctuary. By opening to the public, by the imaginative use of waxwork figures, by letting rooms for private receptions, by giving concerts in the Orangerie – but above all by a constant and meticulous attention to standards, especially in the quality of the guided tours – they have won their way to success – a success crowned in 1975 by the Prince of Liechtenstein with the Medal of Honour for 'threatened masterpieces'. Breteuil – so recently and so gravely threatened – had become, as its owner claims in the title of his book, '*un château pour tous*'.

From Breteuil to **Chevreuse** is a short and pretty drive. The town was fortified at the end of the fourteenth century under Charles VI and again under Henri II. There is a fine old house at 14 rue de Versailles called **la Maison des Bannières** which seems to be late fifteenth-century in date. At 3 rue Lalande was the cabaret du Lys where Racine used to drop in for a drink while helping his uncle supervise the workmen at the château.

The **Château de la Madeleine**, mounted on a high spur above the town, dominates the valley – '*diadème gracieux*' the young Racine described it.

Built in the eleventh century, the keep is a simple rectangular block with tall rectangular buttresses (the sloping ones are modern). This was later surrounded by curtain walls with square towers at irregular intervals. In the fifteenth century two great round towers were added to the north – the vulnerable flank – and these form the most conspicuous features of the ruins today. The north-west tower, with a staircase turret climbing up its inward face, is still complete up to the machicolations. These supported a *chemin de ronde* above which rose a further drum of tower crowned with a pepper-pot roof. The general effect would have been similar to the towers of Pierrefonds.

Round to the west was the main gatehouse, flanked by two low towers which supported a flat platform for the use of artillery.

The whole is built of a curious stone, pitted and pocked like a fossilized sponge, which adds to the impression of extreme and rude antiquity.

From here begins the **Chemin de Racine** which would still form a delightful walk for *'les personnes possédant des qualités sportives'*. Racine, as a young man, lived here with his uncle who, as *Intendant* for the duchesse de Chevreuse, was Governor of the château. In 1661 Racine wrote to his friend Le Vasseur of his life here: 'I pass the time very agreeably. I go to the cabaret two or three times a day; I order about the masons, the glaziers and carpenters . . . I am in the bedroom of a Duke and Peer of the Realm. But I also taste more solid joys. I taste the delights of the solitary life. Except for five or six hours a day, I am quite alone and do not hear the slightest sound.'

His love of solitude accords with his love for his masters the Jansenists, and especially for Monsieur Hamon, *'le plus singulier, le plus pittoresque des Messieurs de Port Royal et aussi le plus poète'*, who walked through life, according to Sainte-Beuve, *'comme dans une forêt enchantée'*, seeing spiritual significance behind each and every object. While he was a pupil here, Racine would walk every day from Chevreuse to St Lambert and then along the valley of the Rhodon where the woods resounded to the bubbling cry of the golden oriole, and thence to Port Royal. In later life he broke with his masters and enjoyed for many years the sweet taste of success as a dramatic poet much appreciated in Court circles. But the early influence reasserted itself. He was reconciled to his master, renounced the secular theatre and when he died, he directed in his will that he should be buried at Port Royal *'au pied de la fossé de M. Hamon'*.

CHAPTER SEVEN

Pontchartrain and the Rambouillet Forest

❧

The obvious route from Paris to Rambouillet is the N10, but a pleasant detour can be made by taking the N12 in the direction of Dreux and seeing the château of Pontchartrain. Another five kilometres along the N12 and we turn south for Montfort l'Amaury, described by Georges Pillement as 'one of the most charming little towns round Paris'. From here we can pass the château of Les Mesnuls before regaining the N10 at St Hubert, or we can take the forest road westwards to Gambaiseul, from which we have a delightful drive by way of St Léger-en-Yvelines to Rambouillet.

To reach the **Château de Pontchartrain** we must take one of the turnings south in the village which converge on its entrance gates. Although a very large house, it has retained throughout that *'belle et noble simplicité'* for which La Bruyère praised it. It is clearly a composite building; the wings and pavilions belong to the early seventeenth century; the entire centre block belongs to the end of that century. The earlier parts are attributed to François Mansart, who is known to have built the Hôtel de la Vrillière in Paris for the same family, the Phélypeaux. It was probably Louis de Phélypeaux, who became Chancellor in 1699, who was responsible for the later rebuildings.

The best known member of the family was Maurepas, one of Louis XV's ministers, who was imprudent enough to write some spiteful verses on the bourgeois origins of Mme de Pompadour. He was exiled to Pontchartrain. It was a long exile, but he was finally recalled to power at the accession of Louis XVI.

In the mid-nineteenth century Pontchartrain acquired a châtelaine of a very different sort, Thérèse Lachmann, a Russian Jewish adventuress who married the Portuguese marquis de Paiva. It was not, however, her husband, but her lover, Count Henckel von Donnersmark, a cousin of Bismarck, who purchased Pontchartrain for her, where she immediately scandalized the country people by dressing like a man.

The house is unfortunately not now open to the public.

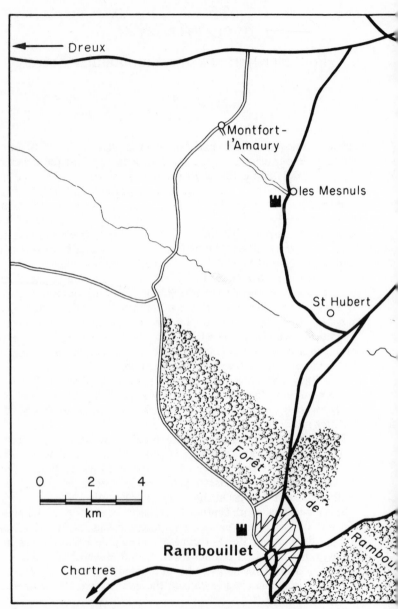

The Chevreuse Valley and Rambouillet Forest

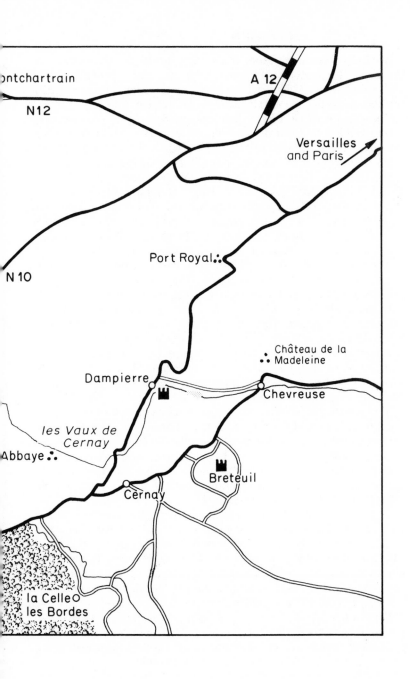

Montfort l'Amaury, more than most towns in this area, has preserved the aspect of antiquity, with its narrow winding streets and cobbled *pavé*. Not many of the houses are architecturally distinguished, but the *tout ensemble* is impressive.

The **Church of St Pierre** does not, at first sight, promise very much; the façade towards the little Place de la Libération is much restored and virtually dates from 1850. Nor is the interior, from an architectural point of view, of much interest. It is an early Renaissance building, started by Anne de Bretagne, but still largely in Gothic idiom. The absence of any triforium is immediately apparent, and the pillars of the nave, which are curvilinear in section, lack any precise profiles – which seems to contribute to the impression of dullness. The aisles, however, are more interesting, with their lierne and tierceron vaulting and their pendant keystones.

The church's supreme attraction is in its really marvellous set of Renaissance stained-glass windows. Almost every aisle window, and many of those in the clerestory of the choir and apse, are filled with glass which is richly colourful in design and rather crude in execution – one feels that they are the work of some provincial artist. The scenes are chiefly from the life of Christ and the characters, apart from one or two clumsy attempts at Roman uniform, are in contemporary costume. With a fine disregard for anachronism St Louis, who died in 1270, is portrayed wearing the Order of St Michael, which was created in 1469.

The south façade has a superb Renaissance **doorway** which incorporates busts of André de Foix, Châtelain of Montfort, and his wife Catherine du Bouchet, whose benefactions to the church made possible the sixteenth-century additions and reconstructions and possibly paid for the windows also. Near this doorway, on the south front, is an inscription dating from the Revolution: '*Respect au Temple de la Raison*'.

Not very far to the north of the church is the **cemetery** with a magnificent cloister surrounding it on three sides and housing two Chapels of Ease. The south range was built in 1598; the other two galleries were added in 1607. An impressive open timber roof covers the whole. There is a beautifully carved Flamboyant doorway in the south gable, but the tracery infilling of the tympanum represents what passed for Flamboyant in the days of Louis-Philippe.

People lived close to death in those days. Today we tend to try to forget about it; but in the past people were continually reminding themselves of its imminent possibility. The inscription in the cloister is by no means an uncommon one:

Vous qui ici passez
Priez Dieu pour les Trespassés
Ce que êtes, ils ont été;
Ce que sont, un jour serez.

There are several old or historic houses in Montfort, including a **fifteenth-century prison** at number 5 rue de Paris; the old **Hôtellerie des Trois Chandeliers,** where Henri IV is said to have slept, at number 6 rue Pétau-de-Maulette; and the **Ravel Museum** in the house called *Le Belvédère* where Ravel lived and composed much of his music. Finally there is the **Maison Valry,** a sixteenth-century house in the rue de la Traille, where Victor Hugo often used to stay.

Victor Hugo was obviously much taken by Montfort l'Amaury. In an Ode written in 1825 he describes the château, comparing its two remaining towers to 'two black giants prepared for combat'. The château was already in ruins by the nineteenth century, and in 1842 many of the walls were in a dangerous condition and were pulled down.

By reason of its situation Montfort had been a most considerable fortress and the comte de Montfort was traditionally among the most powerful overlords in France. He owned in addition the fortresses of Houdan, Montchauvet, Beynes, Gambais, Épernon, Bretoncourt, and Rochefort. One of the most famous members of the family was the Simon de Montfort who as leader of the opposition to Henry III was the chief founder of the English Parliament.

Between Montfort l'Amaury and Rambouillet is the **Château des Mesnuls,** one of the many great houses of France which are situated obligingly by the side of the road and may thus be admired even if they cannot be visited.

The beautiful wrought-iron gate which stands before the château is itself historic. Originally a part of Louis XV's hunting lodge at St Hubert, it was purchased for Les Mesnuls in 1791 where it graced the forecourt until the German occupation in 1940. Admiral Doenitz made Les Mesnuls his headquarters and had the grille removed. Its recovery and replacement after the Liberation acquired a symbolic importance: in the eyes of the local inhabitants *La France Éternelle* had been reinstated.

The château was to play its part in the rehabilitation of France after the war. Its owner, a Rumanian banker named Chrissoveloni, had disappeared into the prisons of eastern Europe. The house was used by the baronne de Mallet as a home for the mutilated

87

orphans who had been left stranded by the tide of war.

The house had known a long and varied history. The oldest portions are the gatehouse towards the town, built by Christophe du Refuge between 1535 and 1571, the left wing of the cour d'honneur and the left half of the main façade, which date from the same period. The façade is saved from dullness only by the extraordinary variety in the brickwork. The rest of the building was added by Achille Courtin, a successful diplomat of Louis XIII who was the first comte des Mesnuls.

Later in the century the château passed through his grand-daughter to the Maréchal de Villars, owner also of Vaux-le-Vicomte. If the victor of Denain showed a greater inclination for Les Mesnuls than for the palatial splendour of Vaux it was probably on account of a village maiden named Choucette who was lodged here in a mezzanine.

Rambouillet is in many ways the oddest of the royal residences. On arrival one is immediately struck by the immense size of the Communs – elegant but undistinguished – and by the smallness of the château, which is undistinguished without being elegant. It is quite a surprise to find within these plain façades a suite of state apartments perfectly proportioned and exquisitely decorated with carved panelling as good as the best work at Versailles.

The reason is, of course, that Rambouillet was never meant for long periods of residence by the Court. It was the forest, not the château, which formed the principal attraction. Stabling for over a hundred saddle horses was the most important requisite. So the comparatively little château was provided with offices big enough for a palace, so long that they were known as 'the Corridor', and so remote that they had to be connected by an underground passage with the royal lodgings.

The estate had belonged, since 1384, to the d'Angennes family. In 1556 it was modernized by a local architect called Ymbert. The summer dining room – a deliciously cool room in red and grey marble – dates from this period.

Charles d'Angennes, who succeeded to the estate in 1611, became the first marquis de Rambouillet. He is more famous for his wife Catherine whose Salon Bleu in their Parisian Hôtel became the centre of a new movement to banish coarseness from the Court of France and to replace it with delicacy and refinement. It was no doubt a necessary reform, but the path could lead to any number of absurdities as Molière demonstrated in his *Précieuses Ridicules*.

In 1700 the estate was purchased by Fleurian, Seigneur d'Armenonville, who began at once to lay out the grounds with the assistance of Le Nôtre. The success was so immediate that the comte de Toulouse, son of Louis XIV and Madame de Montespan, cast covetous eyes on the house and purchased it from d'Armenonville.

The comte de Toulouse was in some respects very odd. He never took his royalty seriously; and when he died in 1737 he stipulated in his will that he should be buried 'like a pauper' at Rambouillet.

His son, the duc de Penthièvre, was one of the few shining lights of virtue in the Court of Louis XV. He devoted one fifth of his immense wealth to the poor, and could be found at his château in cap and apron preparing them an evening meal. His reputation secured his safety during the Revolution up till his death in 1793.

He did not transmit his virtues to his son, the prince de Lamballe, who died at the age of twenty worn out by debauchery. He left a young and charming widow who was to be Marie-Antoinette's companion in suffering until she was butchered during the September massacres.

It was for the princesse de Lamballe that the **Jardin Anglais** was begun. In contrast to the rectilinear formality of the canals and islands south of the château, the area to the south-west of these was recast as a 'natural' landscape of winding rivulets and architectural absurdities. Of these only the **Chaumière des Coquillages** survives. It is what its name implies: externally a cottage, but a cottage which contains a room entirely encrusted with a fantastic variety of sea shells which took ten years to complete. Next to this is an exquisite little **Boudoir**, painted with birds and flowers. Here was another exotic fancy; two little cupboards open and on opening activate two little automatons, originally figures of Negroes, who offered powder and perfume to the ladies.

In 1783 Louis XVI, who coveted the hunting facilities of the forest, bought Rambouillet from the duc de Penthièvre. Marie-Antoinette was not pleased with their new acquisition. 'What am I supposed to do,' she enquired, 'in this Gothic toad hole?'

It is true that the entrance court at that time was of an extremely unprepossessing appearance. A drawing by Rigaud shows a narrow, prison-like yard enclosed by high buildings on either side. The right wing ended in the embattled keep where François I had died; the left wing led to the twin towers of a gatehouse through which one penetrated the court. At the end of this dismal architectural perspective was a façade of only five windows which constituted the entrance front.

The interior, however, more than compensated for the deficiencies of the façades: the state apartments created for the comte de Toulouse are among the finest in France.

The first room, called the **Salle du Méridien**, is of an irregular shape caused by the obtuse angle between the south-west and west façades. It was used as a dining room and commands a magnificent view right down the Grand Canal to the end of the *Tapis Vert*. To the right of this window it opens into a circular **Oratory** contrived by the duc de Penthièvre in the corner tower. Its present decoration, with grey and off-white panelling, dates from 1810 when Trepsat remodelled it for the Empress Marie-Louise. In the next two rooms the panelling was originally in white and gold, but Napoleon III had it stripped down to the bare wood – one of the rare occasions when a nineteenth-century alteration effected what must be regarded as an improvement upon the taste of the eighteenth century. The carvings are of a quite remarkable finesse and are seen at their best advantage in the naked wood. They are mostly the work of Verberkt and can compare favourably with the best of his work at Versailles.

The **Salle du Conseil** has a fine Gobelin tapestry representing Susannah before her Judges. The next room, the **Grand Salon**, contains a remarkable set of chairs upholstered in Beauvais tapestry illustrating the fables of La Fontaine. Among the lovely carved panels of the four seasons can be seen the monogram of the comtesse de Toulouse, Marie-Sophie-Victoire, daughter of the duc de Noailles and great-niece of Madame de Maintenon.

The three little rooms which follow were those accorded to Marie-Antoinette. They hardly come within her term '*gothique crapaudière*'. The end room, her **Boudoir**, was never painted or gilded and the almost lace-like carvings on the oak panels are just as Verberkt left them.

The double glazing throughout this suite was added by Napoleon. His capital N on the handles escaped the fanatical removal of all N's and B's ordered by the royalist comte de Nogent, who became Mayor of Rambouillet the moment the Bourbons returned in 1814.

The only room completely done for the Emperor was his **Bathroom**, which is next in the suite returning on the courtyard side of the wing. It is a rather staccato decoration of Pompeian arabesques and roundels in which are painted some of the many great houses associated with Napoleon. The very small bath is a reminder of that great man's diminutive physical stature.

The next room, in no way distinguished today, was the room in which he slept before leaving for St Helena.

The exterior of the château is too undistinguished to merit much attention. Its final form is largely due to Napoleon's architect Trepsat, who demolished the west wing and rebuilt the entrance front.

But one can look through the ground-floor window of the last room on the west front into the **Bathroom of the comte de Toulouse**. It is entirely tiled with Delft porcelain and incorporates two magnificent panels, each with a vase of flowers surrounded by birds, which are the only known remains of the Trianon de Porcelaine. As this was specially built for Madame de Montespan, mother of the comte de Toulouse, it is wholly appropriate that they should have found their last resting place at Rambouillet.

The cult of the exquisite garden pavilion was one of the great architectural successes of the eighteenth century. One of the last to be built in France under the *Ancien Régime* was the **Queen's Dairy** here at Rambouillet. In 1785 the architect Thevenin began this elegant little structure at a point immediately west of the area enclosed by the formal canals south of the château. It stands at the end of a short avenue approached between two pepperbox lodges, the left hand of which served as a Pavillon de Chasse and was decorated in *trompe l'oeil* by the same Sauvage who did so much delightful work at Compiègne.

The Dairy is a severely classical temple which one might well take for a mausoleum. The first room, in the form of a rotunda, has a marble slab on which the Queen made her cheeses in a series of containers made of Sèvres porcelain. One of these containers still survives at Sèvres. The next room, known as the **Salle de Rafraîchissement**, is conceived as a grotto with little fountains to cool the milk churns and a rocky niche to house the statue by Pierre Julien entitled *La Chevrière*.

While Marie-Antoinette was playing at milkmaids in the Dairy, Louis was occupied in serious stock-breeding in the nearby **Sheepcote**. Wishing to import sheep for the production of fine wool, he purchased a flock of Merinos, forty-two rams and three hundred and thirty-four ewes, from Spain. They were driven up by their own shepherds – a journey which took 119 days. Their descendants can still be seen, and the Merinos of Rambouillet are still famous.

In August 1788 Louis XVI was here for the last time. The following year, during the fateful night of 5 October when the mob was besieging Versailles, it was suggested that the royal family should retreat to Rambouillet. But Louis was pathologically incapable of making decisions and the move was never made.

His brother, Charles X, however, retreated here from St Cloud on 31 July 1830. On 2 August Charles abdicated in favour of his grandson, the duc de Bordeaux. News that the Crown Jewels – regarded as the property of the nation – had disappeared excited new upheavals in Paris and troops were ordered to advance on Rambouillet; every hackney carriage, diligence and omnibus was put into requisition to get them there. The immense, unofficial army arrived and the ex-King had no choice but to yield the jewels back to the people. Late at night on 3 August he left with three unarmed men for Maintenon.

CHAPTER EIGHT

Anet and the Vesgre Valley

✦

Houdan is on the N12 some forty kilometres west of Versailles. It is an attractive and interesting little town with an early twelfth-century keep, some well-preserved timbered houses and a fine church. The **keep** is a little to the west of the church in the rue des Fossés. It is now a water tower and can only be seen from the exterior. It is chiefly interesting for its shape: a cylinder with four projecting towers. This marks an important turning point in the history of fortification. The Norman keep was based on the principle of passive resistance. The walls became thicker, the entrances higher and the internal staircases narrower and more baffling to the attacker, but no attempt was made to provide for covering fire.

Houdan is thought to be the first to attempt to remedy this deficiency, but it did not succeed. The towers do not project far enough for the occupants to see round the bulge of the cylindrical wall. They are also without apertures and therefore offered opportunities of firing only from the topmost parapet.

It is known that Geoffrey Plantagenet had read Vegetius on fortification: it is probable that Amaury de Montfort, the builder of Houdan, had read Vitruvius, but he never quite understood covering fire.

There are four timbered houses of the fifteenth or sixteenth century in the rue de Paris and three more in the rue Docteur-Genret. **Number 66 rue de Paris** is a particularly fine example of what the French call a '*maison à colombages*', so named because of the upright beams.

In the little square in the middle of the town is the imposing **Church of St Jacques and St Christophe**, begun in the late Gothic period and continued throughout the late sixteenth and early seventeenth centuries. We know that important work was in hand in 1517, for in that year the Vicar General of Chartres granted indulgences to all who contributed to the fabric fund. It might be inferred that the sale was not as brisk as was hoped, the sinners of Houdan being either too impenitent or too impecunious, for the building clearly did not progress. The two transepts were meant to terminate in twin towers, neither of which was completed; and the west front also shows signs of having grown slowly. It begins ornately Flamboyant, but, as the façade rises higher, becomes more and more Renaissance in style.

The east end had to wait until the reign of Henri II. The apse is a magnificent example of a Gothic structure built in Renaissance forms. The buttresses have become a ring of correctly proportioned Doric pillars carrying piles – rather like ornate chimney stacks – which receive the thrust from the flying buttresses. The tracery of the windows is entirely in the rounded shapes dear to the Renaissance builder, but retains the love of variety typical of the medieval period.

The interior is magnificent. There are three splendid windows full of Flamboyant tracery on the north wall of the nave, but it is the view from the west end, looking right up the nave, choir and apse which offers the most impressive *coup d'oeil*. The clean white stone makes the high vault stand out like a bleached skeleton, for, owing to the paucity of stained glass here, the church is essentially colourless.

Beyond the crossing the Renaissance takes over. The date 1545 is to be found on the first pillar of the choir on the south side – only four years before the wholly revolutionary chapel at Anet. Only in the roofing does the medieval style survive, culminating in the complex star vault of the apse with its pendants, like swarms of bees, hanging from the intersection of the ribs. The date 1633 is marked on the central boss over the high altar. The vast baroque retable, dated 1672, not only obscures the elegant architecture of the apse but blocks out most of the light as well.

In the last chapel on the north side before the ambulatory is a large mural painting dated 1582 showing pilgrims of the Confrérie Notre Dame de Montferrat in Catalonia.

The furnishing of the church is good, especially the pulpit (1744), the lectern (1747), and the organ case over the west door. This was built in 1734 by Louis-Alexandre Clicquot, son of the more famous Robert Clicquot who built the organ in the chapel at Versailles. The woodwork of the case was done by a local craftsman named Robert Lisant.

North of Houdan, on the N183, is **Richebourg** – an undistinguished village with a most distinguished little church. In the first place the church has an unusual ground plan: a short and simple nave opens into a large double transept of lovely Flamboyant design, which in turn opens into a choir with two aisles and a central apse. This arrangement is clearly articulated on the exterior in the separate roofing of each of the component parts.

The tower is also impressive, with the five little spikes growing out of its pyramidal roof and the staircase turret climbing some two thirds of the way up with its own beautifully tiled *poivrière*.

The church is obviously built of a high quality stone, for the external carving is as crisp in its detail as if it had come fresh from the mason's chisel. The huge gargoyles and richly carved band of foliage under the eaves confer a peculiar distinction upon the south façades.

Inside there is some good sixteenth-century glass, a fifteenth-century Virgin – '*la Madone de Richebourg*' – and some fine woodwork of the eighteenth century, including the high altar and two little credence tables.

At Berchères-sur-Vesgres is the **Château de Herces** – a large square block of late Louis XV style designed by Jacques-Denis Antoine, architect also of the Hôtel des Monnaies in Paris.

The building, in fact, offers an interesting study in the transition from the typical Louis XV of Gabriel, represented by the north façade, to the more classical south front with its attached portico of fluted Ionic columns surmounted by a large, but perfectly plain, segmental pediment. Each façade is distinct in its design, so that in elevation each might belong to a different house. The greatest contrast is between the east front, with its square *dôme à l'impériale* and attached porch, and the west front which is unexpectedly recessed and almost devoid of ornament.

Just to the north of the Forêt de Dreux and standing a little back from one of the meanders of the river Eure is the **Château d'Anet**, once the most important non-royal château in the Ile de France, on account of both its distinguished architecture and its connection with Diane de Poitiers, duchesse de Valentinois, the all-powerful mistress of Henri II.

The nature of her power is not easy to understand. Brantôme, writing after her fall – and therefore with no interest in flattery – could state: 'I have seen the duchesse de Valentinois at the age of seventy as fresh and lovely as at the age of thirty'. She did not, in fact, live to be seventy, so he is guilty of inaccuracy in one respect. But François Clouet has left a very different picture – and all would agree that he was a most faithful draughtsman. He shows us a face as devoid of beauty as it is destitute of character: narrow, vacant eyes; a mean little mouth with a receding jaw; a double chin and far too thick a neck. In order to have won and retained the affections of a boy young enough to be her son she must have had intelligence and charm, but behind this charm there lurked a cold and calculating tenacity in the pursuit of her own material advantage, and she managed her ever-growing estates with a vigilant and stringent economy.

She was the widow of Louis de Brézé, Grand Seneschal of Normandy, and from him she had inherited Anet. On Henri's succession she lost no time in transforming it into one of the most magnificent houses in France.

Although three-quarters of the château have been pulled down, the first sight of Anet can still be an exciting experience. The most dramatic approach is by the N828 from the north-east. The road turns a sudden right angle and there is the whole entrance front in enfilade – a vast array of buildings of different sizes, the more important and imposing of them built in the finest freestone, but with a mixture of very pretty brick in the more menial structures.

Seen in elevation, the central gatehouse commands our immediate attention and respect. Here is a building designed by someone with a real sense of artistic composition. He is clearly a scholar of the antique, for the two wicket gates are framed in a Doric order correct in every detail. But he makes no attempt to copy any classical model; it is a thoroughly original design. The four corners are marked by tall chimney stacks, each in the form of a catafalque raised on a high pedestal. This is a recurrent theme at Anet and expresses the extravagant mourning for Louis de Brézé which his widow always affected.

Over the central arch is a recumbent female figure, a cast of Cellini's famous *Nymphe d'Anet*, now in the Louvre. The whole gatehouse soars to its climax in the high clock tower crowned with the figure of a stag at bay between two hounds. This group is a nineteenth-century reconstruction of the original, which was geared to the mechanism of the clock so that at each chime the dogs barked and the stag stamped out the number of the hour.

The architect was Philibert de l'Orme. While possessing a profound knowledge of proportion and the use of the classical orders, he was more ready to depart from these principles than a lesser man might have been. In his lengthy treatise on architecture he explicitly states that it would be better to be guilty of some error in the rules of proportion than 'in those excellent rules of Nature which concern the commodity, convenience and benefit of the inhabitants'.

His concern for commodity expressed itself at Anet in various ways. Whereas all the rooms of the first floor intercommunicated, they were some of them provided with private staircases which

Rambouillet: the Chaumière
des Coquillages

Château de Breteuil: the
entrance front

Dampierre: enfilade of the State Rooms

gave them a measure of independence unusual at that time. Indoors, a perfect symmetry often resulted in the windows on both sides of a big room being exactly opposite to each other. This caused, as he said, 'darkness and shadow' in the intervals between them, 'which casts a melancholy air over the rooms'. To remedy this defect Philibert de l'Orme often staggered the windows, as he has done in some of the main rooms at Anet.

The finished building occupied three sides of a quadrangle, the fourth being closed by the monumental gateway. The façades were of a noble simplicity against which the elaborate central feature of the main façade stood out by contrast. Here de l'Orme accentuated the focal point of his design by means of a tall portico of three superimposed orders which thus rose a full storey above the façade. The portico may still be seen in the courtyard of the École des Beaux Arts in Paris. The orders are applied correctly and according to reason. They may be said to represent simplicity in the Doric, elegance in the Ionic, and enrichment in the Corinthian. So the ground floor, for everyday usage, is proportioned to the Doric, the first floor, for the State Apartments, to the Ionic, and the topmost storey – a purely ornamental feature which framed in its archway a statue of Louis de Brézé – to the Corinthian.

In the seventeenth century the duc de Vendôme made his own entrance in the **west wing**. This entailed the new frontispiece with coupled Ionic pilasters on the façade and the large and lovely staircase hall within, designed by Desgots.

The other side of this wing, which faces the gardens, although truncated, has retained the original dispositions of Philibert de l'Orme. It will be noticed that the windows are not regularly spaced but arranged in groups. This not only served the 'commodity' of his internal arrangements, but saves the façade from monotony.

The corresponding wing on the east side of the cour d'honneur has disappeared except for the **Chapel**, which was originally a projection from it. The western façade of the chapel was therefore a part of the interior decoration of the galleries in front of it, and only received its present form in 1844 from the architect Caristie.

It is from the east that the chapel is best appreciated. From here it can be clearly seen that there is a central core which is cylindrical in shape and covered by a dome and cupola and from which there project three chapels with curved façades. A ground plan would show that these façades are all arcs of the same circle, so that the central core is inscribed in an outer, but incomplete, circle; the interstices towards the east are filled by two square sacristies.

In this de l'Orme shows himself a true follower of the Italian Renaissance. Himself a contemporary of Palladio, he drew his inspiration from the same sources – Alberti and Bramante. These would both have agreed that the circle was the perfect shape and white the appropriate colour for a church. Palladio wrote of the circle: 'it is enclosed by one circumference only, in which is to be found neither beginning nor end . . . its parts correspond to each other and all of them participate in the shape of the whole; and moreover every part being equally distant from the centre such a building demonstrates extremely well the unity, the infinite essence, the uniformity and justice of God'.

The interior of the chapel is of a chaste and almost puritanical beauty, of a lovely white stone, '*la belle pierre blanche de Vernon*', with the main lines of the architecture delicately pencilled in with a fine black marble inlay. The low relief figures in the spandrels and in the vaults of the window embrasures are generally accepted as being the work of Jean Goujon and add a gentle enrichment to the theme. But it is the dome, a network of coffers, diminishing in size as they spiral up towards the opening beneath the cupola, which is the supreme glory of the chapel. Its pattern is reflected two-dimensionally in the marble inlay of the floor. It is a deeply – some would say coldly – intellectual approach to religious architecture.

There is another chapel at Anet to the west of the château which is the **Mausoleum of Diane**. It was built immediately after her death in 1566 by Claude de Foucques. The tomb of Diane, saved by Alexandre Lenoir at the time of the Revolution, has been pieced together again in recent years. It is ascribed to Pierre Bontemps. Either side of the door, two statues by Gougeon – not to be confused with Goujon – represent Faith and Charity, two causes to which Diane, like many royal mistresses, devoted the years of her retirement.

The only other vestige of the original château is the **Cryptoportico** – a vaulted undercroft to the central block which opened on to the vast enclosed gardens to the north. The galleries which surrounded and protected this garden were demolished by the duc de Vendôme.

Louis-Joseph de Vendôme was the great-grandson of Henri IV and Gabrielle d'Estrées. Cynical, arrogant, gluttonous and homosexual, he was a man to whom posterity is reluctant to attribute a single virtue; 'filthy in the extreme', wrote Saint-Simon, 'and proud of it'. When not on campaign he held court at Anet where he and his brother 'lived in open debauchery'.

The duc de Vendôme added the tall arched screen known as the

Hemicycle between two new pavilions to link the château with the governor's house. It was in the courtyard thus enclosed that the Fontaine de Diane, by Jean Goujon, used to stand. It was taken by Lenoir to the Louvre where it can still be seen. Contrary to popular belief the Diana is not a likeness of the duchesse de Valentinois.

From the House of Vendôme, Anet passed through the female line to the duc du Maine; and its fortunes were linked from then on with those of Sceaux. Thus it passed to its last owner before the Revolution, the duc de Penthièvre, who died here in 1793. Considering that this was the year of the Reign of Terror, his obituary is somewhat remarkable. 'Citizen Penthièvre is dead,' it ran; 'History will relate that he was a Prince, that he was born near the throne, that he lived peacefully in obedience to the law when the Monarchy was overthrown. But the voice of the poor will penetrate across the ages to proclaim him the Father of the Needy.'

Diane de Poitiers, Vendôme, Penthièvre – a rapacious mistress, a filthy bastard and a saintly duke: these have been the principal owners of Anet.

In the Revolution the château was sold, and passed into the hands of a speculator called Demonti who proceeded to pull the buildings down and sell the materials; but in 1811 the death of one of the workmen who fell from the ruins caused an outbreak of local indignation and the destruction was arrested. For twenty years the west wing, with its gaping wound towards the north, stood empty and desolate. It was not until 1841 that the comte de Caraman began the first campaign of reconstruction. He restored the gatehouse; he secured the fabric of the now isolated chapel and provided it with a façade and portico.

In 1860 a more important reconstruction was undertaken by M. Moreau who set about the redecoration and refurnishing of the surviving wing in its original style. He must have the credit for a considerable amount of success.

In the **Salon Rouge**, to the north of the staircase hall, the ceiling could be reconstructed from the old designs. Some of the original doors had survived – now at the École des Beaux Arts – and could be copied, as for instance in the **Library**. Here, too, are assembled fragments of the original *grisailles* windows, mostly thrown out by Vendôme.

Upstairs in the huge **Salle des Gardes** the magnificent tapestries, rare survivals of the workshops of Fontainebleau, were specially woven for Diane de Poitiers and very probably for Anet. The pediments of the doors are carved to the original designs of Philibert de l'Orme for the Orangery.

Finally in the **Chambre d'Honneur** at the end of the wing, where the central panel of the ceiling comes from that of the demolished gallery, there is a splendid four-poster bed known as the **lit de Diane** which was recovered from a hotel in the town of Anet. It is undoubtedly part of the original furnishing of the château and remarkable in still possessing its original hangings and counterpane. From its size and richness it must have come from one of the main bedrooms, and was possibly the bed slept in by Diane de Poitiers.

The **Church of St Cyr and Ste Juliette** at the other end of the town is worth a visit also. It was largely built at the expense of Diane de Poitiers, between 1547 and 1581 – the last date marked on the keystone of the unfinished bay of the north transept. The exterior is frankly Flamboyant with a good west portal, but the interior is in Gothic translated into Renaissance with the rather unusual feature of sexpartite vaulting. Otherwise the formula is that of the late Gothic, when it was common to omit the clerestory at a great sacrifice of light to the interior. The furnishing of the church is good. The retable, dated 1642, was made by a mason from Nancy called Claude Mahieur. The churchwarden's seat is from the eighteenth century and unusually ornate. But it is the pulpit which is the special glory of the church. It dates from 1678 and was the direct result of a legacy from François Loret, concierge of the château.

On the southern fringe of the Forêt de Dreux is the **Château d'Abondant**, an attractive, if severe, example of the Louis XIII style with the brick decorations to the façade which were so common at that time. It was enlarged and redecorated in the early eighteenth century and has some extremely fine panelling and furniture in the voluptuous style of the *Régence*. At the end of the nineteenth century it was sold by the comtesse Lafond to M. Harjes who completely renovated the interior and laid out formal gardens to the design of André Duchesne, who worked for the Duke of Marlborough at Blenheim.

The most distinguished person to inhabit Abondant was the duchesse de Tourzel. In the second half of the eighteenth century the family du Bouchet de Sourches was held in the highest esteem, and when her husband was killed in a riding accident Louis XVI took the unprecedented step of appointing her son, still under age, to succeed his father as *Grand Prévôt de France*, saying: 'The Sourches family are never minors'.

When the Bastille fell the duchesse de Polignac, Governess to

Marie-Antoinette's children, was among the first to abandon the sinking ship and Madame de Tourzel was appointed to succeed her. 'Madame,' the Queen said to her, 'I had entrusted my children to Friendship; now I entrust them to Virtue.' Her devotion was absolute. She played the principal role – of 'baronne de Korff' – in the flight to Varennes. She accompanied the royal family to their prison in the Temple until she was taken, with her daughter Pauline and the princesse de Lamballe, to La Force. In the September Massacres she and her daughter were rescued by a strange Englishman who must have been the original of the Scarlet Pimpernel. At the Restoration she was made a duchess (her husband had been marquis de Tourzel) and devoted her long retirement to writing her memoirs and looking after the poor and needy. In 1832 she died at Abondant and her tombstone in the little sixteenth-century church records:

Ici repose
L. E. F. F. A. A. M. J. J. de Croy
Duchesse de Tourzel
Gouvernante des Enfants de France
Courageuse dans l'adversité
Fidèle à Dieu et au Roi
Véritable Mère des Pauvres
Elle a passé en faisant le bien
Vénérée de tous
Ardemment aimée de ses enfants
Elle mourut à l'age de 82 ans
Qu'elle repose en paix

The initials stand for Louise-Elizabeth-Félicité-Françoise-Armande-Anne-Marie-Jeanne-Joséphine. One can imagine the scene at her baptism: 'Name this child . . .'.

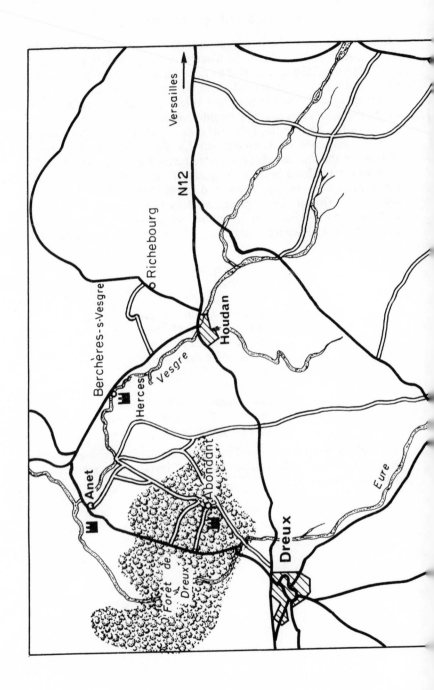

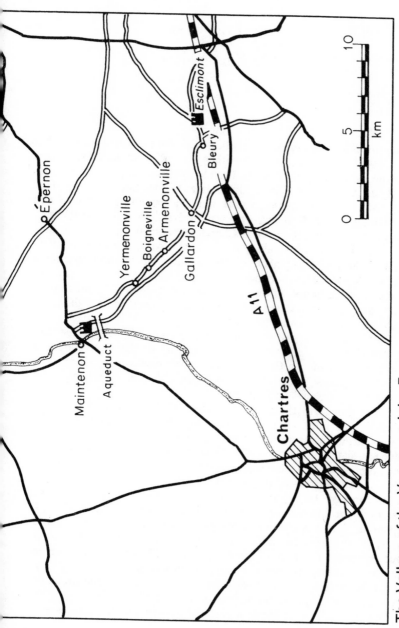

The Valleys of the Vesgre and the Eure

CHAPTER NINE

The Eure Valley

✲

Nogent-le-Roi, as its name implies, was once a royal manor, but in 1444 it was given, together with Anet, to Pierre de Brézé as part of the dowry of Charlotte de France, natural daughter of Charles VII and Agnès Sorel. The family de Brézé seemed fated to be involved with the royal mistresses, for it was the grandson of Pierre and Charlotte, Louis de Brézé, who was husband to Diane de Poitiers. It was to him that the present **Church of St Sulpice** was largely due.

From the rue de l'Église, to the north-west, the church offers one of the finest fragments of Renaissance church architecture in the whole area. The short nave looks as if it has been truncated, but the age of the house on the corner opposite the west front implies that the church can never have extended any further. It is therefore unfinished rather than truncated.

The rude masonry of the tower suggests an antiquity greater than it can claim. It dates from 1671. Standing at the west door and looking up at the north face of this tower one can see, beneath a filled-in window, a curious figure of an old man – perhaps some apostle or prophet – let into the wall.

From the north there is a fine view of the choir and transepts built in an admirably restrained Flamboyant Gothic, with the combination, not uncommon in the Ile de France, of the severely efficient slates of the upper roofs with the homely brown tiles of the ambulatory. This latter has an unusually shallow slope resulting from the disposition of the interior façades.

In contrast to the untidy mixture of styles presented by the exterior, the interior of St Sulpice has a unity which is at once apparent. But it is a unity of design and of materials rather than a unity of style, for the nave takes up the same theme as the choir but expresses it in terms of the Renaissance. The lierne and tierceron vaulting is continued over the nave, but in wood, stained and gilded. It can be dated from the bosses which bear the arms of the comte de Beautru, who acquired the seigneurie of Nogent in 1628.

The choir and apse create a pleasing impression of openness and luminosity which is greatly enhanced by the handsome cage of wrought iron with which the choir was enclosed in 1763. It was the work of two local ironsmiths. In order, presumably, to obtain a maximum area of glass, the tall arches of the choir arcade were made to support the clerestory without the mediation of a triforium. It was this arrangement which necessitated the shallow gradient of the ambulatory roof which let the water in. The consequent re-sloping of the tiles occasioned the filling in of the lower lights of the clerestory windows.

The choir and ambulatory contain some very interesting examples of sixteenth-century stained glass. Unfortunately the painting on some of the windows cannot have been properly fired, for in many of the lights the features of a face or the modelling of a torso have been washed out, leaving a luminous blank. This is all the more regrettable because, where the painting has survived, the faces are extremely vivacious – obviously real portraits of ordinary people. The scenes depicted give much information about the customs and costumes of the age. It only needs a little imagination to realize that this was for them 'the Bible in modern dress'. In this way the artists of the sixteenth century made Christianity contemporary.

The **town** of Nogent has retained some of its most picturesque features and some of its most primitive sanitation – the little stream of the Roulebois contributing largely to the picturesqueness and catering largely for the sanitation. In the little square west of the church is a fine timbered house with overhanging storeys – the top-most used for the storage of salt – and fine carved beams which are much defaced. Just round the corner in the rue Général de Gaulle is another splendid brick and timber house.

The Eure Valley provides a delightful drive from Nogent to **Maintenon**, the mere name of which must evoke in all lovers of history the memory of Françoise d'Aubigny, better known as Madame de Maintenon.

Born in almost total penury in the *conciergerie* of the prison at Niort in 1635, she became, nearly fifty years later, the morganatic wife of Louis XIV. In worldly terms it was an almost incredible destiny, but worldly welfare was never uppermost in her mind. '*Je meurs de tristesse,*' she admitted to a friend, '*dans une fortune qu'on aurait peine à imaginer.*'

Through their mutual connection with the Maréchal d'Albret she became the close friend of Madame de Montespan who was at the height of her power as *Maîtresse Déclarée* of the King. In due course the mistress became a mother and needed a person '*sûre et discrète*' to whom she could confide the care of the children with whom Louis so regularly provided her. Thus Françoise d'Aubigny came into contact with the King.

In order that the new governess could have a place of her own to which she could take the royal children, Louis purchased the Château of Maintenon from the marquis de Villeray and presented it to her. From henceforth she was known as Madame de Maintenon.

She was delighted with her new domain: 'I have spent the last two days at Maintenon,' she wrote to her brother, 'which seemed like one moment. The house is beautiful enough, though a little too big for the way of life I intend.' Nevertheless she proceeded to enlarge it.

The castle of which she had become the châtelaine dated back at least to the year 1200 when the stone keep was built. At the other corners of the square quadrangle the three brick towers, dating from the fourteenth century, are surprisingly robust, the small, square chambers inside them allowing for a massive solidity of wall.

The north range of the quadrangle had been rebuilt in the first quarter of the sixteenth century by Jean Cottereau, *Surintendant des Finances*. It must be said at once that for the holder of so lucrative a post, this was an extremely modest building.

The style is typified by its tall roof – nearly half of the total elevation – against which the elaborate dormers make their distinctive patterns of white stone against blue slate. The principal feature of the front is the entrance pavilion. Framed between slender turrets, its steep roof rising considerably above the rest of the skyline, the gatehouse offers a delightful example of an architecture which still disdained symmetry. The vertical flight of windows is left of centre because it is directly above the larger of the two entrance arches. The logic of the façade has been obscured by the disappearance of the smaller of these entrances, but it is perfectly clear from the masonry that there was originally a wicket gate to the right of the main arch which was slotted for a drawbridge.

Having built his gatehouse in a resolutely French vernacular, Cottereau made his solitary concession to the Italian Renaissance in the elegant dormer window which crowns the whole.

The charming quadrangle, open towards the south, is built in a simple mixture of brick and stone reminiscent of Blois in the days of Louis XII. The obverse side of the gatehouse, to which is added an octagonal entrance and staircase tower, forms one of the most delightful of architectural compositions, while the façade beyond the tower shows a strong resemblance to the contemporary Hôtel de Ville of Orléans.

To this château Madame de Maintenon added the modest wing, which contains her own apartments, on the west side of the courtyard, between the gatehouse and the *donjon*. It was she who demolished the curtain wall, thus opening up the quadrangle to the south. The wide prospect of meadows which it thus commanded was described as 'beautiful *and* ugly'. There was but one remedy possible at that date. The King sent Le Nôtre to 'adjust' the landscape.

He laid out a formal parterre on a formal island immediately south of the château and he brought the waters of the Eure round both sides of his island to meet in a long, straight canal. The canal was lined by two noble avenues, that on the left being named after Le Nôtre himself and that on the right after Racine who spent some time here while writing *Esther* and *Athalie* for the young ladies of St Cyr.

At the end of the canal can be seen today the majestic ruins of one of Louis' most colossal undertakings – the **Aqueduct of Maintenon**. It was the most ambitious item in a most ambitious design, for it was nothing less than to divert the waters of the river Eure and to bring them the 110 kilometres to Versailles. The greatest obstacle to this enterprise was the considerable drop in the ground level where this artificial river was to recross its own valley, just south of Maintenon. The negotiation of this necessitated the building of an aqueduct more than four and a half kilometres long. At its highest point it would have been seventy-two metres above the river level. It was to have had three tiers of arches. We must imagine another row of arches of nearly the same height surmounting the present arcade and a further storey, half the height of the lower ones, on top of that.

In 1684 a task force of thirty thousand men, two thirds of them soldiers, was set to work on this gigantic enterprise, but in 1688 war broke out and the troops were withdrawn. The work was never to be resumed. Eight million livres had been spent on it and according to Vauban its success was assured.

After the abandoning of the aqueduct Louis never again returned to the scene of his failure and Françoise seems to have lost interest in Maintenon. She transferred her estate to her niece, Françoise-Charlotte d'Aubigny. Backed by such a dowry, to which the King added 800,000 livres from his private purse, the new Françoise was married to the duc d'Ayen, Adrien-Maurice, later Maréchal de Noailles. The château has remained in their family ever since.

The hand of the Revolution was heavy upon the house of Noailles.

At the end of July 1794, the old Maréchale, her daughter-in-law the duchesse d'Ayen and her granddaughter were sent to the guillotine on a trumped-up charge of conspiracy. The old lady's plea that, being deaf, she would have embarrassed conspirators by requiring them to talk at the top of their voices was brushed aside by the brutal Dumas: '*alors, tu conspirais sourdement!*'

The Château of Maintenon survived unharmed, but like so many buildings of its sort the period of enforced neglect necessitated extensive renovations in the middle of the nineteenth century. The architect Parent has left us a house in which each century has clearly left its mark. The magnificent long gallery, originally a corridor built to connect the château with the church, is frankly nineteenth-century pastiche. There are lovely 'Chinese' wallpapers from the eighteenth century as well as some beautiful panelling brought from the Château de Mauny. But from the seventeenth century is preserved intact the private **suite of Madame de Maintenon**.

It is just what we would expect of her. It has real charm, much dignity and little or no ostentation. The tall *lit à la duchesse*, hung and upholstered with pale blue silk, fringed and tasselled in gold, is firmly insulated behind its balustrade. Beside it an open archway offers a glimpse into an inner sanctuary – '*ce petit trou où je prétends écrire.*' Here, and here only, could she retire '*dans une douceur et un repos d'esprit incroyables*' for a brief respite from the almost unbelievable position to which Fortune had elevated her.

It was at Maintenon that the last scene of the Bourbon dynasty was destined to be played. In the night of 3 August 1830 the ex-King Charles X arrived here from Rambouillet, where he had abdicated in favour of his grandson, the duc de Bordeaux. 'At two in the morning all was ready for the reception of the sad little cortège. As he got out of his carriage, the King looked overwhelmed. With difficulty he mounted the staircase which Louis XIV had mounted before him, and was conducted to the apartment of Madame de Maintenon.' The next morning, after the flag of the Cent Suisses – the King's personal bodyguard – had been torn up and divided amongst the officers, the last descendant of Louis XIV to wear the Crown of France took the road for Cherbourg and for exile.

The best view of the aqueduct is to be had by taking the road for Épernon and then, after crossing the river, turning right into the rue de la Gare. This brings us to the minor road which is almost immediately crossed by the aqueduct. It then follows the little valley of the Voise for Yermenonville and Gallardon.

Just beyond Yermenonville is a delightful example of the fortified

108

farm or smaller *Gentilhommière* called the **Manoir de Boigneville**.
Its features are soon listed: an octagonal entrance and staircase
tower with an exceptionally tall pointed roof on the south-west
front and two corner towers with exceptionally flat pointed roofs on
the north-east side. It is worth persevering along the rue de l'Arsénal
and over the bridge to get this latter view and to follow the pretty
little valley through its ancient poplar plantations to **Armenonville**,
where there is a charming village church. It is a simple thirteenth-
century nave with no aisles to which a modest onion dome was
added in the seventeenth century.

It is impossible to be within sight of **Gallardon** – and the plain of
la Beauce offers some fairly distant prospects – without becoming at
once aware that here is a **church** of unusual distinction which is in
some ways distinctly unusual. The broadside view shows clearly the
widely different levels of the nave and choir.

At the short range imposed by the closely packed houses of the
village, this duality is not so much in evidence; but if, having viewed
the west front with its severe Romanesque façade, the visitor explores
the little narrow streets to the south-east of the church he will come
suddenly upon a very different building.

The great height of the clerestory windows has imposed the
use of double flying buttresses – thin slices of masonry which
present an elevation resembling the narrow spine of a slender
book. Notice the colonettes at the head of the lower arches, a feature
borrowed from Chartres, as is also the balustrade on the north
side of the apse at the top of the ambulatory wall.

It is an exciting church to explore because of the continual
contrasts it offers. We enter from the west into a vast nave, offering
a huge expanse of dull, plain wall only slightly relieved by the presence of dull, plain round-arched windows. It seems quite unworthy
of its marvellous painted wooden barrel vault, with its carved centre
posts and tie-beams, which received its decoration in 1708.

At the east end of the nave a flight of steps leads up to a broad
dais. From here four more steps, semicircular in shape, give access
to the chancel arch, which frames a vista of the noble architecture
of the apse. The whole thing seems to have been conceived by
someone with a wonderful sense of theatre.

The chancel arch gives access to a truly wonderful choir and apse,
which clearly owe much to St Denis and Chartres but which have
certain original features of their own. The architect has put considerable emphasis on the height of the clerestory windows, which
take up approximately half of the total elevation. An unusual feature

109

is the alternation of broad and narrow bays in the apse. It is most evident in the triforium level.

From the east end, as one looks back, a most odd effect is produced, for the large blank wall which contained the chancel arch almost completely cuts off the nave. Nave and choir seem to be two separate buildings, as indeed the first, remote view of their respective roofs would have immediately suggested.

In the rue Porte Mouton, opposite the west front of the church and a little further along towards Maintenon, is one of the best **timbered houses** in the area. Each beam has been carefully carved, some showing the latest taste in Gothic decoration and others, notably those flanking the upper windows, reflecting the earliest Renaissance.

The distant views of Gallardon also offer the perplexing silhouette of a tall, top-heavy remnant of masonry known as the **Épaule** – the Shoulder of Mutton. It is all that remains of a twelfth-century *donjon* which Dunois recaptured from the English in 1442 and slighted.

At **Bleury**, to the east, there is a charming early Renaissance house, with a nearly complete cylinder of staircase tower capped with a *poivrière*, which is now the **mairie**. It was a modest house with only one flight of windows either side of the tower and entrance. Right up by the church, whose roof seems to be almost a part of the farmyard buildings, is another similar house, but older and distinguished by the ornament of its front door. Some of the windows retain their original mullions and transoms with a delicate linear moulding to the frame. The staircase tower rises well above the roof ridge and must have been built for look-out purposes. The façades are extremely attractive, being covered with a much weathered pink plaster.

No distance at all east of Bleury is **Esclimont**, a fine château in an even finer park. The old fourteenth-century *donjon* has become the gatehouse and preserves a tone of rough-hewn grandeur which is no longer to be discerned in the **château** proper. Built in 1543 by an Archbishop of Tours, it passed through his sister to the Hurault family which at that time provided Lords to Vibraye, Cheverny and Gallardon. In 1648 Henri Hurault sold it to a son of Claude de Bullion – a name curiously appropriate to a Superintendent of Finance.

It was under a Bullion that the château was recast in an eighteenth-century mould. Contemporary prints do not suggest that it gained in elegance through this metamorphosis. The nineteenth century, for once, was more successful. By 1865 the château had passed to the family of La Rochefoucauld, and its owner, the duc de Doudeauville, had it completely redecorated, within and without, by the architect Parent in the style of the French Renaissance – that is, of the châteaux of the Loire. The towers, simple cylinders with shallow conical roofs, regained the medieval formula of machicolations and *chemin de ronde*, into which were cut elegant dormers which borrowed something from Azay-le-Rideau and something from Le Lude; the plain pediment of the east front gave place to an elaborate frontispiece, again recalling Azay, while the insignificant little windows of the second storey were dignified as dormers and set in a chessboard pattern of brick and stone which seems to derive directly from Les Réaux.

Inside – and the interior may be visited on application – there is some extremely good panelling of the early eighteenth century, some magnificent tapestry and some fine historical paintings.

The **park**, which is open to the public, was laid out in 1875 by Bühler in the 'English' style – Doudeauville was for many years Ambassador in London – and is now fully matured. The parterre before the east front was designed by the comte Ernest de Ganay who was a frequent guest. He has left his Testament of Hospitality. 'Esclimont remains, in France, one of the very rare Châteaux where a charming welcome, where genuine high standards, where old fashioned courtesy, transmitted by a noble tradition, still preserves [in 1919] the image of the once legendary "*douceur de vivre*" of the eighteenth century.'

CHAPTER TEN

Chartres

On 11 July 1144, a ceremony took place which was to be of decisive importance for the architecture of Europe – the consecration of the new choir of St Denis. The Abbot Suger was the first man to realize the full potential of the cross-ribbed vault and pointed arch. He was obsessed with a deeply theological theory of light. He had to hand glaziers who possessed, in Viollet-le-Duc's words, 'such a sureness and experience of touch that we needs must credit them with a long continuity of observation'. If Suger's choir was, in his own words, 'flooded with a new light', it was to be light filtered through the loveliest windows the world has ever seen.

The consecration of St Denis not only inaugurated the new style which we call Gothic; it announced in its ceremonial that the King of France 'bears in his person the living image of Christ'. The new style therefore had a considerable dynastic importance. 'Precisely because it evoked the mystical archetype of the political order of the French Monarchy,' wrote Otto von Simson, 'the style of St Denis was adopted for all the Cathedrals of France.' Among the many important persons present at the consecration was Geoffroy de Lèves, Bishop of Chartres.

The association, also, of the Virgin Mary with Chartres was very early established. In 878 Charles the Bald presented to the Chapter one of the most breathtaking of all relics – the chemise supposedly worn by the Virgin on the occasion of the Annunciation. In due course Chartres came to be regarded as her chosen residence on earth: no pains could be spared to provide a worthy palace for such a Queen.

The first building with which we need concern ourselves is that of Bishop Fulbert, begun in 1020. It was Fulbert's successor Thierry who saw this Romanesque cathedral dedicated on 17 October 1037.

A century later it was decided to build a square bell tower some distance to the west of the church but in line with its north aisle. The desire for symmetry led to the construction of a twin tower in line with the south aisle. This in turn suggested the idea of prolonging the nave to meet the towers, and a new west front was built, deeply recessed between them. Finally this same façade was taken down stone by stone and re-erected flush with the towers. The west front as we see it today, up to the rose window, had been created.

Because of the somewhat haphazard process by which the façade evolved, the three portals of the **west front** of Chartres all open into the nave and are therefore closely grouped together. At St Denis and most of its derivative cathedrals the portals correspond with the ends of the nave and aisles and are consequently set further apart. Here at Chartres the three portals form a single decorative whole, the **Portail Royal**. Although the work of a number of different artists, they express a unified theme.

To the right, the south portal represents the first coming of Christ. He is seen in the place of honour, the tympanum, seated on His mother's knees. To the left, the north portal depicts His ascension into Heaven. In the centre He is seen coming again to judge the world, an image taken from the Apocalypse. In each group He is supported by His precursors of the Old Testament (the famous statue-columns) and surrounded by scenes of everyday life – for without the humanity that He redeemed His redemptive acts would seem a little pointless.

This humanity is seen in terms of man's labour – the labours of the body, in the north portal, where the ceaseless, seasonal struggle with Nature is intermixed with the signs of the zodiac – and the labours of the intellect, in the south portal, where the seven sciences are depicted together with some of their more distinguished exponents. Look at the top right-hand corner of the north door: there are the shepherds with their rather stylized sheep. Next to them Aristotle bends frowning over his little writing desk; above Pythagoras, who discovered the mathematical intervals of the musical scale, is hammering out a chime on some bells, while next to him Grammar presides grimly with book and birch over two cowering pupils.

Such are the broad outlines of the scheme. A secondary theme is provided by the **capitals** above the statue-columns which form a continuous frieze of sculpture depicting incidents in the life of Christ. A few of the subjects are from the apocryphal Gospels and are not easily recognized, but the familiar scenes are there as well, In the south portal, on the left-hand side above the central statue-column, is a particularly lively representation of the betrayal by Judas and the arrest at Gethsemane. It is strange that in all this there should be no direct reference to the Crucifixion.

Several sculptors collaborated in the production of the **statue-columns**. Those of the central bay have a pre-eminence all their own. There is no canopy overhead to break the upward movement; their feet rest upon the slightest of supports; their elongated figures and closely pinioned arms accentuate their architectural allegiance.

It is supremely in the female figures that the artist has shown his genius; taller and more attenuated than the men, their pendent sleeves and plaited tresses reaching almost to the ground, these noble ladies epitomize the cult of chivalry: with their high necklines revealing only the face and their delicately fluted draperies betraying no trace of underlying anatomy, they are almost sexless.

As late as the nineteenth century vestiges of paint and gold leaf could still be discerned on these statues. The historical imagination should see the Portail Royal brightly coloured and richly gilded.

Today not only the original colouring but often the original surface of the stone has weathered away; some of the figures are having to be replaced with facsimiles. This operation is only possible because a hundred years ago mouldings were made from which the accuracy of these copies may be ensured. The new carvings can be distinguished fairly easily by their yellower colour.

In 1194 Bishop Fulbert's cathedral, with the exception of the west front and towers, was destroyed by a terrible fire. For two days it continued to burn and the inhabitants, many of whose houses had also been consumed, were in agonies about the fate of their sacred relic. On the third day the heat abated somewhat and there emerged from the crypt a procession of clergy who had been trapped in it throughout the conflagration. On their shoulders they carried the reliquary. It was decided to rebuild.

It is often objected today, as it was objected by St Bernard then, that 'the Church clothes its stones in gold and lets its sons go naked' – an aphorism which does scant justice to the immense work of charity undertaken by the medieval Church. But the decision to rebuild Chartres must not be seen narrowly as an unwarrantable extravagance on the part of a 'triumphalist' Church with no social conscience. The commercial welfare of the people of Chartres depended largely upon the success of its four great fairs; the customers at these fairs were mostly pilgrims attracted by the sacred relic. Economy and religion worked, in fact, hand in glove. The City of Chartres was not economically viable without its cathedral. It was the butchers, the bakers, the drapers, the cobblers and wine merchants of the town, just as much as the royal family and dignitaries of the Church, who paid for the new building.

Nevertheless, it would be a mistake to attribute mercenary motives to those whose zeal carried through the campaign. The building of Chartres Cathedral was both the occasion and the result of a great upsurge of faith. Men and women, high and low, old and young, harnessed themselves to the carts which brought the stone from the quarries of Berchères. These convoys were conducted with reverent and almost liturgical discipline, either in silence or to the accompaniment of psalmody. Unable to complete their arduous journey in one day, they would encamp for the night and the great plain of La Beauce would twinkle with the constellations of their many fires.

In the centre of all this pious activity the new cathedral rose rapidly from its forest of scaffolding. The architect – to use the word in its modern sense – had been given a task which was at once daunting and exciting, for to meet the challenge he had at his disposal the full resources of a new technique. His problem arose from the fact that he was obliged to build on to the surviving west front and to use the existing foundations. Since Fulbert's cathedral had only a wooden ceiling it could afford a span of nearly sixteen and a half metres to the nave, whereas the widest nave so far vaulted in stone, that of Sens, aspired to only fifteen metres. The vault at Chartres would need to be proportionately higher, and at thirty-seven metres it broke all records.

In order to tackle this problem the architect adopted a plan of campaign which was at once bold and simple. Inspired by Suger's brilliant pioneering at St Denis he went all out for a maximum area of stained glass. To achieve this he did away with tribunes, leaving only a modest triforium between the nave arcade and the greatly enlarged clerestory windows.

Nearly everything that was done at Chartres had been done before, but it had been done in a tentative, more or less experimental fashion. Now at last the new style, shaking off all traces of the Romanesque, steps confidently into its own.

The first, fantastic fact to be grasped was that walls could be abolished. The old style, represented by the west front, is still conceived as wall space into which windows, however large, could be inserted. But in the **choir and nave** there are no walls. The structure consists of a series of stone canopies upheld by tall piers and stabilized by a series of flying buttresses which carry the thrust from the stone vault out to a further set of piers which form the buttresses between the aisle windows. These flying buttresses – perhaps the first to be thought of as an integral part of the design – consisted originally of only the lower two arcs joined by the charming cartwheel arcades.

Piers, buttresses and arcading made up a vast open-work stone skeleton, devoid of walls, which could stand on its own – and no doubt for some time it did. But the open spaces between these ribs and bones were destined to receive what is undoubtedly the finest set of **stained-glass windows** to have survived so nearly complete. Anything which might be taken for wall at Chartres is simply the framing or infilling required by this fantastic fenestration.

When walls had been a structural necessity the medieval builder had sought to obtain the rich effect which he desired by mural painting. But the smallness of the windows so reduced the lighting as to render most of his efforts disappointing. With the disappearance of the wall it became possible to replace the flatness of pigment with the lovely luminosity of glass. It was Abbot Suger who first grasped this opportunity at St Denis, and in the three **west windows** of Chartres – those immediately above the Portail Royal – we can see what Suger's glass was like, for these were made by the same master glaziers and reflected the same subjects. In particular the right-hand light, the Tree of Jesse, shows what the mutilated remnant at St Denis must have been like in its perfection. It has been called by Émile Mâle 'the most beautiful window ever made'. The happy survival of these three windows – for twelfth-century windows are rare – is one of the many miracles of Chartres.

To enter the cathedral, especially on a day of splintering sun, is to enter Aladdin's cave. It appears at first to be in darkness; but its darkness glows with opalescent colour. One hundred and seventy-three windows – a total area of over two and a half thousand square metres – contribute to this overwhelming impact. As the eye becomes accustomed to this darkness, the architecture begins to emerge – clustered columns shooting upwards to the spring of the arch where they part company and splay out into the ribs of the great vault thirty-seven metres overhead, framing the lovely galaxy of glass.

To see the windows thus is to appreciate them at one level – as a glowing, vibrant constellation of colour; to gaze at them is to be transported, like St John the Divine, to a paradise where the streets are 'pure gold, as it were transparent glass', to a city whose foundations are garnished with sapphire and emeralds and amethysts and pearls, which had 'no need of the Sun, neither of the Moon, for the glory of God did lighten it'.

But with a pair of binoculars – an equipment necessary for a visit to Chartres – one can see the windows at another level, the detailed viewpoint of the master glaziers who made them. For this paradise, this translucent evocation of the Heavenly City, is made up of tiny scenes of humdrum daily life. It was in his routine chores that Christian man was taught to glorify God.

Take for instance the **second window from the west in the north aisle**. It was given in memory of a Bishop called Lubin by the publicans of Chartres on the somewhat slender pretext that when Lubin was a monk he was reputedly cellarer of his monastery. Most of the window is descriptive of the production of wine; the rest depicts the life story of Lubin. In the circular panel in the centre of the light we can see the cellarer drawing his wine from a green barrel. Two circles up from the bottom on the right, in an incomplete roundel framed in red, is a scene from Lubin's childhood. When he was a shepherd boy, a monk, thinking him to be rather bright, decided to educate him. In order to give him his alphabet he cut the letters into his belt – and the actual letters can be seen (with binoculars) in this roundel.

The windows were all gifts to the cathedral. Many of them came from the richer clergy – and some of these were very rich. Lord Clark has reckoned that the Dean's private income would have been some £250,000 a year in modern money. Forty-four windows were given by the royal and noble families of France; forty-two by the trades guilds of the city. These guilds have all appended their 'signature' in the form of a few scenes of their typical activities at the foot – that is to say the most easily visible part – of the window. Thus a lady is seen trying on a dress in the drapers' window and in another a cobbler is depicted threading the laces into a new-made shoe.

In the **Chapel of the Blessed Sacrament**, formerly the Chapel of the Holy Martyrs, the extremely lovely central window shows the stoning of Stephen. The window to the left of this was the gift of the stonemasons: at the bottom, on the right hand side, they can be seen at work on the cathedral; above their heads are the models from which the profiles of the architecture are to be copied.

Some of the windows have a particular interest for the English. The **fifth from the west in the north aisle** can be judged from its style to be by the same hand as one of the windows in Lincoln Cathedral. At the east end, immediately right of the entrance to the Chapel of St Piat, is an **apsidal chapel** of which the right-hand window commemorates St Thomas à Becket. When he was murdered some of his blood fell upon a young cleric who accompanied him. This young cleric was John of Salisbury, later to be Bishop of Chartres. He brought with him the precious relic of the new saint's blood.

There is no overriding theme to which donors of windows were asked to conform. Each was allowed to express his own personal faith in the way he chose. What matter that among so many there should be five windows dedicated to St Nicholas and four to St Martin – not to mention the twenty which rendered homage to the Virgin Mary?

But in the great **rose windows** of the transepts, each with its five lancets beneath it, we do find a coherent iconography. This is no doubt due in part to the fact that each ensemble is the gift of a single donor. The windows of the north transept were given by Blanche de Castille, mother of St Louis; those of the south transept by Pierre, comte de Dreux.

The **north rose**, with the loveliness of a water opal and the complexity of a snowflake, is distinguished by the bold and effective introduction of squares into its design. In the very centre are the Virgin and Child surrounded, in the inner ring, by doves and angels. The square panels depict the kings of Judah and the half circles round the circumference the minor Prophets. Beneath the rose, in the central lancet, the infant Virgin is seen in the arms of her mother, St Anne. Time has dealt harshly with the latter; it has so darkened her visage as to make her resemble some Parsee princess.

On either side of St Anne, Melchisidek, with his bread and wine, prefigures the Eucharist and Aaron, with his budding staff, the Virgin birth; David predicts the Passion, and Solomon, inside right of the row, the Adoration of the Kings. It was an opportunity to present Solomon in all his glory. In fact he is represented in the full glory of a French king at his coronation – and he bears a suspicious likeness to the known portraits of St Louis at the age of about sixteen. His mother, Queen Blanche, who paid for the window, was not going to miss the opportunity of eternalizing the son she adored and of glorifying the Capetian dynasty which he represented.

In the **south rose** window the risen Christ occupies the centre roundel encircled by the worshipping chorus described in the Book of Revelation. In detail the twenty-four musicians provide important information on the state of evolution of musical instruments at that time. In the lancets below is a deeply theological statement expressed by the mounting of the four Evangelists upon the shoulders of four Prophets. Outside left, as one looks at them, is Luke on Jeremiah; inside left Matthew on Isaiah; inside right John on Ezekiel and outside right Mark on Daniel.

It is a strange theology which seems almost to invert the importance of the Old and the New Testament. It was an attitude, however, not uncommon in the School of Chartres. Of their respect for Greek philosophy the Portrail Royal bears witness; but looking at these Evangelists riding upon the Prophets one is reminded of the words of Bernard[1]: 'if we can see further than the Ancients, it is not because of our own strength of vision, but because we are borne up by them and carried to a great height. We are dwarfs mounted on the shoulders of giants.'

In the **first window of the south choir aisle**, as one enters it from the transept, is another miraculous survival of the fire in 1194 – a portion of a window dating from the early twelfth century. It occupies the top three squares of the left-hand light and can be identified easily by the pale sapphire blue which predominates. It represents a large Virgin and Child who has for centuries been known as *Notre Dame de la belle verrière*.

It would be convenient now to go outside again and inspect the north portal or **Portail de la Vierge**. It was begun in 1197, only three years after the great fire. It shows a considerable evolution of style, technique and thought since the days of the Portail Royal. The statue-columns show a new conception of the sculptor's art. Essentially the move is towards a greater realism. The figures are no longer motionless and mummified like those of the west front; the postures are more varied, the folds of the drapery more natural, for the underlying anatomy has been considered. From left to right they present a progression from Patriarchs to Prophets to Apostles; from Melchisidek to St Peter.

Look at Melchisidek, fifth on the **left**: there is a wonderful sense of strangeness and dignity about this representative of the eternal order of priesthood as he stares out into the future, holding his chalice and his loaf close to his breast. Note the simple, harmonious lines of his loose, light raiment and the rhythmic furrows of his curling beard. Next to him is Abraham with Isaac, still bound, in front of him. Both are looking past Melchisidek towards the Divine voice which saved Isaac and condemned the ram, depicted at their feet.

Answering them on the **right** of the doorway are John the Baptist and St Peter, who used to hold a chalice reflecting that of Melchisidek. What a wonderful contrast this pair affords – the weird, wild look of the 'voice crying in the wilderness' and the solid respectability of the Rock upon which Christ was to build His Church. There is something almost baroque about the sweep of John the Baptist's

[1] Not St Bernard, but Bernard of Chartres who was head of the School and Chancellor of the Cathedral 1114–19.

beard, while Peter bears a strong and surely intentional resemblance to Melchisidek; his brow is slightly furrowed and he has the same faraway look.

Against the **central** doorpost is a figure of St Anne with the infant Virgin in her arms. In 1204, the year before the completion of the north portal, the comte de Blois had sent from Constantinople to Chartres another breathtaking relic – the head of St Anne. '*La tête de la mère*,' runs the account in the cartulary, '*fut reçue avec grande joie dans l'église de la fille.*'

On either side of the central door the left-hand bay is devoted to the Annunciation, Visitation and Nativity, to the accompaniment of a procession of virtues and vices; while to the right a selection of worthies from the Old Testament gives the place of honour in the tympanum to Job. The artist seems to have chosen for his text chapter 2 verse vii: 'so went Satan . . . and smote Job with sore boils from the sole of his foot unto his crown'.

These two flanking bays are the last sculptural ensemble of the cathedral, for between the completion of the central bay of this north porch and the beginning of its side supporters the whole of the **south portal** was undertaken. This, like the rose window above it, was the gift of the comte de Dreux.

The theme is the Last Judgement, with the Martyrs of the Church in the left-hand bay and the Confessors in the right. These figures mostly seem just to lack the vital spark of inspiration, but one scene is a work of genius – the separation of the sheep from the goats immediately above the central doors. It is not without humour. The figures of the condemned seem more disappointed and disgruntled than dismayed, let alone appalled, at their predicament. Significantly they number in their throng a king, a bishop and a monk. But the impact of the scene derives from the dynamic rhythm of the harvesting angels above their heads. Moving with the unison of a well-coached crew they sweep their victims to their damnation.

The glories and intricacies of Chartres provide a seemingly inexhaustible fount of interest and delight. One can return again and again and always find something new, always find the same thrill in what one had found before. It is impossible not to wonder who was the author of this dream-made-real. If he ever signed his name it has long since been effaced. It might have been placed in the centre of the **labyrinth** – the marble miz-maze which is inlaid in the nave floor. This labyrinth, 294 metres long, was also called 'the Road to Jerusalem'. It is thought to have been one of the penances of the pilgrim to negotiate its entire length upon his knees. It is possible that in achieving this so-called work of piety they have obliterated the signature of one of the greatest architects the world has ever known.

His great work has inspired the tributes of men throughout the ages, but perhaps the most perceptive compliment was that paid by Napoleon. 'Chartres,' he observed, 'is no place for an Atheist.'

Only the eighteenth century was blind enough to fail to appreciate Chartres and it was the cathedral chapter that did the greatest damage to the building, though fortunately only to the choir. They clothed the inner surfaces of the choir screen with marble reliefs of the most astonishing mediocrity and faced the inside of the arcades with classical ornament of the most indifferent quality. In order that no detail of this inferior decoration should escape the eye, they increased the lighting by removing the stained-glass windows. They also destroyed the thirteenth-century rood screen which had closed the west end of the choir. Some of its exquisite carving, used for rubble beneath the paving stones, has been recovered and is on exhibition, together with some of the few remaining treasures of the cathedral, in the **Chapel of St Piat** which forms an appendix to the apse.

Compared with this act of vandalism, the damage caused by the Revolution was almost negligible. It did, however, see fit to destroy the statue in the crypt of the *Virgin about to have a child*, so named although she has manifestly already produced the child. It was, in any case, of dubious authenticity.

The **crypt** gives a wonderful sense of the massive solidity of the underbuilding and incorporates much of Bishop Fulbert's original work. The old well can be seen, which determined the site of the shrine, and in one of the south chapels, dedicated to St Clement, are some twelfth-century murals. The upper portions are largely intact and show a number of animated figures, both human and animal, reminiscent of the Bayeux Tapestry.

At the north-east corner of the cathedral, approached through a massive wrought-iron gate which in the eighteenth century formed the entrance to the choir, is the Episcopal Palace, now the **Musée de Chartres**. If the collection is of a somewhat miscellaneous character, it is at least greatly enhanced by its gracious setting.

From the thirteenth century come the delightful statuette of St John the Evangelist, an enamel processional cross from Château-neuf-en-Thimerais and the armour worn by Philippe IV at the battle of Mons-en-Puelle – a sinister reminder of 'le Roi de Fer' who promised this armour to the cathedral if he was victorious. From the Renaissance are the twelve remarkable enamel plaques of the Apostles, the work of Leonard Limosin ordered by François I two years before his death and given by Henri II to Diane de Poitiers for the decoration of Anet. From the sixteenth century also is the Brussels tapestry of Moses and a magnificent Holbein of Erasmus in old age. From the seventeenth century, the Gobelin copies of the famous tapestry *Les Chasses de Maximilien* and Rigaud's portrait of the duc de Saint-Simon who lived near Chartres. He has the pouty expression of a spoilt child and his large eyes, which we know from his writings missed little or nothing of what went on, are those of one who regards from a detached standpoint. Chardin, Fragonard and Hubert Robert represent the eighteenth century.

There is also a room devoted to photographs and paintings of the city of Chartres, with a particularly interesting view of the siege in 1568 – an occasion when a cannon ball passed through the west rose window of the cathedral. Henri IV, having successfully taken the town, had himself crowned here and not at Reims.

Chartres has retained enough of its **old houses** to be a delightful place to walk round, but the gradients are steep and there are many flights of steps to negotiate. North of the cathedral is the rue du Cardinal Pie. Here, at the end of a courtyard, at number 5, is the **Cellier de Loëns**, the thirteenth-century wine cellar of the dean and chapter, consisting of three magnificent 'naves' supported by two rows of pillars.

Turning left at the museum, we now turn right into the **rue Chantault**, where there are some fine half-timbered houses and a Romanesque house, number 29, with two grotesque Norman faces carved in the tympanum of a round arched window.

A little to the south of this is the **Church of St André**, now sadly dilapidated. Rebuilt immediately after the fire of 1194 it is almost wholly of twelfth-century origin.

The **rue de la Tannerie**, on the other side of the river Eure, affords many delightful views of the cathedral. In times of peace the inhabitants installed themselves here outside the ramparts and set up the *métiers de la rivière*, the fulling, tanning and currying of leather, and innumerable riverside laundries. Many of these old buildings survive and provide the foreground for these glimpses of another world.

If we recross the Eure at the rue du Bourg we come to one of the finest of the old houses, number 35 rue des Écuyers, a half-timbered structure with an apsidal staircase from which it gets its

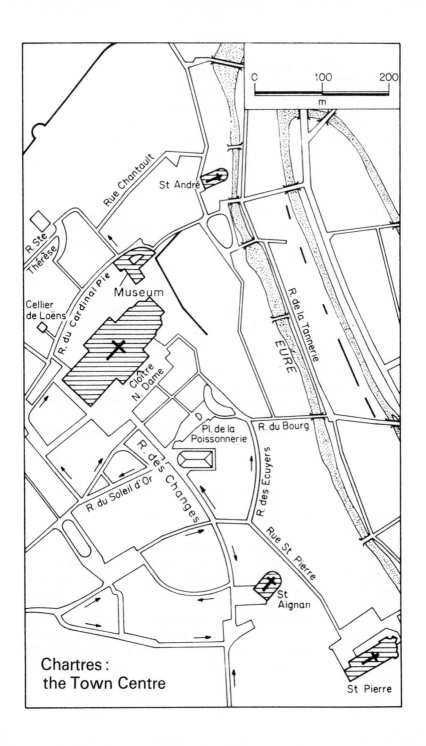

Chartres :
the Town Centre

name **Escalier de la Reine Berthe**. This lady was a dowager countess of Chartres who became Queen to Robert the Pious in 992. As the house only dates from the sixteenth century it is difficult to know what connection it can have had with her.

A little further to the south, the rue des Écuyers becomes the rue St Pierre and at number 16 is another house of Renaissance date, the **Maison des Trois Pigeons**, behind which looms the *abside* of the **Church of St Aignan**. This building suffered from a succession of fires which left it a patchwork mostly of the fifteenth and sixteenth centuries. There is an elegant Renaissance porch dated 1541 on the west front. The interior, not particularly distinguished in the first place, has been rendered hideous by nineteenth-century stencil work. St Aignan has some interesting glass of the early sixteenth century which creates a pleasant kaleidoscopic effect of bright blues, purples, reds and yellows. The painted wooden vaulting is dated 1625.

One might suppose that a cathedral of the importance and magnitude of Chartres would have absorbed the potential for architecture and stained glass in a city this size. The reverse, however, is true: the cathedral set a standard which is reflected pre-eminently in the **Church of St Pierre**, which is south-east of the cathedral, quite near the point at which the N10 enters the town.

The **east end** of St Pierre is truly magnificent, with its full fan of light and elegant flying buttresses, their two tiers of arches enabling the maximum elevation to the clerestory. It is a superb example of how the medieval builder made an aesthetic virtue out of a structural necessity.

The upper part of the apse was rebuilt at the beginning of the fourteenth century when the Gothic style had reached its highest perfection. It was built on to the original thirteenth-century ambulatory which is contemporary with the nave. This heightening of the choir produced an awkward junction of roof levels, to remedy which no serious attempt was made.

Inside, St Pierre is exactly what the exterior would lead one to expect: a nave strongly reminiscent of the cathedral, its later date only noticeable in the ornament of the triforium and the tracery of the clerestory, and an apse that is beginning to suggest the total luminosity of Amiens or Beauvais.

Advantage was taken of the large spaces available for glazing to provide St Pierre with a set of **stained-glass windows** second only to those of the cathedral itself. Dating from the early fourteenth century, they are in paler colours and provide a more ample illumination to the vessel of the church. On the north side of the nave the subjects are taken from the Acts of the Apostles, on the south side the Confessors and Martyrs of the Church are depicted, while in the choir the Saints and Prophets are grouped round the person of Christ. The high windows of the choir are of sixteenth-century workmanship, made by Robert Pinaigrier and transported here from the church of St Hilaire.

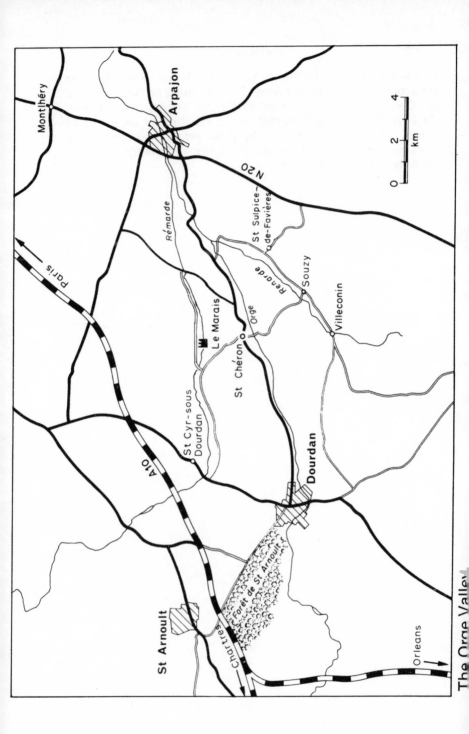

The Orge Valley

CHAPTER ELEVEN

The Orge Valley

The N20 follows a very old road from Paris to Orléans. The approach to the capital has been guarded since the year 991 by the important **fortress of Montlhéry**. It soon became part of the Capetian domain and was among their most highly prized possessions. '*Garde bien cette tour,*' said the dying Philippe I to his son Louis le Gros; '*elle m'a fait vieillir avant l'age.*'

Although originally conceived as a protective device, a fortress was an ever-present threat to the inhabitants of the bourg. Military operations gravitated towards the great castle and they were the first to suffer. In 1591 they had had enough. They successfully petitioned for its demolition. Only the tower of the *donjon* survives.

The road joins the river Orge at **Arpajon,** which has little to interest a visitor today except for its great **Halle** or covered market place. This is of seventeenth-century construction and affords an interesting comparison with the one at Milly-la-Forêt which is two centuries older. Their construction is remarkably similar.

The Halle at Arpajon was built in connection with the 'Foire des Haricots' which still takes place in September. The wealth of the region largely depended on the success of this fair and the seigneur who built the Halle naturally took his percentage. It was finally bought from the duc de Mouchy by the commune in 1821 after fourteen years of negotiation.

A remarkable feature of Hurepoix is that so much real country survives so close to Paris. West of Arpajon is a delightful area watered by three confluent rivers – the Renarde, the Orge and (confusingly) the Rémarde.

The first sight of the church at **St Sulpice-de-Favières**, south-west of Arpajon, is one of the great experiences of the Ile de France. It was described in the seventeenth century by the Abbé Chastelain as 'the most beautiful village church in the whole kingdom'. Over the low roofs of a hamlet of some two hundred souls rises the choir and apse of a church capable of holding two thousand.

For Favières was a place of pilgrimage. Sulpice was a seventh-century Bishop of Bourges who is said to have resuscitated a child who had drowned in the Renarde. There may, however, have been a reason several layers deeper in the folk memory of the country, for here, as at Chartres, was one of the sacred wells which attracted pagan pilgrims for centuries before Sulpice.

No doubt it was the pilgrims who contributed the funds necessary for so fine a building, which progressed steadily from 1260 till about 1320. St Sulpice comes, then, at the moment of full maturity of the Gothic style. Beauvais and the Sainte Chapelle had both been begun less than twenty years before.

From the outside the effect is chiefly built upon the contrast afforded between the lofty elegance of the choir and apse, with their three storeys of windows surrounded by the scaffolding of slender flying buttresses, and the more solid aspect of the nave – a simple alternation between sturdy buttress piles and exquisite Geometric tracery.

The west portal was once very fine, though it has been badly defaced and carefully restored; but the niches are empty and the central figure of Sulpice armless and decapitated. There are two tiers of carvings over the doors, one representing the Last Judgement, with souls being weighed in the balance, and the other the resurrection of the bodies. Above these in the tympanum the Christ stands between two angels and the kneeling figures of His Mother and St John.

Inside, one is immediately struck by the airy lightness of the building resulting from the great height of the vault, which measures twenty-five and a half metres to the keystone, nearly as high as that of Salisbury Cathedral. The impression is greatly enhanced by the very beautiful stone of which it is built. The architecture is today amply illuminated, but it is tempting to try to imagine the building with its full complement of stained glass. There is a perfectly lovely window at the east end of the south aisle to guide our imagination. Although presented by Blanche de Castille, and therefore contemporary with some of the glass at Chartres, it is lighter and more translucent, so that amid the blaze of colour the beauties of the architecture would still have been apparent.

Unfortunately, towards the end of the seventeenth century the nave roof was destroyed by fire and the vaulting replaced by a timber ceiling. The date 1697 over the bay to the right of the pulpit obviously refers to this.

There is some good furniture in the church: a monumental churchwarden's seat, which makes one feel that a churchwarden

Dampierre: Grand Salon

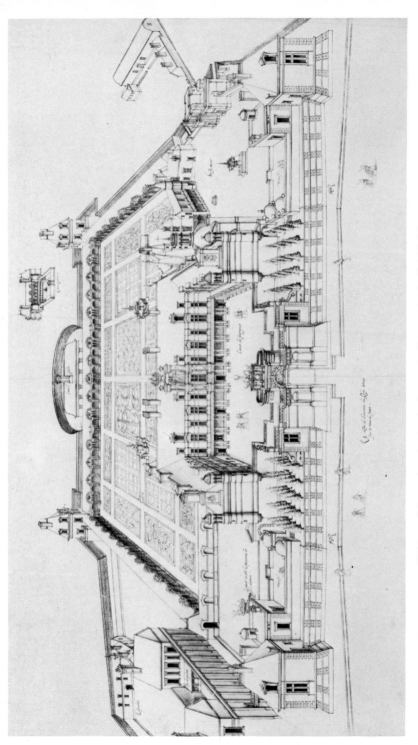

Château d'Anet: drawing by Androuet du Cerceau in the British Museum

Château de Maintenon: the garden front

Maintenon: the aqueduct and château

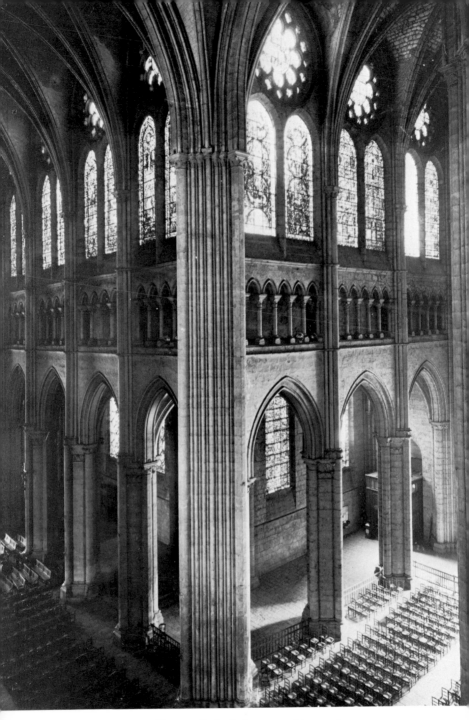

Chartres Cathedral: nave and transept

must have been a very important figure in eighteenth-century France; and a fine set of stalls. In the Revolution the church was stripped of all its treasures. The reliquary of Sulpice, which had been credited with so many miracles, was taken off 'to work a few miracles at the Mint'.

The north aisle opens into the much smaller Chapelle des Miracles, which is all that remains of the previous church built in 1180. It contains an interesting series of rather crude paintings of the life and miracles of Sulpice – not unlike the hand-coloured illustrations in an early nineteenth-century children's book.

From St Sulpice the charming little valley of the Renarde leads to **Villeconin**, a pleasant village with a delightful country church dedicated to **St Aubin**.

A slightly odd effect is produced by the crowding in of flying buttresses – surely not needed here – where there is hardly room for them. For the church, having no clerestory, offers only an extremely narrow gap between the aisle roof and that of the nave. The church dates from the fifteenth and sixteenth centuries except for the tower, which is clearly older.

From the Place de l'Église one can see the brown roof of one of the towers of the **château**. This is a fourteenth-century castle with obvious Louis XIII alterations and additions. It was built by either the father or the grandfather of the Jean Montagu, a high officer of state under Charles VI, who was beheaded in 1409 by order of Jean sans Peur. From the Montagus it passed to the family Malet de Graville whose most distinguished member was Louis, *Amiral de France* under Louis XII.

The west front is the most attractive, with the old *donjon*, heavily machicolated and slotted for a drawbridge, adapted as the entrance porch to a more homely dwelling. Inside there are some fine timber ceilings and handsome vaulting to the Salle de Montagu.

We now retrace our steps to Souzy and cross over the Vallée de l'Orge to **Le Marais** in the valley of the Rémarde. This is by far the most important château in the area.

There is a splendid view of it from the road, looking straight up the long canal at the entrance front. Here is one of the few great country houses to be built in the Ile de France under Louis XVI and certainly the finest. The architect was Barré, known in the Loire Valley for the beautiful Château de Montgeoffroy and for the classical wing of Le Lude.

Neither of those buildings, however, prepares one in the least for Le Marais. There is here none of that homely simplicity which characterizes those provincial dwellings, but a piece of conscious architectural design. Thought out in every detail, with almost every stone considered, Le Marais is a more sophisticated, more urbane achievement – more like some *hôtel particulier* from Paris suddenly transported to the depths of Hurepoix. Barré has clearly been influenced by Gabriel, but this is a step further in the 'return to Antiquity' which became so much the fashion towards the end of the century.

Barré has put considerable emphasis on the centre of his composition by crowning it with a dome which could be regarded as disproportionately high for a building of this size. Beneath the dome a recessed portico makes a square of deep shadow against which the pillars – impeccably Doric – stand out white and naked. On the garden side this emphasis is much reduced. The dome is replaced by a raised attic storey, and the portico consists only of four attached pilasters.

Built in 1770 for the architect's uncle Pierre-Henry le Maître, it passed in 1786 to his young niece the comtesse de Briche. She immediately set herself to entertain her tenants. '*L'amour de mes paysans*,' she wrote, '*le désir de les rendre heureux, me causaient une joie intérieure.*' She kept open table in the park; there was an abundance of food and there was music for those who wanted to dance it off and – delightful, optimistic phrase – '*vin à discretion*'.

Her devotion to the peasantry secured her survival of the Revolution and until her death in 1844 Le Marais was the centre of a charming and cultivated *vie de Château* which has been all too rare in French history.

In 1897 there was a sudden revival of the glories of Le Marais. The marquis de Castellane, the exotic, aesthetic spendthrift of the *belle époque*, and his American millionaire wife purchased the château. There was much about 'Bony' de Castellane which would pass as affectation. 'An exile, not from my country but from my epoch, I amused myself by living in another age, as much from a taste for beauty as from a distaste for my own times.' He had, however, a perceptive mind and understood the art of patronage. His relations with his workmen were excellent. It is often the mark of the true artistocrat that he reaches the artisan without passing by way of the bourgeoisie – and Castellane was an outrageous snob. When he managed to produce a genealogy tracing his ancestry back to the Carolingian kings a kinswoman of his, the old comtesse de Beaulaincourt, commented: '*Vous avez oublié de mentionner un certain Adam de Castellane qui épousa Eve de Je-ne-sais-trop-quoi.*'

Such was the new châtelain of Le Marais. 'Its architecture is perfect and logical,' he wrote, 'the Salon d'Honneur is central to the plan. It is preceded by rooms which are decorated simply because they are rooms through which one simply passes, whereas those which come after them are more sumptuous because they are designed for habitation.' The salon and the dining room are both heavily architectural rooms, with coupled columns and richly wrought entablatures, but the Salon Blanc is delicate in its refinement.

Typically, the new owner had to consider the decor in relation to the costumes not only of his servants but of his guests. 'The interior is of a pale mignonette green,' he wrote; 'our red liveries from Paris jarred with it. I had special ones made.' The new liveries gave the house 'an atmosphere that was deliciously faded. One could imagine oneself in an eighteenth century of silver and blue.' Outside in the courtyard he stationed a porter in a scarlet coach-man's surcoat. 'Who is this Cardinal here?' asked the Grand Duke Wladimir on his arrival. 'He is there,' replied Castellane, 'to provide a splash of scarlet against the white of the château.'

Men like the marquis de Castellane are not likely to be seen again in Western civilization and there is no splash of scarlet to distinguish Le Marais today.

At **St-Cyr-sous-Dourdan** is a charming ensemble composed of the church and a fortified farm which was once a priory. From here it is a matter of five kilometres south to **Dourdan**, capital of Hurepoix.

In 1222 Philippe-Auguste built the **castle** of which the lower half of the outer walls still largely remains. It was clearly based on the plan of the Louvre, which was built some twenty years earlier, and it was very nearly as large. The plan is simple and logical: an approximate square with a tower at each corner and a further tower marking the centre of each side, making it about thirty metres from tower to tower – an easy bowshot. On the south-east side the middle tower is replaced by the gatehouse; the north corner tower is con-siderably larger than the others and forms the keep.

This **keep** still stands some twenty-five metres high. It is of a very high quality masonry with walls over three and a half metres thick. The spiral staircases within these walls are alternately right- and left-hand thread – presumably a device to counteract giddiness. The keep marks a new conception of defensive architecture in having its entrance doors openly at ground floor level. Earlier castles were entered often as high as the third floor, but this was found to impede the defenders as often as the attackers. The principle that 'attack is the best method of defence' found its first expression in the easier access to and from the keep at Rouen and here at Dourdan.

There is not very much about Dourdan today from which we might reconstruct in our imagination the fairy castle which forms the backcloth for the month of April in the *Très Riches Heures du Duc de Berry*. The view is obviously taken from the south, for the gatehouse is to the right and the keep diametrically opposite, rising high above the rest of the building, and capped with an impressive conical roof.

When a castle was not being used for war it was frequently in use as a prison. It was here that Jeanne de Bourgogne was locked up by her father-in-law, Philippe le Bel. When her husband succeeded as Philippe V he came with a great cavalcade to release her and bring her back to be Queen.

Immediately opposite the château is the **church**, which has undoubtedly suffered through its proximity to a military target. Built originally in the early thirteenth century, it was partly destroyed when Dourdan was besieged in 1428. Rebuilt in the late fifteenth century, to which it owes its beautiful vaulting and Geometric windows, it was again damaged during the Wars of Religion. Among other things the south tower was partly demolished by order of the captain of the castle who felt it a threat to his security which it overlooked. It was again restored and completed in the seventeenth century. Perhaps its most beautiful feature is the north porch, a fifteenth-century addition by Amiral de Graville.

Inside, the overwhelming impression is of the great height of the vaults – an impression which is somewhat enhanced by the narrowness of the arches.

North-west of Dourdan stretches the Forêt de St Arnoult, and north-west of the forest is **St Arnoult** itself, a large village with an interesting church containing what is thought to be the oldest crypt in the Ile de France.

It must have been originally a façade of almost Cistercian austerity, its vertical accent very much emphasized by the uninterrupted lines of the buttresses which rise to their full height with no break. The Romanesque arch of the central doorway shows remains of rather interesting carving in the capitals, but retains the note of rude simplicity. Above it, in place of the narrow lancets, the fourteenth century opened a large Geometric window of an alien yellow stone.

The north-west door, which forms the present entrance, has a low four-centred arch with badly disfigured Flamboyant decorations. The west front thus exhibits three phases of medieval architecture.

The south-east door, only recently re-opened, belongs to the

original twelfth-century building. It is called the Porte des Caté-
chumènes and it is noticeably narrow. It appears that the builder
was taking literally the text of Matthew, chapter 7, verse xiv: 'strait
is the gate and narrow is the way which leadeth unto life'. Through
this door came those who were to be baptized. The font is, appropriately enough, in the south aisle near this entrance.

Inside, this is a most impressive church. A rough-hewn nave
in pure Romanesque, the pillars round with squared capitals of
a simple, bold design. There are rather tall clerestory windows
and a dark wooden barrel vault built on ornately carved beams
which date from the sixteenth century.

By contrast to the magnificent nave the apse looks tall and
dull; and it has some very indifferent glass. There are two aisles
to the north, almost like another church, where the pillars, entirely
cylindrical, splay out with no capitals into the many sheaves of the
lierne and tierceron vaulting, so that they resemble palm trees.

Beneath the altar is the **crypt of St Arnoult**. It shows in its walls
the herring-bone pattern of masonry used by the Romans and may
be as old as the sixth century. It was constructed to house the mortal
remains of Arnulph, bishop and martyr.

We have today almost wholly lost sight of the cult of the relic.
It needs all our historical imagination – and a crypt such as this to
stimulate our historical imagination – to recapture the sense of
being in the presence of eternity which was fostered by this cult.
This sense is admirably evoked by Pierre Lechaugette, writing of
crypts in general and St Arnoult-en-Yvelines in particular: 'there
lies sleeping the member of the mystical body, already in glory, now
finally united to the Head, bearing witness to every member of the
living body in this place now on earth of their common faith, their
common hope and their single love'. For centuries after his death,
Arnulph was responsible for this atmosphere of devotion which still
communicates a numinous quality to the building he inspired.

CHAPTER TWELVE

Fontainebleau

❧

Fontainebleau is only sixty-five kilometres from Paris and by using the A6 one can reach it in under an hour. But if it is possible to make a more leisurely approach the gain is considerable. We visit Fontainebleau only because of its château, and the château exists only because of the forest and the hunting which it afforded. A deliberate diversion through this strange and lovely woodland provides an appropriate overture to our arrival at the palace.

Fortunately for our purpose Henri IV created the requisite ring road in order to enable his courtiers to follow the hunt. The visitor from Paris can turn off the N7 at the roundabout called La Table du Roi and take the **Route Ronde** circling anti-clockwise round the château and its town. The road leads through a picturesque landscape of rocky outcrops, sandy wastes and slopes described by François I as '*nos délicieux déserts de Fontainebleau*'. They provided the perfect habitat for the stag, the wild boar, the heron and the kite which were the quarry most prized by the royal huntsmen and falconers.

So delightful is this overture that it would be worth completing the half circle to the **Croix de St Hérem**. It was at this point, in 1804, that Napoleon met Pope Pius VII whom he had summoned to France to crown him Emperor. Napoleon decided to evade the problems of precedence imposed by a formal reception at the palace and met Pius 'accidentally' here while ostensibly hunting a wild boar.

In many respects it is good to approach Fontainebleau with Napoleon in mind, for our first sight of the château is likely to be from the Place Général de Gaulle and the view of it thus obtained was his creation. It was he who pulled down the long, dull wing which screened the forecourt from the town and opened up the whole magnificent vista. The historical associations with Napoleon, also, are strong and moving.

It was in October 1807 that he wrote to Duroc, his *Maréchal du palais*, saying: 'it is our desire to use the château de Fontainebleau as a residence, keeping every part for its original destination'.

In associating his Imperial court with Fontainebleau and not with Versailles, Napoleon was identifying his own regime with the main line of French kings rather than with the last three Bourbons. Here he could claim Henri IV and François I among his predecessors and even St Louis; for, true to the traditions of the French château, Fontainebleau retained embedded in its Renaissance fabric the old medieval keep. '*C'est la maison des siècles*,' said Napoleon; '*la vraie demeure des rois*.'

'The real home of our kings.' It was to Fontainebleau that François I usually referred when he said '*allons chez-moi*'. The royal family was *at home* here more than anywhere else. As always happens to a favourite seat, each generation made its own alterations and additions with the result that the palace presents a pleasant medley of architecture of widely differing styles. There is always homeliness amid its magnificence.

A walk round the exterior provides an opportunity to unravel the complex history behind this medley, but the ground plan should be studied first. It shows that the palace itself is composed of two separate blocks, the huge forecourt known as the **Cour du Cheval Blanc**, because it once contained a statue of the white horse of Marcus Aurelius, and the irregular **Cour de l'Ovale**, so named because there was once an oval guardroom where there is now a gatehouse. The two are connected by the Galerie François I, to the south of which another open court, the **Cour de la Fontaine**, has been contrived.

In April 1528 François I commissioned Gilles le Breton to undertake a massive programme of reconstruction. He had found upon the site an old castle, roughly the shape of a magnet, and a small convent whose situation had been determined by the pure waters of the Spring of Bliaud or Fontaine de Bleau as it came to be spelt. The ground plan of the castle dictated the shape of the Cour de l'Ovale, while the Convent of the Mathurins provided consecrated ground for the Chapelle de la Trinité on the north side of the Cour du Cheval Blanc.

The Cour du Cheval Blanc was intended for tournaments and military reviews and needed to be extremely large. On the left, as we enter it, is the long, low **Aile des Ministres** built by François I in 1528. We can still see on the chimneys the capital F's with which he so often left his signature upon his buildings. The extreme simplicity of the style reflects the original use of the wing, for it was here that the King rehoused the Mathurin monks whose convent he destroyed to make room for the courtyard.

135

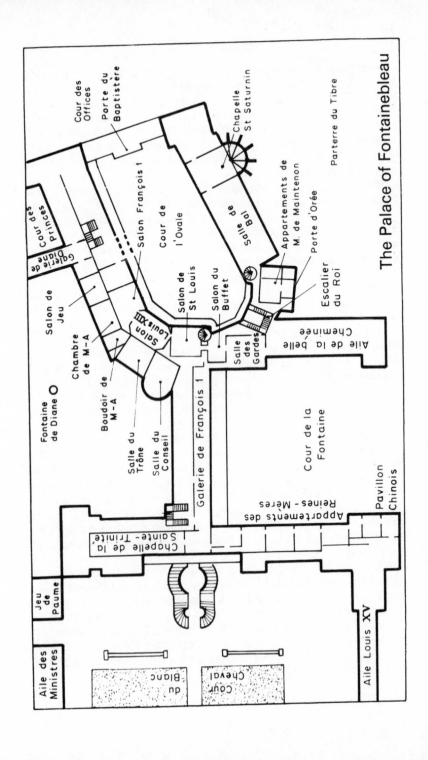

The Palace of Fontainebleau

Cour des Offices

Porte du Baptistère

Cour des Princes

Galerie de Diane

Salon de Jeu

Chambre de M-A

Boudoir de M-A

Fontaine de Diane O

Salle du Trône

Salle du Conseil

Salon Louis XIII

Salon François 1

Cour de l'Ovale

Chapelle St Saturnin

Salon de St Louis

Salon du Buffet

Salle de Bal

Appartements de M. de Maintenon

Porte d'Orée

Parterre du Tibre

Escalier du Roi

Salle des Gardes

Aile de la belle Cheminée

Galerie de François 1

Chapelle de la Sainte-Trinité

Appartements des Reines-Mères

Cour de la Fontaine

Pavillon Chinois

Jeu de Paume

Aile des Ministres

Cour du Blanc

Cheval

Aile Louis XV

Opposite the entrance grille is the **west front** with its great horse-shoe staircase. We can at once detect the presence of two different styles. To the left of the staircase the windows, which are framed by stone quoins, are separated by a single pilaster in the rather coarse grey stone of the district. This stone does not lend itself to the sculptor's chisel and dictates its own austerity of style. In contrast to these rather homely façades the first floor to the right of the staircase is faced with the finest ashlar and the pilasters frame the windows. This refacing was done under Henri IV who thus transformed much of the original work of Le Breton.

It is interesting to note that the building to the left of the staircase is in fact the **Chapel**. Usually a chapel was given a distinctive treatment which made it at once identifiable from the exterior; but there is almost no indication of the chapel's existence here except the absence of dormer windows, which upsets the apparent symmetry of the façade. François I was no lover of exact symmetry and the more we look at this front the more we see that each part balances but does not reflect the other.

The work started by François I was continued under Henri II by the architect Philibert de l'Orme. It was he who designed the first stone staircase to the central pavilion. In spite of his proud claim that it was 'one of the most beautiful pieces of work that you could possibly see', it was less elegant than the present one and almost useless as there was at this time no door in the pavilion.

It was not until 1614 that a door was opened in this façade and this began to be used as the main entrance. Twenty years later du Cerceau rebuilt the **stone staircase** with the beautiful flowing lines which we see today, but it was reserved for Napoleon to open up the courtyard to the town. He thus provided the palace with its most sumptuous approach.

It was, alas, for his departure rather than his arrival that the court is chiefly famous. On 6 April 1814 he signed the deed of abdication. Whatever we may think of Napoleon, there is something infinitely pathetic about the spectacle of a great man broken. His agony during the ensuing days is better imagined than described. He learnt of the defection of Ney and Berthier; even his attempted suicide was unsuccessful. But in the end he mastered himself and on 20 April, the day fixed for his departure for Elba, he rose magnificently to the occasion. With the soldiers of the Old Guard sobbing in the courtyard, he descended the great horseshoe staircase, embraced General Petit and kissed the flag on which were recorded so many of his victories. 'May this kiss pass on into all your hearts,' he cried

137

and then, promising to write a book on all their great achievements together, he bade them farewell with the words '*Adieu mes enfants!*' and threw himself into the carriage which awaited him. From that moment the Cour du Cheval Blanc has been known also as the 'Cour des Adieux'.

The third wing of the courtyard, on the south side, is obviously of later date than the others. It was built in 1739 by order of Louis XV to provide seventy-two new apartments. It was built with an eye to economy. It was, for instance, specified in the contracts that the marble used for the mantelpieces should be of inferior quality – '*commun*' or '*non du beau*'. Not surprisingly the façade that went with them is devoid of architectural distinction, which makes it all the more deplorable that in order to build this wing Louis XV destroyed one of the real glories of Fontainebleau, the Galerie d'Ulysse. This gallery, 150 metres long, was decorated in fresco by Primaticcio and Nicolo dell' Abbate with fifty-eight scenes from the *Odyssey*.

Its passing was not unmourned. An Italian named Algarotti went to take a last look at the frescos at the very moment that the demolition started – 'we had to beseech the workmen to suspend for an instant their work of devastation'. He found that the paintings 'still had the freshness, the relief and vigour of colouring' they had always had. The duc de Luynes, however, dismissed the gallery as '*mauvaise et inutile*' and he spoke for his century. The Galerie d'Ulysse was replaced by the pedestrian **Aile Louis XV**.

In 1854 Napoleon III installed a **court theatre** in the west end of this wing, which is worth a visit, The architect, Hector Lefuel, drew his inspiration from the theatres of Versailles and Trianon – doubtless a reflection of the Empress Eugénie's own enthusiasm for Marie-Antoinette.

At the extreme end of the wing there is a passage which leads us out into the gardens and brings us to the only survival of François I's building – the grotesque façade of the **Grotte du Jardin des Pins**. It dates from 1543, when Serlio was in charge of the works at Fontainebleau. The figures of *Atlantes*, whose abdominal muscles form part of the rustication of the masonry, are typically Italian and presumably designed by Serlio.

From the grotto there is a pleasant walk through the **Jardin Anglais**, laid out by Hurtault for Napoleon, in the middle of which can still be seen the original **Fontaine de Bleau** from which the palace takes its name. From here the path leads back along the side of a triangular lake, the **Étang des Carpes**.

The lake has, since the days of Henri IV, been well stocked with these enormous, gluttonous fish. It is still sometimes claimed that the oldest date back to the *Ancien Régime*. It cannot be true, for during the Revolution the lake was drained and the consequent sale of fish lasted for eight days. Under Louis XIII and XIV one member of the palace staff held the title '*Gouverneur des Cormorants*'. His job was to train cormorants for a sort of aquatic falconry, an art learnt from the Chinese.

The path leads us back to the Cour de la Fontaine – the most beautiful part of the palace, the inmost sanctuary of the royal court.

Under Henri II the King's apartment was at the south-west angle of this courtyard in a block known as the Pavillon des Poëles. The *poëles* were porcelain stoves which provided the royal rooms with the nearest equivalent to central heating. This pavilion was replaced by Louis XV with the heavy, square block which we see today. It reflects the architecture of Versailles, but lacks the elegance of the tall first-floor windows of its august prototype.

The façade adjoining this pavilion contains the **Appartement des Reines Mères**, so named because it was inhabited by Catherine de Medici, Marie de Medici and Anne d'Autriche successively. The simple, dignified façade was the design of Philibert de l'Orme.

At right angles to this, across the end of the courtyard, runs the **Galerie François I**. It was refaced in the beautiful stone of St Leu d'Esserent under Henri II and Charles IX, but the loggia owes its present form to Henri IV. François I had his **Appartement des Bains** on the ground floor – a series of rooms corresponding approximately with those of a Roman bath – with a sumptuous fresco decoration which made it 'a very pleasing and delicious place'. The stoves for heating the water and thermal chambers necessitated chimneys which have since disappeared, leaving the serried rank of dormers which we see today.

The remaining façade is known as the **Aile de la Belle Cheminée** after the huge mantelpiece which adorned the **Grande Salle** within. It was built by Primaticcio in 1568 and is the only façade in this part of the palace to retain its original appearance. It is, perhaps for this reason, the most distinguished piece of architecture in the whole ensemble. The Cour de la Fontaine, seen across the waters of the lake, presents one of the most lovely views in the Ile de France.

Through the central archway of Primaticcio's wing we can gain access to the **Avenue de Maintenon**, which was the approach to the original main entrance – **la Porte d'Orée**. François I was as likely to have come to Fontainebleau from the Loire Valley as from Paris and was more interested in having access to the forest than the town. *Orée* is the French for the verge of a forest and provides a possible etymology for the name.

The architecture of the Porte d'Orée is pure Le Breton, translating a feudal gatehouse into a Renaissance entrance pavilion, but with a typical disregard for symmetry. The square tower to the right of the archway is broader than the one to the left and the main roof is eccentric. Le Breton is true to the French tradition in his vertical treatment of the flight of windows on either side.

In detail, however, the gatehouse has suffered various changes. The frescos in the loggias were so heavily restored by Picot in the nineteenth century as to have lost all historical interest. The doors were ordered in 1664 by Colbert for Louis XIV. Above them is a segmental tympanum for which Cellini designed his famous *Nymphe de Fontainebleau*, now in the Louvre. It never reached its proper destination, for Diane de Poitiers, the all-powerful mistress of Henri II, appropriated it for her own château at Anet.

Next to the gatehouse are the huge windows of the **Salle de Bal**. The original plan had been for a vast open loggia with a high vault painted in fresco – a very Italian and Renaissance conception which we owe to Serlio. Philibert de l'Orme, who succeeded him as architect, decided to replace the vault with a coffered ceiling and to glaze the arches, thus creating the large apartment which we see today.

Beyond the ballroom are the two superimposed chapels dedicated to the Virgin Mary and St Saturnin. The original chapels had been consecrated in 1169 by Thomas à Becket. They were entirely rebuilt in 1541 by Le Breton. The arrangement was a frank acceptance of class distinction, the **chapelle haute** being reserved for the King and his courtiers while the **chapelle basse** was provided for the domestic staff. In 1882 the cupola had to be renewed and the architect Boitte gave way to a petty republicanism by inverting the initials FR (*Fransiscus Rex*) to RF (*République Française*).

We are now well placed to view the King's Garden or **Parterre du Tibre** laid out for Louis XIV not, as might be expected, by Le Nôtre, but by the architect Le Vau. There is nothing distinguished about the design; it has neither the peaceful poetry of Courances nor the animating profusion of Vaux or Versailles. From the far side, however, there is an admirable view of the château with its seemingly endless succession of high pavilion roofs and tall red chimneys.

The terrace at the eastern extremity of the parterre overlooks the **Cascades**, also a creation of Louis XIV's, which used to accommodate the fountains of Francini, the hydraulic engineer who did so much for the waterworks of Versailles. Today the fountains are silent, but the terrace provides a vantage point from which to admire the **Grand Canal**.

This was the most important addition to the gardens made by Henri IV, who took an almost childish delight in its construction. Malherbe records how he would sit sometimes from five or six in the morning until midday watching the workmen. When it was finally completed it took eight days to fill with water.

Under Louis XIV the Canal was the centre of much of the pageantry of the Court. In 1664 Sebastian Locatelli described an evening excursion of the royal family with the Queen and the Queen Mother in a barque 'richly gilded and of wonderful stateliness' and the King driving along the bank in a *calèche*, a vehicle which combined the ease of a bath chair with the elegance of a Roman chariot.

To the north of the Parterre du Tibre lies the vast **Cour des Offices**, built by Rémy Collin in 1609 for Henri IV. It is a most accomplished piece of architecture. By the alternation of doors and windows on the ground floor he has introduced a pleasing rhythm which is reflected in the spacing of the dormers above. In the north and south ranges he has inserted a complex central pavilion with high roofs and lofty chimney stacks which lend a great distinction to the whole. Especially magnificent is the colossal niche which frames the entrance from the **Place d'Armes** and seems to reflect an idea of Bramante's for the Belvedere.

From the Cour des Offices we can approach the palace as Henri IV intended it to be approached. It was he who straightened out the wings of the Cour de l'Ovale and erected the gateway known as the **Porte du Baptistère**, re-utilizing a triumphal arch by Primaticcio and capping it with a square-based dome.

Through its arch we can look into the courtyard, the nucleus around which the rest of the château was built. At the far end is the old twelfth-century **keep** in which François I made his bedroom. To either side of it the buildings of Le Breton follow the odd, irregular angles of the original foundations. To their sober façades Serlio added the colonnade, as much to provide a connection between the rooms at first-floor level as to embellish the courtyard. The portico, often attributed to Serlio, has been shown by Sir Anthony Blunt to be the work of Le Breton and therefore part of the first design. It was moved to its present position and deprived of its stone staircase by Henri IV.

141

From the Porte du Baptistère there is a path which follows the line of the old moat, leading north round the **Cour des Princes**, which brings us into the **Jardin de Diane**. This takes its name from the statue of Diana in the fountain, which dates from 1603. The hounds, cast in bronze by Pierre Biard, have recently been returned from the Louvre to their proper position.

The façades of the royal apartments, reconstructed during the eighteenth century, look out on to this garden. They lack any architectural pretensions and might be those of a large town house rather than of a palace. This need not surprise us for it was here, more than anywhere else, that members of the royal family could feel themselves at home.

From the Jardin de Diane we can return between the **Tennis Court** and the Aile des Ministres into the Cour du Cheval Blanc. This walk round the courts and gardens could take upwards of one hour and might be used to stimulate an appetite for lunch. The gardens, the banks of the canal or the rocky outcrops of the forest provide many opportunities for a picnic.

* * *

A visit to the **interior** of the palace is a formidable undertaking for a single afternoon; ideally one should make several visits. The tour divides naturally into three main parts – the Grands Appartements, the Appartement des Reines Mères and the Petits Appartements. Even more than the exterior, these endless rooms reflect the truth of Napoleon's description – *la maison des siècles*. Since all the rooms have been subject to frequent restoration and redecoration, the visitor is continually passing from one period to another and then back. It is useful to start with a general historical outline in mind.

François I invited two Italians to Fontainebleau – Gian Battista Rosso, a Florentine who emulated Michelangelo, and Francesco Primaticcio of Bologna, who was more influenced by Raphael and Correggio. Both were financed in a manner typical of the age – by preferment in the Church. Primaticcio became Abbot of St Martin and Rosso a Canon of the Sainte Chapelle. A considerable number of artists, some French, some Italian and some Flemish collaborated under their direction and thus was formed the First School of Fontainebleau. Its distinctive feature was the combination of fresco panels with high relief stucco frames incorporating human and grotesque figures. The Galerie François I, the Escalier du Roi and the Salle de Bal are the most important survivals.

Under Henri IV was founded the Second School of Fontainebleau. The great names were now French or Flemish – Toussaint Dubreuil, Ambroise Dubois (whose real name was Bosschaert) and Martin Fréminet. The most important ensemble to survive is the Chapelle de la Trinité.

We start our tour of the **Grands Appartements** with one of the earliest creations, the **Galerie François I**. It is still a very pleasing ensemble. The subdued, rather pink colouring of the paintings accords beautifully with the brown and gold of the woodwork. The general impression is satisfying, but in detail much of the decor is open to criticism; some of the stucco figures are not only grotesque but absurd. Rosso's full-length figures, however, are extremely elegant.

But the gallery has not retained its original appearance. The windows on the north side were filled in by Louis XVI in 1785. Already in 1731 Van Loo had done a considerable touching up of the frescos. Unfortunately the technique of fresco painting, which is done while the plaster is still wet, makes restoration virtually impossible. In 1837 a report by the architect Fontaine describes the paintings in the gallery as 'almost entirely effaced'. Louis-Philippe ordered a 'restoration' which was little less than a total repainting, based on the original designs.

The Galerie François I had an effect even on the architecture of England. In 1540, when Henry VIII was building Nonsuch, he had in his employment a certain Nicolas Bellin of Modena. From 1533 his name occurred frequently in the *comptes des bâtiments* for Fontainebleau. Henry often discussed architecture with his Ambassador at the Court of France, Sir John Wallop, who found François I equally interested in what Henry was doing at Whitehall, Hampton Court and Nonsuch. 'He heard say,' writes Wallop to Henry, 'that your Majesty did use much gilding in your said houses, especially in the roofs, but in his buildings he used little or none, but made the roofs of timber finely wrought with divers colours of wood natural.'

In 1834 there was an interesting opportunity for inspecting the ceiling of the Galerie François I. Louis-Philippe had started his great work of restoration and the ceiling had been taken down in sections and was lying on the floor. The comtesse de Boigne describes it in her memoirs: 'we were able to admire the perfection of this example of the work of the cabinet maker – I almost said "the art of the goldsmith" – executed with the precision with which one might make a snuff box'.

The comtesse de Boigne was a member of Louis-Philippe's first house party at Fontainebleau. Her observant eye soon detected the influence which the great palace began to exert upon the 'Bourgeois King'. There was, during this voyage, she writes, 'a certain *parfum de trône*; at least there was evidence of a slight inclination to mount the bottom step of the ladder of royalty. It was the first time since the Revolution that I saw the King dare to remember that he was a descendant of Henri IV. This residence, so very aristocratic, of Fontainebleau recalled the blood of the Bourbons to his veins and he developed a taste for it.' But if Fontainebleau exercised a subtle influence over Louis-Philippe, Louis-Philippe made an unmistakable impact upon Fontainebleau. In order to save the place from ruin he was obliged to make a thorough renovation. The Fontainebleau of François I can only be dimly sensed behind the restorations of Louis-Philippe.

From the Galerie François I we can reach the apartments on the south side of the Cour de l'Ovale where the most important remnants of his decoration survive.

The first room, the **Salle des Gardes**, is a typical Louis-Philippe composition. Only the fine Louis XIII ceiling remains intact from the past. The fireplace is pieced together from oddments found in the Garde Meuble – a bust of Henri IV from the Orangerie, the framework of the overmantel in Henri II's bedroom and the two statues from the famous 'Belle Cheminée' in the adjoining wing.

Beyond this is the **Escalier du Roi**, built by Louis XV in 1747. He retained at first-floor level what had been the decorations of the bedroom of François I's mistress, the duchesse d'Étampes. The decor was designed by Primaticcio and consisted of a series of frescos representing the life of Alexander the Great. These scenes of exalted masculinity are as it were held in place by stucco figures of idealized femininity. The attenuated ladies afford an interesting comparison with Rosso's figures in the gallery.

The frescos were restored by Pujol in the nineteenth century. Whenever possible the original design was made the basis for the reconstruction, but the slender females are probably the only genuine survivals of Primaticcio's ensemble.

From here a narrow passage leads to the **Salle de Bal**, which has already been described from the outside. This also was the design of Primaticcio and was carried out by his assistant Nicolo dell' Abbate. It was praised by Vasari as one of the most distinguished achievements of the First School of Fontainebleau. Louis Dimier, one of the chief historians of the palace, is less favourable in his judgement. 'The figures,' he writes, 'are lacking both in solidity and in life; heads that are too small alternate with bodies that are too long.' One example will demonstrate the justice of his criticism. In the spandrel between the third and fourth windows on the court-yard side are represented the Three Graces. Never have three figures done less to deserve that title. Their tiny heads serve only to emphasize the largeness of their lumpy and misshapen anatomy. It would have been bad enough to leave such uncomely coarseness naked: Prima-ticcio has gone one worse and clothed them only with a ring of bells half-way up the calf – the most inelegant point at which to divide the human leg.

All these frescos were virtually repainted in the nineteenth century by Alaux. He had the original designs to inform him and by the application of heated wax he was able to bring to the surface colour which had almost disappeared. Thus he had the double guide of Primaticcio's lines and Nicolo dell' Abbate's colours. His restoration was no mean achievement and the Salle de Bal, like the Galerie François I, creates a general impression of rich and noble harmony.

Next to the Salle de Bal, in the square block of the Pavillon de la Porte d'Orée, are **Madame de Maintenon's rooms**, redecorated by Louis XIV and recently meticulously restored. From here we retrace our steps to the Salle des Gardes and proceed in a clockwise direction round the rooms overlooking the Cour de l'Ovale.

The **Salon de St Louis** or **Salon du Donjon** occupies the oldest part of the château and served usually as the King's bedroom until Henri IV moved into what is now the Salle du Trône. It was Louis-Philippe who placed the most conspicuous ornament in the room – the huge bas relief of Henri IV on horseback which was carved by Mathieu Jacquet for the centrepiece of the 'Belle Cheminée'.

The next room is variously known as the **Cabinet de Théagène**, from the subject matter of its paintings, or the **Salon Louis XIII**, from the fact that he was born here. Painted by Dubois, it is one of the best survivals of the Second School of Fontainebleau, but Louis XV upset the decorative scheme by removing four of the paint-ings to make room for his doorways, some of which are false and serve only the interests of symmetry.

It was in this room, on 27 September 1601, that Marie de Medici's first son was born. It is usually the penalty paid by those who marry titles that a male child is expected of them as soon as possible and the poor Queen was tormented by the fear that this child would be a girl. The King made a private arrangement with the midwife that if it were a boy her first order would be 'warm me a towel'. The words were uttered but the child born was so puny that the midwife's expression caused the King to doubt the message. She gave the baby the kiss of life; and then in order to reassure the King as to its sex she uncovered the appropriate portion of its anatomy. The King rushed to his wife's bedside. '*Mamie!*' he cried, '*réjouissez-vous. Dieu nous a donné ce que nous désirons. Nous avons un beau fils!*'

The birth of Louis XIII was a great turning point in the life of his father. The morals of the Court, following the example set by the King, were little short of disgraceful. The King's mistress, Gabrielle d'Estrées – commonly known as *duchesse Ordure* – provided him regularly with what he most wanted, which was children. In 1599 he obtained from Rome the annulment of his marriage with Marguérite de Valois and all feared he would be fool enough to marry Gabrielle. She openly boasted that she could only be robbed of the crown by the death of the King. She forgot to reckon with her own. On Good Friday she was struck down by some horrible and then unknown disease. The King, who had set out from Fontainebleau to be with her at the last, was met on the road by the Marshals Bassompierre and d'Ornano with the news of her death. Alone with his two friends in the great Salle de la Belle Cheminée, Henri wept for his worthless mistress while France rejoiced.

The coming of Marie de Medici and her prompt production of a Dauphin brought a new propriety to the Court. One of the most attractive qualities of Henri IV was his paternal affection. In the galleries and gardens of Fontainebleau the King could be seen playing endless tomfooleries with the young Prince. 'I want to be always with Daddy!' was the Dauphin's ecstatic cry. At the age of nine he had to face the tragic loss of his father and succeed to the throne. He was to adorn Fontainebleau with its magnificent horseshoe staircase and the two sumptuous ceilings in the **Salle du Trône** and the **Chambre de la Reine**.

The ceilings, which are the work of Jean Gobert, are heavily ornate and richly gilded. It was the fashion of the age in architecture as in furniture and in clothing. At the wedding of the prince de Condé to Mlle de Montmorency the Queen had to retire from the ball after one hour because she was so weighed down by the jewels that adorned her lavish costume.

Fontainebleau was probably at this time at the height of its glory. The works of Primaticcio and Rosso were still in their prime; the paintings of Dubois, Dubreuil and Fréminet were fresh upon the walls. Saint Germain, nearer to Paris, was the official seat of the Court, but Saint Germain could never compare with Fontainebleau for beauty, spaciousness and richness of decoration. Until the building of Versailles, Fontainebleau was the brightest jewel in the crown of France.

With the completion of Versailles Saint Germain fell into disuse while Fontainebleau retained its second place. The custom of bringing the entire Court here for four or five weeks' hunting in the autumn – known as the '*Voyage de Fontainebleau*' – became an annual event under Louis XIV and his successors.

Right at the end of his reign, Louis XIV decided on an enlargement and redecoration of the **Chambre du Roi**. This room backs on to the Salon Louis XIII and overlooks the Jardin de Diane. Louis retained Gobert's ceiling and the oval medallions above the doors, but he replaced the panelling in a style which was already beginning to take on the sinuous lines associated with his successor. Over the mantelpiece he kept the portrait of his father, Louis XIII, painted by Philippe de Champaigne. One of the excesses of the Revolution was to burn this painting in front of the statue of Marat along with forty-eight other royal portraits.

Napoleon turned the Chambre du Roi into his Throne Room. He put his own portrait by Gérard over the mantelpiece. Louis-Philippe removed this in favour of another Champaigne of Louis XIII.

Louis XIV also redecorated the **Salle du Conseil** next door, but only his ceiling survives, for in 1753 Louis XV determined on a further redecoration. It is a most attractive ensemble, though perhaps more suited to a drawing room than to a council chamber. Boucher, Van Loo and Jean-Baptiste Pierre have an equal share in the credit. It is a wonderful example of artistic collaboration; it needs the evidence of the *comptes des bâtiments* to reveal that the pink panels are by Pierre and the blue-grey ones by Van Loo.

Louis XV also made costly redecorations for his mistresses. Madame de Pompadour was more interested in her private house at Fontainebleau, the Hermitage, which is a gem of the period but not opened to the public. Madame du Barry's apartments were for the most part deliberately effaced by Marie-Antoinette.

The memory of Marie-Antoinette is mostly preserved in the three rooms adjoining the Chambre du Roi. On her first arrival as Dauphine at Fontainebleau she spent three hours being shown round the palace by the marquis de Marigny and it was here that she first captivated the Court and scored a number of triumphs against du Barry with the King. In the Court theatre – at that time situated in the Aile de la Belle Cheminée – etiquette forbade applause, but when the duc d'Aumont inserted into a piece some verses complimentary to the Dauphine she received a spontaneous ovation.

Her **Salon de Jeu** was entirely redecorated in 1786. It was the last year that the Court went to Fontainebleau before the Revolution. It is not known in which month the decor was completed, but it is reasonable to suppose that it was done before the *Voyage*. The Queen probably had one season's enjoyment of her salon.

The ceiling was painted by Berthélemy, the panelling by Rousseau and the overdoors by Sauvage, who did so much beautiful work at Compiègne.

When the list of the furniture was drawn up during the Revolution, the Salon de Jeu was found to contain thirteen different gaming tables – each game in those days requiring a special sort of table. None of them is there now, but the two beautiful commodes by Benneman have found their way back.

The **Boudoir of Marie-Antoinette** is usually acclaimed as the most perfect interior decoration at Fontainebleau. It was completed between 1785 and 1786 and therefore also served for one season only.

The word *bijou*, as applied to architecture, has become debased. It is unfortunate, because the exquisite refinement of this room belongs to the art of the jeweller. The overall colour scheme is of silver and gold. Almost all the surfaces are covered with decoration, but with so light and delicate a touch that it is never ornate. As so often at Fontainebleau, it is a work of artistic collaboration. The design was by Mique, the ceiling painted by Berthélemy, the Pompeian arabesques by Rousseau; the beautifully modelled overdoors are by Roland and the bronze ornaments to the fireplace and windows by Gouthière.

Recently the room has recovered two of its most precious furnishings – the little bureau and the mother of pearl work table, both by Riesner. If harmonious surroundings ever brought peace to a human soul, perhaps this marvellous little room afforded a few weeks' solace to that unhappy Queen.

The **Chambre de la Reine** also dates largely from her time. The ceiling, as we have noticed, is Louis XIII, and the doors and overdoors and the gilded carvings of the bed are what she knew. Only the *meuble d'été* – the lovely Lyons silk hangings and upholstery –

the last ever ordered under the *Ancien Régime*, were never seen by her. They were first put up for Joséphine in 1806.

Napoleon did not make any significant additions to the structure of Fontainebleau. But he found the palace unfurnished. His influence is chiefly to be sought in the decoration and furnishing of the Petits Appartements.

We have now completed the tour of the Grands Appartements and return to the vestibule at the head of the horseshoe staircase. It is a convenient opportunity to look into the **Chapelle de la Trinité**. The decoration of this chapel was the most important achievement of the Second School of Fontainebleau. It is related that it owed its origin to the visit of the Spanish Ambassador, Don Pedro, in 1608. Henri IV personally conducted him all round the palace and finally asked his opinion. 'All that is lacking,' came the answer, 'is for God to be as well housed as your Majesty.'

The whole design is due to Fréminet, under whose directions the sculptors and stuccatores worked. Except for the replacement, during the eighteenth century, of the oval paintings between the windows, the decor has survived unaltered. Fréminet painted in oils on dry plaster and his work has proved more durable than that of Rosso or Primaticcio.

The altar was not completed until 1633, when the two statues by Bordoni were set on either side. They represent Charlemagne and St Louis, but their features are unmistakably those of Henri IV and Louis XIII.

From the vestibule we gain access to the **Appartement des Reines Mères**, also known as the **Appartement du Pape**, which occupies the first floor of the west side of the Cour de la Fontaine.

The third room, the **Grand Salon**, has the most remarkable ceiling originally made for the bedroom of Henri II in the Pavillon des Poëles. It is the work of two wood carvers named Perret and Chanterelle and incorporates the theme of the seven planets. The Gobelin tapestry *Alexander and the family of Darius* is of special interest since Le Brun executed the design here at Fontainebleau.

The next room, the **Chambre d'Anne d'Autriche**, had another very rich ceiling painted in 1660 by Cotelle de Meaux. Portraits of Anne and of her niece and daughter-in-law Queen Marie-Thérèse ornament the overdoors.

In the centre of Gabriel's block, which replaced the Pavillon des Poëles, is the bedroom of Princess Helen of Mecklenburg-Schwerin who married the eldest son of Louis-Philippe, the duc d'Orléans, in

1837. There was a double ceremony, the Catholic service being conducted in the Chapelle de la Trinité and the Protestant one in the Galerie des Colonnes – a creation of Louis-Philippe's on the ground floor beneath the Salle de Bal.

The **State Bedroom of the duchesse d'Orléans** contains some of the most notable furniture in the palace. The light, fanciful frieze and the fireplace survive from Gabriel's original decor. The bed and chairs come from Louis XVI's bedroom at St Cloud, for which they were made in 1787. The commode, not unlike that in the Queen's bedroom, is by Benneman and comes from Compiègne. On it stands the princess's jewel casket with porcelain plaques by Revelly depicting her reception at Fontainebleau.

This room also served as the bedroom for Pope Pius VII, once in 1804 for the coronation of Napoleon and again in 1812 when he came as a prisoner. Napoleon, having got the temporal power of Europe into his hands, wished to control the spiritual power also and to make Paris the Holy See. He succeeded in forcing upon his captive the signature of a *concordat* which deprived the Supreme Pontiff of the right to create any bishop not nominated by the Emperor. The signatures on the document tell all that needs to be told – the Pope's pathetic scrawl and the Emperor's triumphant flourish. Pius was so overcome with shame afterwards that for days he would not even say Mass. But time was on his side. The star of Napoleon was setting fast and the Allies were advancing on Paris. It was soon the Emperor's turn to taste the bitter humiliation of defeat.

A touching sequel to the whole painful episode was added three years later when Pius learned of Napoleon's approaching death at St Helena and with truly Christian generosity pleaded his cause. 'He can no longer be a danger to anyone; we would wish that he might not be a subject of remorse to anyone either.'

The memory of Napoleon is chiefly to be sought in the **Petits Appartements** which occupy the ground floor behind the Galerie François I and beneath the King's and Queen's apartments on the first floor. Built by Louis XV and Louis XVI, the rooms have mostly retained their original fireplaces, panelling and other architectural ornaments. To this framework were added the silk hangings and draperies, the tables, chairs, sofas, consoles and *guéridons* of Marcion, Bélanger and Jacob Desmalters.

One of the best examples is the **Salon Jaune** of Joséphine's suite. The cornice, decorated with swags and garlands, is identical with that of the **Salon d'Étude** which can be dated to 1772. The marble fireplace, also, is plainly Louis XVI. In contrast to these the panels of gold silk, hung here for Joséphine, are plain rectangles. The furniture, by Jacob Desmalters, is plain and rectilinear also. It stands on a magnificent Aubusson carpet specially designed for this room.

Everything was done to the precise instructions of Napoleon. He had, by his own admission, *'le goût passionné du détail'*. In Joséphine's **Cabinet de Toilette** he ordained every fitting. 'It is desirable,' he wrote, 'that the bath should be sunk so that there are not more than eight or nine inches above floor level in order to accommodate the sofa which is to cover it.' The sofa, which conceals the bath when not in use, opens out to form a screen round it when it is needed.

Poor Joséphine did not have long to enjoy these new luxuries. In October 1809, Napoleon arrived at Fontainebleau straight from Schönbrunn and the victory of Wagram. The Court was summoned and Joséphine hastened here from St Cloud. She found the door between her bedroom and her husband's had been walled up. Two months later her dismissal was announced and preparations made for Marie-Louise of Austria to succeed her.

Beyond Joséphine's rooms were those of Madame Mère, who kept herself rather apart from the Court saying: 'in public I call you *Sire* and *Majesté*, but in my own rooms I am your mother and you are my son'. These rooms were part of the **Galerie des Cerfs**, which had been partitioned off under Louis XV and was only restored to its original state in 1863. This was one of Napoleon III's main contributions to Fontainebleau. It had been built by Henri IV and as its name implies was devoted to the chase. The decoration, inspired by the Gallery of Maps at the Vatican, consisted of a series of aerial views of the forests belonging to the King together with the châteaux attached to them, all painted by Dubreuil. It would have provided a priceless document for the architectural historian, but the old story has to be told again: the paintings had so deteriorated as to be largely unrecognizable. Two painters, Guiaud and Lassone, using such prints and drawings as were available, repainted the scenes. The portrayals of Montceaux and Madrid are extremely good, but they do not represent contemporary documents on the appearance of those two important châteaux.

The Galerie des Cerfs is always remembered as the scene of a semi-judicial murder. In 1648 Christina of Sweden was lodging at Fontainebleau. She had abdicated her throne and embraced the religion of Rome without becoming thereby any less dictatorial or any more Christian. She had among her suite a certain marquis

Monaldeschi whom she accused of having betrayed her, though whether his offence was of a political or a gallant nature is not known. He was arraigned before her in the Galerie des Cerfs, condemned and forced to make his confession before being stabbed to death then and there. Barbaric executions did not normally shock Frenchmen of the seventeenth century, but this action caused widespread indignation.

Above the Galerie des Cerfs is the **Galerie de Diane**, originally painted by Dubois as an apotheosis of Henri IV. It had to be rebuilt under Napoleon and its decoration was only achieved under Louis XVIII who made it a gallery of French history. The pictures, however, were mostly dispersed by Napoleon III when he installed the library here.

In 1868 the Emperor appointed Octave Feuillet librarian, and it is through his letters to his wife that we get our last picture of Fontainebleau as a royal palace. Feuillet was deeply impressed by the place – 'very far removed from what we have seen at the Tuileries, at St Cloud and at Compiègne. All the glory of the Valois dynasty stands out in full relief in these galleries with their wallpaintings, their woodwork and their ceilings, all elegant and superb. The uniformed officials and the ladies in court dress were dwarfed by this overwhelming decor.'

Dinner was served in the Salle de Bal – 'the most beautiful Banqueting Hall in any palace in the world'. After dinner the company went down into the Salon Chinois on the ground floor of Gabriel's pavilion. Its windows opened on to the lake, where a fleet of pleasure boats and gondolas awaited the guests. Eugénie always used to declare that nothing was more conducive to conversation than the gentle rocking of a boat. '*La nuit tombait, mais magnifique, et ces barques, ces toilettes, ces lumières dans l'eau, ces verdures sombres dans le fond, tout cela avait un véritable aspect de fête de cour.*'

We should end our tour of Fontainebleau with a visit to the **Musée Chinois** which now occupies these rooms. The exhibits, which were mostly looted from the Summer Palace at Peking, are of interest to the connoisseur, but for the average visitor it is the memory of Eugénie that is important. Here Feuillet describes her, seated on a large sofa with her back to the huge windows, open on to the garden and the lake. Fontainebleau, with all its historical associations, seems to have dictated the conversation of its inhabitants. 'We talked till midnight on every subject – the palace and the memories that it recalled of Marie-Antoinette, of Monaldeschi and of Mme de

Motteville. We were gay – the Emperor more than usual.'

The moment of calm is often precursor to the storm. It was during this visit to Fontainebleau that the first results of the election came in. In the Jura the imperial candidate had lost to the republican by eleven thousand votes to twenty-two thousand.

The fête continued with the typical mixture of magnificence and informality cultivated by the imperial couple. Eugénie loved to lead walking parties into the forest; she walked fast, '*son pas élégant et intrépide, la tête haute*', talking with animation on her favourite topic – history. To Feuillet she seemed 'like some fantastic memory of Diane, of La Vallière, of Marie-Antoinette'. Marie-Antoinette. The Empress was always haunted by that figure of tragedy in whose steps she so often trod and was subject to premonitions that she would share her fate.

One day in July Mme Miramon came to Fontainebleau and had an audience with Eugénie. Her husband had been shot at the side of the Emperor Maximilian of Mexico.

A little later Napoleon and the Prince Imperial went to Paris for a distribution of prizes. They returned late and in sombre mood. All that evening Eugénie was seen applying smelling salts to her nose and murmuring '*mon petit garçon; mon petit garçon*'. The prince had had a hostile reception by the crowd.

Feuillet began to be apprehensive. 'I do not know if my imagination is deceiving me,' he wrote, 'but I see difficult times advancing with great strides towards us.'

The visit of the Court to Fontainebleau was due to end on 5 September. Already Eugénie had noticed a change in the temperature. 'Autumn has come,' she said; 'I feel sad.'

On the last day there was a display of fireworks and all the inhabitants of Fontainebleau were invited to attend. The courts, the terraces, the parterres were invaded by an immense crowd. Only the Jardin Anglais was reserved for the members of the Court. Eugénie was at the balustrade talking happily to members of the populace.

When darkness fell the Emperor appeared bearing a flaming torch with which he lit the first rocket as a signal for the display to begin. Suddenly the whole scene was illuminated. Red, blue and silver flares lit up the walks and alleys and threw the bosquets into dramatic relief of brilliant highlight and cavernous darkness. Fountains of coloured fire rose and fell in cascades of gold and silver rain. Rockets streaked into the air and burst into great petals of light with a roar that made the ground tremble. Suddenly, as the fires died down, there was a fanfare of trumpets and the Avenue de Maintenon was seen to be filled with ghostly figures on horseback. The regiment of Imperial Dragoons was conducting a torchlight retreat. Everyone followed them into the Cour du Cheval Blanc where they executed a carousel. Feuillet was ecstatic: 'it was like one of the magnificent fêtes of the Valois,' he told his wife.

The next day the Court left for Biarritz. They were never to return. Three years later Feuillet returned to a hotel in the rue de Rivoli from which he could see the blackened ruins and gaping windows of the Tuileries. The royal and imperial regimes of France were gone for ever. '*C'était un monde disparu.*'

CHAPTER THIRTEEN

Excursions from Fontainebleau

A number of excursions may be made from Fontainebleau which have the added attraction of taking us through the forest. If we travel west for about twenty kilometres on the N837 we come to **Milly-la-Forêt**, described in a recent article as '*un bourg rural qui devient snob*'. Jean Cocteau and Christian Dior made their habitation here and the church became a fashionable place for weddings. But it retains its rural life, especially the cultivation of *les simples* – medicinal herbs – the gathering of which brings a seasonal influx of workers from Brittany not unlike the hop-pickers of Kent.

There is a covered market or **Halle** at Milly, as fine as that at Arpajon but considerably older. Licence to build it was granted by Louis XI in 1479 at the request of Louis Malet de Graville, Seigneur de Milly. It was not until 1858 that it became the property of the town. Its timbers are of chestnut which has acquired over the years '*une dureté extraordinaire*'.

Graville built the Halle to encourage trade and restore the fortunes of Milly after the devastations of the Hundred Years' War. It was he who gave Milly its distinctive features. The beautiful boulevards follow, as so often, the lines of his fortifications. The château and the church were rebuilt. The gatehouse to the château has lost its high pavilion roof and *poivrières*, leaving only the silhouette of the rather oddly-shaped and serrated crenellations. Another gatehouse in the rue de Lau became the home of Cocteau while the water mill was converted into a residence by Christian Dior.

The **Church of the Assumption** has happily retained its tall and elegant tower dating from the turn of the twelfth century, to which Graville appended his new nave and choir in 1475. The choir stalls with their misericords are those originally made for this choir. The south aisle is later still, dating from the seventeenth century. There are thus three different epochs represented, but all blended into one pleasing harmony of style.

Jean Cocteau has left his mark on Milly-la-Forêt in his decorations of the **Chapel of St Blaise des Simples**. The chapel is all that is left

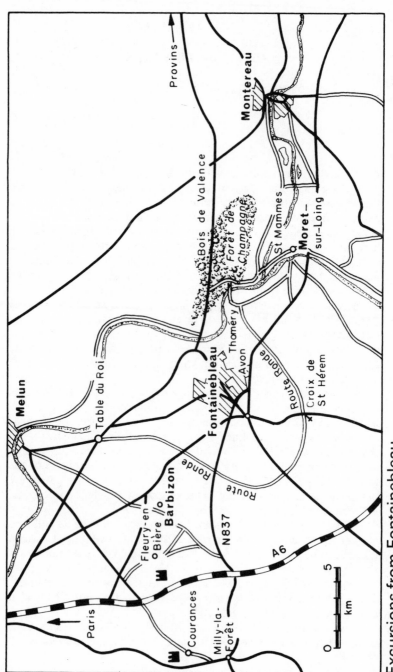

Excursions from Fontainebleau

of a leper hospital or *Maladrerie* built in the twelfth century and dedicated to St Blaise, the bishop and doctor who specialized in cures effected by herbs. Cocteau therefore made his walls the pages of a gigantic herbal.

Five kilometres north of Milly is the **Château de Courances**, perhaps the best maintained private estate in the Ile de France. The first sight of it from the road is a never-to-be-forgotten experience. A long, straight drive, set between the long, straight canals overhung by two double avenues of the most magnificent plane trees that one could wish to see – they were planted in 1782 – leads to the tall, handsome façade of brick and stone against which can be seen the flowing lines of the *fer-à-cheval* staircase copied from Fontainebleau. '*L'arrivée de Courances est l'une des plus belles arrivées de château que l'on puisse voir en France.*' So wrote the comte Ernest de Ganay, himself a son of the house and in his time the foremost authority on the châteaux and gardens of the Ile de France.

After this imposing overture, the **gardens** continue to open up new and ever lovelier perspectives on all sides. A huge area of grass, neatly mown, containing a number of *pièces d'eau* on slightly different levels, surrounds the château. The luxuriant foliage of the trees, their lower members cut back and underlined with trim box hedges, with a few statues at regular but widely spaced intervals, completes the scene.

It is interesting to compare the gardens here with those of Vaux-le-Vicomte, which are on the same scale. There is at Vaux a great elaboration of fountains and statues and gravel paths, while here at Courances is a green and peaceful landscape to which man has given a symmetrical and ordered shape. Above all there are no fountains. The water, which comes from a number of local sources, forms a series of small cascades and gentle overflows, providing a sweet and constant music to the ear. Presiding over the whole scene from the slight elevation of the Vertugadin, to the left of the main axis, is the figure of Arethusa, brought here from Marly.

To this classical lay-out has been added in more recent years a delightful little 'anglo-japanese' garden to the north of the alley which leads to the village, full of colourful and exotic trees.

The château was built in the middle of the sixteenth century for Cosme Clausse, Secretary of Finance to Henri II, but was largely rebuilt in the seventeenth century by Claude Gallard who laid out the gardens in the style of Le Nôtre. In the eighteenth century it passed to Aymar de Nicolay. His descendants owned Courances until 1870, but from 1830 it was abandoned. When it was bought by the Baron Haber there was a sizeable tree growing in the Salon. It was Haber and his descendant, the marquis de Ganay, who so successfully restored both house and garden.

After the Second World War, Field-Marshal Montgomery made his headquarters here in convenient proximity to Fontainebleau. John Hopkins, who was his ADC at the time, relates how bats used to emerge from the panelling as soon as they had started dinner. The Field-Marshal would then give the order: 'tell the butler to keep the soup hot and fetch your squash racket'. He then armed himself with a billiard cue and the two would proceed to do execution on the bats. 'For a man in his late sixties,' says Major Hopkins, 'his aim with a billiard cue was uncanny.'

Another château which has been closely connected with Courances is **Fleury-en-Bière,** some six kilometres to the north-east. Built also by Cosme Clausse, it is now in the hands of the de Ganay family which owns Courances.

The forecourt of Fleury is one of the best period pieces in the Ile de France. The vast area enclosed clearly reflects the Cour du Cheval Blanc at Fontainebleau – in its original state – especially in the use of brick ornament, but Fleury is far better. The façades and curtain wall are divided by slender pilasters into panels, the heads of which are alternately round and square. This is entirely achieved by outlining in brick against a plaster wall. The more ornamental features, with broken pediments and tabernacle windows, are clearly inspired by Serlio's drawings. The gatehouse pavilion in the centre of the curtain wall presents towards the roadway an elaborate Renaissance design of niches and panels, framed in brick and stone, but it has retained the paraphernalia of defence. Each niche has an arrow slit and there are in fact six apertures through which the unwanted visitor might be shot at.

The château proper was largely rebuilt in 1624 but retained the gallery and the chapel painted by Primaticcio.

At the time of the Revolution, Fleury belonged to the prince de Talmont who was guillotined at Laval. His widow remained here and in the early nineteenth century destroyed much of its interior decoration. The chapel was turned into a kitchen and the murals of Primaticcio almost wholly defaced. It was only in this century that the comtesse de Behague, grandmother of the marquis de Ganay, restored the interior using the panelling and staircase from the Château de Vitry.

From Fleury it is about five kilometres east to **Barbizon.** Apart from its place in the history of art, there is nothing about Barbizon to distinguish it from a dozen other villages in the region. It was the very ordinariness of the place which originally attracted the artists who have made it famous. There is therefore something contradictory about making a refuge into a place of pilgrimage. If Rousseau, Millet or Daubigny could see the place today they would avoid it.

For the whole movement associated with the term 'École de Barbizon' was a retreat from the conventions and restraints of the world of art in the 1840s. The works of these artists were consistently refused by the jury of the Salon and ignored by the bourgeois public of Paris. In order to be true to their artistic inspiration, Rousseau and his associates wanted to get back to a completely unsophisticated country life. *'Paysan je suis,'* Millet declared; *'paysan je mourrai. J'ai des choses à raconter comme je les ai vues.'* He was as interested in the labours of the peasant as the others were in the structure of the rural scene. Their works are now in all the great galleries of the world. The Louvre has opened its doors to many.

The houses occupied by Millet and Rousseau can be visited and the *auberge* which was patronized by the artists and run by le Père Gannes, with the paintings which they left on the walls and furniture. It cost them fifty-four sous a day with *'vin à discretion'*. In 1859 Millet sold his *Angélus* for 1200 francs. For years afterwards Adèle Moscher, who posed as the peasant woman, lived on at Barbizon and was known always as 'la Mère Angélus'.

*　　*　　*

An excursion to the east of Fontainebleau takes us first to **Moret**. If we approach it by way of Avon, Thoméry and St Mammes, we obtain a view across the Loing to Moret that is one of the most perfect pictures in the Ile de France.

The river here opens out into a wide area of shelving ground whose different levels form a complex of weirs and islands. Between them the water flows in every possible direction, bringing an animation to the scene which is pleasing to the eye and delightful to the ear.

Across this waterscape the long bridge – blown up in the last war but rebuilt to its old design – leads to a medieval gatehouse to the right of which are some old houses, built out over the river on long wooden props, and the fairly considerable remains of a watergate. To the left of the gatehouse rises the church of Notre Dame de Moret, and to the left of the church the square, decapitated block of the old keep. The town, with its tall brown roofs and pointed gables, provided frequent subject matter for Sisley, who lived and painted here for twenty years.

The old medieval curtain wall can be traced along the river front and north across the car park known as the Champ de Mars, to where another gatehouse answers the first at the other end of the main street. From here the rue des Fossés follows the line back towards the castle.

Within the constricting confines of these former defences the streets are narrow and tortuous and the houses crowd closely in around the church. For the medieval Church was at close quarters to the people, following the rhythm of their daily lives and matching with her ceremonies the important occasions of agriculture and commerce, so that her holy days were their holidays and their feasts her festivals. What more natural than to find amid the carvings of the west portal of Moret a sow suckling her piglets while she herself is nourished with acorns. The scene was not extraneous to popular piety.

It may have been the very closeness of the surrounding houses which imposed upon the builders the omission of the ambulatory. Such an omission is by no means unusual in the Ile de France, but with a building so clearly influenced by Notre Dame de Paris as **Notre Dame de Moret** one instinctively looks for the radiating lines of the flying buttresses as they fan out round the apse. At Moret the buttresses are all at right angles to the choir and form the strictly parallel pattern of the oars of a galleon.

Another link between Moret and Notre Dame de Paris is in their mutual connection with the House of Capet. The early Gothic, which emanated from St Denis, was a royal style and its first flourishing was within Capetian territory. Moret has been a royal town since the days of Louis VI in the early twelfth century. This status is expressed in the decoration of the west front, where the containing arch of the **portal** rises above the cornice to support the royal arms against the balustrade.

It is a very striking and original feature, this twin doorway framed in a single arch which combines in its decoration a great boldness of conception with an astonishing delicacy of execution. By a happy fortune the original statue of the Madonna still stands between the two doorways.

Entering through this Flamboyant portal one is immediately confronted by the full perspective of the church; one is also looking back down two and a half centuries of architecture. For Moret is

Fontainebleau: Marie Antoinette's Boudoir

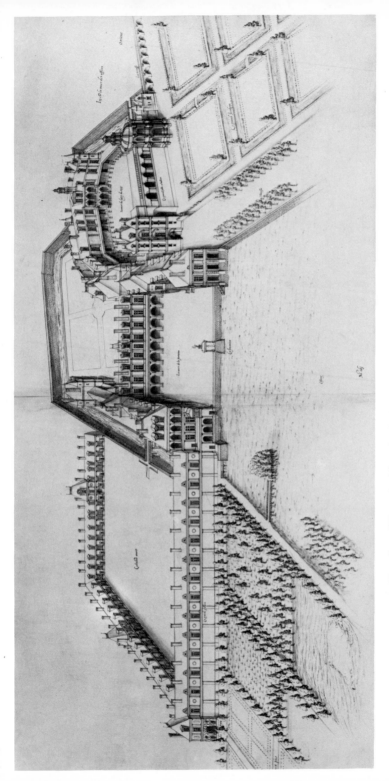

Drawing of Fontainebleau by Androuet du Cerceau in the British Museum: view from the south, showing the former Galerie d'Ulysse (centre left)

the result of long and leisurely campaigns of building. The apse and choir were started at the end of the twelfth century and it is here that the influence of the mother church of Paris is chiefly felt. Unfortunately the **choir** has been badly disfigured. When, in the fifteenth century, the upper storeys were added to the belfry the whole north side of the choir was walled in by way of abutment.

It is therefore the south side of the choir only which merits our attention. It has all the airy elegance of the new-born Gothic style. An interesting fact may be deduced from a close inspection: the ribs of the vaulting are continued down to the capitals of the main pillars by means of slender colonettes; it will be seen that these alternate between a single colonette and a sheaf of three. This can only mean one thing: the architect had originally intended sexpartite vaulting, but had, following the example of Paris, dispensed with the *pile forte – pile faible* formula. In fact a quadripartite vault is more logical for supporting an oblong canopy of roof, as was proved at Chartres.

The choir had to wait a century for its transepts and for the first three bays of the nave. In the former the Geometric style comes into its own in the huge windows that open north and south. Finally in the fifteenth century, the west bay of the nave was added. This end of the church is distinguished by one of the finest organ lofts in the Ile de France, contemporary in style with the Galerie François I at Fontainebleau. It was built to house an organ presented by Blanche de Castille. This instrument, however, was replaced in the nineteenth century by a new one.

The stained glass, which was of no distinction, was blown out by the same explosion which destroyed the bridge. It has been replaced by slightly garish modern glass which would perhaps be more effective if it comprehended the clerestory as well as the ground-floor windows.

It is obvious from the sturdy strength with which the west end of the church was constructed that twin towers were intended for this façade. They were never built.

Near the church a few of the old fifteenth-century timbered houses are still to be seen; in one of them – the **logis Bon Saint Jacques** – the barley sugar for which Moret is especially esteemed can be bought. The **Grand Rue** also has two good Renaissance houses at numbers 26 and 28, but above all, in the garden of the *mairie*, is the so-called **Maison François I**. There is no known connection between the house and the King other than the style to which he gave his name.

In 1822 a certain Colonel de Brack bought the house and had it transported to Paris, where it was set up in the Cours la Reine. In 1956 the comte d'Ussel sold the site to developers on condition that the house was returned to Moret, where it can now be seen once more.

The twelfth-century **castle** was originally a royal bastion against the counts of Champagne, but when Philippe le Bel received Champagne as his wife's dowry the strategic significance of Moret dwindled. The castle was more often used as a prison. Philippe filled it with the wretched Templars and Louis XIV sent Fouquet here, under the custodianship of d'Artagnan, to await trial.

Its last moment of glory was on the occasion of the marriage of Louis XV to Marie-Leczinska. She had come from Wissembourg in Alsace by easy stages. On 3 September she slept at Provins and on the next day made her way to Montereau. The Court was at Fontainebleau and Louis fixed on Moret for their first meeting. It was raining as it had never rained before as he set out with his brilliant cortège. The muddy roads were almost impassable and at one point in Marie's journey no less than thirty horses had to be harnessed to her great *Berline*.

The meeting was planned to take place on the hillside behind Moret. A dais had been prepared and bales of straw laid down to insulate the magnificent carpet from the all pervading mud. Louis greeted Marie with a boyish enthusiasm which won all hearts. As he did so the weather dramatically cleared and the sun, piercing through the rain, crowned the scene with a rainbow. The young pair got into the King's coach and drove back over the bridge into Moret where the bride spent her last night before the wedding in the old keep. The keep has now been incorporated in a private house and has lost all of its character and most of its interest.

Napoleon also spent a historic night at Moret, but not at the castle. It was the last stage in his return from Elba. Everyone was in confusion and the authorities did not know which way to turn. Orders arrived from the Emperor that they were to prepare a night's lodging for him. Orders arrived from Paris that they were to arrest him. He turned up at midnight and went to the Mayor's house, number 24, Grande Rue. At four next morning he was off again and was back in the Tuileries by the end of the day.

The road which follows the north bank of the Seine from Moret to **Montereau** passes through heavily built up and industrialized territory; but it has the merit of bringing the visitor in over the two bridges at the point where the Yonne 'falls' into the Seine from which the place derives its name. The old town is thus clearly defined, engulfed in the new high-rise buildings. The bridges were built in the eighteenth century but have been much restored. The one which crosses the Yonne was the scene of the murder of Jean-sans-Peur, duc de Bourgogne, who was having a parley with the Dauphin, the future Charles VII, in 1419. They were supposed to be forming an alliance against the English but a quarrel broke out and one of the Dauphin's supporters took the opportunity to avenge the murder, some fourteen years previously, of the duc d'Orléans, by felling the Burgundian duke with his battle axe. Reprisals and counter-reprisals followed and Montereau was the scene of much bloodshed. Charles finally hanged all those accused of complicity with Burgundy.

From the bridge the **Church of Notre Dame and Saint Loup** rises magnificently, dominating the old town by virtue of its exceptionally tall nave. A closer inspection, however, is something of a disappointment. The nave in itself is very fine and has even been attributed to the workshops of Philibert de l'Orme. Its rather severe Renaissance design links it with the work being done at Fontainebleau and at Anet in the mid-sixteenth century. The architect, however, has made no attempt at all to tie his building in with the towers, which are lower than the roof ridge. It is possible that the rebuilding of the towers was part of his original intention which was never realized.

Inside, there is something cold and unwelcoming about the nave. It is built in a rather displeasing stone and needs the complement of a set of really colourful stained glass in the tall clerestory windows. The modern glass in the apse fails somehow to accord with the architecture or to enliven it. The east window of the Lady Chapel however is a good example of modern glass with an interesting colour scheme of bright blues and reds against a background of umber and ochre.

The rest of the church divides into two periods. The ambulatory and its chapels date from the early thirteenth century as also do the main arcades of the nave where the supporting piers each consist of a sheaf of fourteen colonettes. The double aisles were added or rebuilt in the fifteenth century, as their Flamboyant tracery suggests. On one of the pillars of the nave hangs the sword of Jean-sans-Peur.

From Montereau we can return to Fontainebleau through the Bois de Valence and the Forêt de Champagne, or continue north-east to Provins.

CHAPTER FOURTEEN

Provins

~~

There is always something deeply moving about ruins. Perhaps it is their very incompleteness which provides the stimulus needed to set the mind at work on an imaginary reconstruction and makes it more receptive to the strange power of an old and crumbling wall to throw back across the centuries the distant echo of a bygone age.

There is no place in the Ile de France which illustrates this more clearly than Provins – once the flourishing capital of Brie and favourite seat of the counts of Champagne, but for centuries a pleasant backwater where the stream of life has been sluggish and the echoes of history have been allowed to linger. In house after house we may find some architectural survival, some vestige of tracery, some buttress or arcade immured as in a fossil. 'Even although we do not know the monuments to which they belonged,' wrote André Hallays, 'they are so numerous and so evocative, in the silence of the dead city, that they cannot fail to communicate to us the glory and the opulence of the city that was.'

To recover a sense of the glory and the opulence, we need to turn back the pages of history to the early medieval period, for by the end of the thirteenth century Provins had already started upon an irretrievable decline. But from 1048 until then, under Thibault le Grand, Henri le Libéral and Thibault le Chansonnier, counts of Champagne and Brie, it ranked, next to Paris and Rouen, as the third greatest city of France, boasting some fifteen thousand inhabitants and famous throughout Europe for its fairs.

The importance of these fairs in the economy of the country was considerable and it was part of the business of the ruler to see that they were properly policed. They lasted for some six weeks each, in late spring in the Upper Town and in early autumn in the Lower.

From time immemorial there had been a *place forte* on the high spur of land known as the Ville Haute. Clovis and Charlemagne were here. In the ninth century the monks of St Benoît-sur-Loire, fleeing from the Norman invader, concealed in the marshy ground at the foot of the citadel the relics of St Ayoul, the martyr of Blois. A century later these relics, forgotten but now miraculously rediscovered, became the centre of a cult and the Ville Basse grew up around the nucleus of the church and monastery. Upper and Lower towns were encircled by a great girdle of stone, pierced by many gates and set about by a multitude of towers above which the skyline was pinnacled with the belfries and steeples of innumerable churches.

By the eighteenth century the depopulation of Provins had achieved its nadir, the effects of which may still be observed in the Upper Town. To walk along the **rue de Jouy** today is more like walking along the street of some rather ramshackle country village.

First and finest of its architectural remains is the old *donjon* known as the **Tour de César,** a great octagonal tower rising head and shoulders above its four attendant *poivrières*. The keep is known to have existed in 1137. Captured by the English in 1432, it was surrounded by a circular platform of masonry from which artillery could operate. This platform is still known as the 'Pâté aux Anglais'. The single entrance to the *donjon* was on the south side, some five metres above ground level and reached from the Pâté aux Anglais by a removable plank bridge.

In the Grande Salle of the first floor the vaulting overhead encloses an aperture, similar to those found in bell towers, which enable ammunition and provisions to be hoisted up to the top floor. The extreme narrowness of the staircases would have made them almost useless for this purpose.

From the first floor these staircases lead directly to the gallery which Viollet-le-Duc had reason to suppose was originally a covered *chemin de ronde*. Each of the four towers is hollowed out at this level into a sort of niche for the rough accommodation of the soldiers and watchmen.

Above this level the structure of the Tour de César has been significantly altered. We know that in 1282 there was a *tour de guette*, or look-out tower, right at the top, for in this year there was hung here a curfew bell. A painting on the ceiling of the church of Sainte-Croix shows a small cylindrical tower with a conical roof standing in the middle of the platform. We also know that the present roof, a magnificent timber structure, was only built in 1693 when the bells of St Quiriace were hung here.

Saint Quiriace was the Bishop of Jerusalem credited with the discovery of the True Cross. It would be interesting to try to piece together the reputed fragments of this precious relic; it would also be interesting to know how to account for the three heads supposedly

165

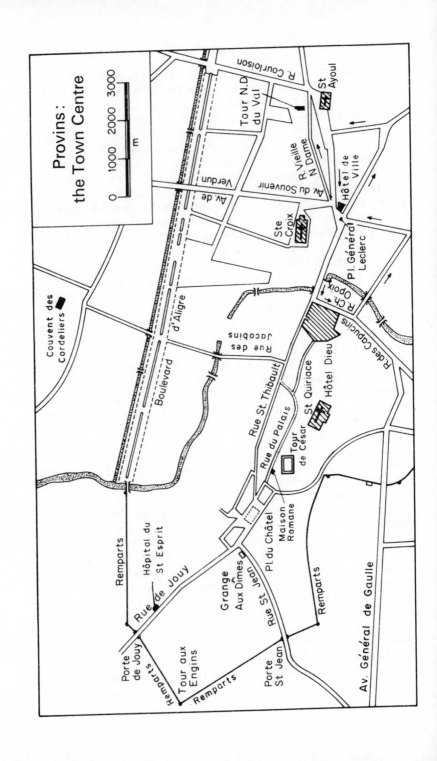

Provins : the Town Centre

0 1000 2000 3000
m

Couvent des Cordeliers

R. Courloison

St Ayoul

Tour N.D. du Val

Hôtel de Ville

R. Vielle N. Dame

Av. du Souvenir

Av. de Verdun

Ste Croix

Pl. Général Leclerc

R. Ch. Oporix

R. des Capucins

Boulevard d'Aligre

Rue des Jacobins

Hôtel Dieu

St Quiriace

Rue St. Thibault

Rue du Palais

Tour de César

Maison Romane

Pl. du Châtel

Remparts

Hôpital du St Esprit

Rue de Jouy

Grange Aux Dîmes

Rue St Jean

Porte de Jouy

Remparts

Tour aux Engins

Remparts

Porte St Jean

Remparts

Av. Général de Gaulle

belonging to Saint Quiriace. Sens and Orléans each claimed one; the third was brought to Provins by Milon de Breban from Constantinople.

At first sight the **Church of St Quiriace** is unattractive – a gaunt and graceless building crowned by a slate dome which is as inappropriate to the rest as it is uninteresting in itself. Once inside the building, however, the visitor has the impression of having just entered a cathedral. The whole is open and spacious and built of a light, honey-coloured stone with a marvellous luminosity.

The choir and apse, built mostly in the reign of Henri le Libéral between 1157 and 1185, is in a transitional style, half Gothic and half Romanesque. There is a beautiful little arcade running along at triforium level which gives way, in the slightly later transepts, to a distinctly Geometric tracery. The capitals on the sturdy pillars of choir and apse, directly inspired by the Cathedral of Sens, are typical of the region. Typical also of their age are the rather amusing faces carved into the corbels on the south wall of the south choir ambulatory.

It was not until 1238 that the vast octopartite vault of the choir was achieved – an unusual formula which was tried out first at Voulton, not far to the north of Provins. The nave, begun about the same time, was to have extended westwards for forty-six metres, which would have greatly enhanced the impression of being in a cathedral. It was conceived in the *pile forte – pile faible* formula, but only one double bay was ever built, for by the second half of the thirteenth century the days of prosperity were over. Edmund of Lancaster, who married the widow of Henri le Gros, learning of a riot in which the mayor had been assassinated, deprived the city of its privileges. The fairs were abandoned and with them the building of St Quiriace. Returning to England, Edmund took with him the red rose of Provins which became in due course the red rose of Lancaster. Finally, in 1285, with the marriage of Philippe le Bel to the daughter of Henri le Gros, Brie and Champagne were united to the royal domain: Provins became an ever more obscure provincial city.

In 1662 a fire destroyed the central belfry which was replaced by the slate dome. From outside the effect is deplorable; from within it manages to harmonize with the architecture of the crossing and contributes much to the general impression of lofty and luminous grandeur.

North and east of St Quiriace was the palace of the counts of Champagne; the site is now occupied by a college which still incorporates the palace chapel.

Leading westwards from the college and St Quiriace, the rue du Palais passes beneath the walls of the Tour de César and opens on to the **Place du Châtel**. The whole area is rich in vestiges of its architectural past. Half-way down the rue du Palais on the left is the **Maison Romane**, parts of which date from the tenth century. On the north-east corner of the square a single capital, originally belonging to the south porch, recalls the church of St Thibault, which drew its revenues from the sale of horseshoes.

Continuing west from the Place du Châtel we come to the rue St Jean. Here, on the right, is a very fine old tithe barn, **la Grange aux Dîmes**, known from documents to have been here since before 1176. The ground-floor façade was clearly once in the form of an open arcade, above which the projecting corbel stones supported the timbers of a large penthouse roof. The windows of the upper storey are original, each divided into two lights by a slender column-mullion.

Inside is a vast open vaulted chamber, which once served as a covered market. It can be dated by its style at about 1320. The first impression is of a coarse and rough-hewn architecture, the ribs of the vaults being in a crude, rectangular form, which contrasts oddly with the finely-chiselled capitals beneath. But an attentive inspection will reveal at the base of many of the ribs the beginnings of carved profiles. This reminds us that carving of this sort was very often only done after the stones had been positioned in the structure.

Underneath is another great vaulted chamber, with high raised arches just beginning to be in the pointed style, and curious capitals incorporating a sort of inverted scallop shell in their foliage. In one corner is an entrance into the immense network of underground passages which is such an outstanding feature of Provins – described by Georges Pillement as 'a city of catacombs beneath a city in the open air'.

Continuing along the rue St Jean we come to the **Porte St Jean**, an archway between two flanking towers, which has suffered much at the hands of time. An early nineteenth-century watercolour shows a far more elaborate structure, with slots for a drawbridge and the remains of machicolations and a *chemin de ronde*. The existing stone-work towards the west is what is known as *en bossage*, each stone having a convex surface for the better deflection of projectiles.

The guardrooms in the towers interconnect both above and below street level, and by a series of winding stairs lead to the platform on top, from which is a magnificent view along the **ramparts**. These are mostly thirteenth-century building, though the defences were certainly begun a century before that and frequently modified afterwards. There is a most interesting and attractive walk along the bottom of the moat as far as the corner tower, **La Tour aux Engins**, and round to the next gate, **la Porte de Jouy**. It leads us back into the Ville Haute, and by turning immediately right we can walk along inside the ramparts and see into some of the towers in which the remains of old vaulted chambers are still visible. At the end of the walk the inside of the Tour aux Engins forms the backdrop to an outdoor theatre.

Along the rue de Jouy, on the left, are the much restored remains of the **Hôpital du St Esprit**, founded in 1177 by Henri le Libéral as almshouses for the poor, the old and the foundling. He was justly named 'le Libéral', for he founded or endowed no less than thirteen such charitable institutions.

The Church of St Ayoul, as we have seen, was the nucleus around which the Ville Basse had grown. In 1048 the Benedictine priory was established by no less a person than St Robert, the founder of Cîteaux. By the end of the eleventh century his buildings were complete, and the transepts and crossing remain to this day.

In 1157 a terrible fire ravaged the priory and church, and the relics of St Ayoul were sent on tour to England to raise funds. The success of this appeal led to the construction of what was the greatest glory of the church, its **Portail Royal**. As its name suggests this is a miniature version of the west portal of Chartres. There was a strong dynastic connection, for Henri le Libéral was brother to Robert, Count of Chartres and Blois.

Unfortunately the statue-columns of St Ayoul are in very poor condition today. But it is clear that their style is anterior to those of the nearby St Loup-de-Naud, which can be dated to 1167. At St Ayoul the features are simply engraved on to the stone, the eyes and hair being merely represented by lines. At St Loup they are already being carved three-dimensionally.

The central bay was grievously disfigured in 1792 by the insertion of a window into the tympanum. This act of vandalism was perpetrated in order to compensate for the loss of light occasioned by the blocking of the clerestory windows by the organ, which was salvaged from the abbey of Jouy.

The building served as a parish church as well as a chapel for the Benedictines. At best they were uneasy bedfellows; at worst they were at loggerheads. In the middle of the sixteenth century they agreed to the building of a partition wall which gave the south aisle and

169

transept, together with their dependencies, to the monks, while the nave and north transept were made over to the parish.

It was a timely move on the part of the Benedictines; for no sooner had the parish assumed full responsibility for the nave than its roof fell in. It was replaced by a wooden barrel vault. At the same time the parishioners built the apse and a second aisle to the north. The capitals to the columns, in this aisle ornamented with triglyphs, and the pendent keystones betray the influence of the Renaissance; but the rib vaulting might well pass for thirteenth-century if we did not know that it was built three hundred years later.

The little belfry over the west end bears further witness to the hostilities between the two owners. The bell was needed, the Abbé Pasques informs us, for when the monks were *en mauvais humeur* they would refuse to ring the great bells.

At the Revolution the church was sold. The Benedictine chapel 'with its stalls on which were painted the most beautiful actions of St Benoît, in which so many saintly monks were buried' became a butcher's shop and the parish church a stable.

One of the most celebrated inmates of the priory was Peter Abelard, who sought refuge here in 1120. Although he was one of the greatest minds of his century, and certainly one of the most reputed teachers in Europe, he is chiefly famous for his love affair with Héloise. His misconduct so scandalized her uncle, Canon Fulbert of Notre Dame, that he hired ruffians to break into Abelard's cell in the middle of the night and castrate him – a mutilation which deprived him, *inter alia*, of any prospect of preferment in the Church.

At Provins he attracted so many pupils that he had to do his teaching in the open air; and the rue du Pré aux Clercs, parallel to the Boulevard d'Aligre, enshrines in its name the memory of these outdoor lectures.

Not far from St Ayoul is a fine, slender gatehouse surmounted by a fine, slender cupola – the only remains of the collegiate church of **Notre Dame du Val**. Founded outside the city in 1196 by the comtesse Marie de Champagne, it was removed, after the Hundred Years' War, to the greater security of the Ville Basse. The fourteenth-century buildings, however, were completely destroyed at the Revolution, leaving only this gatehouse, dated 1544 but incorporating some of the much older city gate, 'la porte Bailly'.

The rue Vieille Notre Dame leads us to the other important surviving church of the Ville Basse – **Sainte-Croix**. The east end, seen from the Avenue du Souvenir, makes an exciting architectural composition, the steep, pointed roofs of the tower, nave and Lady

Chapel rising one behind the other, while the odd, irregular roof of the ambulatory winds its way somewhat uncertainly round the east end.

The west front is a complete jumble in which two separate façades are juxtaposed without the least attempt having been made to unite them. The left-hand side has an elaborate sixteenth-century doorway. Most of its intricate carvings are flamboyantly Gothic, but at the base of the pinnacle is a delicate low relief design which is unmistakably italianate. Above the door the cockleshell, emblem of the pilgrim, is much in evidence.

The twelfth-century crossing and tower are the chief survivals of the original church, which suffered from a disastrous fire in 1509 followed two years later by a flood which reached the top of the high altar. In 1635, after further floods, the floor level was raised by one metre, which accounts for the church's truncated proportions. Between 1511 and 1581 the choir and ambulatory were rebuilt and a second north aisle was added, as at St Ayoul; as at St Ayoul also there was continual friction between the parish and the priory. Arguments over the temporalities flared up at frequent intervals, the partisans not hesitating even to interrupt Divine service to gain their points.

In 1718 it was decided to raise the east and west arches of the crossing in order to open up the prospect along the nave into the choir. Only one workman could be found to undertake so perilous a task. His name was Durand and his fellows promised to give him a white blackbird if he succeeded. He presumably won his bird.

During the Revolution the nave became a manufacture for saltpetre. The choir was dedicated to the Goddess of Reason, who represented – curiously enough – by a statue of St Margaret taken from the Cordelières.

No distance at all from the church of Sainte-Croix is the Hôtel de Ville in the little **Place Général Leclerc**. This used to be known as the Place du Val, and was where public executions took place.

The executioner's house, traditionally outside the confines of the town, is still to be seen on the right of the Route de Paris just where the road used to pass the Porte de Paris. The last to use this as his official lodging was Cyr-Charlemagne Sanson, who operated the guillotine at the execution of Louis XVI.

The Route de Paris becomes the rue des Capucins, which in turn becomes the rue Christophe Opoix, named after the famous historian of Provins. The rue Saint Thibault, at right angles to this, leads to the old **Hôtel Dieu**. This was begun in 1160. Only the doorway, which dates from the thirteenth century, and the vestibule, where the groined vaulting betrays its origins in the twelfth, survive of the medieval building. It contains an interesting sixteenth-century retable depicting the donor of the retable kneeling before the Virgin Mary with scenes of pilgrimage on either side.

From here, on Sundays and holidays, the **subterranean passages** can be visited. This network of tunnels, opening from time to time into wide vaulted chambers, provides the humidity needed for weaving, and some of it dates back to the Franks.

The Hôtel Dieu used to serve as a *maison de plaisance* for the countesses, an appendage to the château proper which towered above it. From its high windows it looked across the valley of the Durteint to the opposite slopes of Les Dameries and Fontaine Riante.

There is a tradition that Thibault IV, known as Le Chansonnier, comte de Champagne, looked out one day from these windows to these slopes. There, in a pool of supernatural light, a woman of surpassing beauty was tracing with a naked sword the outlines of a building on the ground. As the result of this vision he founded the nunnery known as **Les Cordelières**. In the refectory of the Lycée which now occupies the site of the château there is a statue of Thibault looking out of the window.

The building was started in 1247 and continued by Thibault V, who succeeded in 1253. It fared very badly during the Hundred Years' War and the church, which originally completed the quadrangle, was destroyed. In 1505 the buildings were restored and the cloisters rebuilt. In 1843 the south range of the cloister was demolished and, but for the intervention of Prosper Mérimée, the east and west ranges would have disappeared also.

The **Chapel** is a most unexpected building – a vast barn with a huge wooden barrel vault. There is no architecture worth the name and the interest lies wholly in the furnishings. These include a fine set of Renaissance stalls, dated 1621, with a little return at each extremity finished with a fluted column. On the north wall, with no apparent means of entry, is an elaborate pulpit. It is decorated with a Corinthian order, the lower parts of the columns wreathed in vines, with gilded figures in the panels and adorned with ears of corn and bunches of grapes, which also festoon the sounding board. The symbolism is, of course, eucharistic, but at first sight it looks more appropriate to bacchanalian festivity. Most interesting of all is the little monument that contained the heart of Thibault V, who died in 1270. It is an exquisite piece of thirteenth-century sculpture, executed in a white stone that was capable of receiving the most delicate carving. It is hexagonal in shape with the figure of a monk framed in a Gothic arch in each panel. There are traces of poly-chroming still to be seen. A little pyramidal roof of copper supports a crystal dome through which the heart of Thibault could be seen.

There are four important churches in the neighbourhood of Provins: Voulton, Rampillon, St Loup-de-Naud and Donnemarie.

Voulton, some seven kilometres to the north, is both interesting and unusual. It was saved from demolition in 1847 by Mgr Allou, Bishop of Meaux. Dating from about 1180, when the choir and first bay of the nave were built, it had to wait until 1220 for the completion of the nave and west front.

It is exceptionally tall for its date and size, the windows of both storeys being the same height, which gives a considerable dignity to the edifice, especially from the east.

Inside it has a character all its own. A ground plan, showing the alternation *pile forte – pile faible*, would suggest sexpartite vaulting. It is in fact quadripartite, but in each bay, instead of a single arch between each pier, there are twin arches upheld by squat, cylindrical columns. As there is no triforium, this leaves a large space of blank wall between the nave arcades and the clerestory.

The glory of Voulton, however, is in the great octopartite vault of the choir which immediately links it with St Quiriace at Provins. These are the only two examples known.

One of the most worth-while excursions from Provins is to **St Loup-de-Naud**, some nine kilometres to the south-west. Once a fortified village dominating the road from Sens to Meaux, it stands attractively in a pretty little wooded valley. The houses, with their pleasant medley of brown roofs, climb the little hill where there are still vestiges of fortification, and the whole is crowned by one of the rare churches in the Gothic Ile de France to have retained its Romanesque ensemble almost intact. St Loup-de-Naud is second only to Morienval.

The church was built in two phases – the choir, crossing and first two bays of the nave are late eleventh-century. But in 1167, owing to a generous donation from Henri le Libéral, the nave was extended and the wonderful west portal created.

It is this extension which first confronts the visitor, offering at the west end a huge porch, like a *porte cochère*, in very early pointed style, which shelters an exquisite miniature *portail royal*, obviously inspired by Chartres and dating from 1170–75. In the centre, between the two doors, is St Loup himself. The artist has combined

173

Environs of Provins

km

Melun

Paris

Rampillon

Montereau

Donnemarie—
Dontilly

Thénisy

St Loup-de-Naud

Provins

Voulton

Nogent-sur-Seine

a love of bold, angular shapes with an apparent dislike of plain surfaces: every square centimetre is textured except the face of the bishop, which thus stands out rather effectively. On his left are St Paul, the Queen of Sheba and Jeremiah; on his right St Peter, Solomon and (perhaps) Isaiah. They appear to be by the same hand. The treatment of the right hand and sleeve is almost identical in each statue.

Above St Loup, in the lintel, is the Virgin attended by Apostles, only eight of whom have been accommodated, while in the tympanum is a Christ in Majesty surrounded by the emblems of the four Evangelists. It is probably thanks to the protection afforded by the porch that this delightful group is so well preserved.

Inside one is immediately struck by the dramatic effect of the steady recession of rather flattened transverse arches which form the perspective up the nave. It was unusual for Romanesque churches in the Ile de France to have stone vaults, but St Loup-de-Naud was probably influenced by Burgundy and Vézelay.

The nave is *pile forte* – *pile faible*, but lacks the usual sexpartite vault which usually accompanies that formula. It is built of a white, almost chalky stone. The clerestory windows have been filled in, making it darker than was probably intended, for the windows originally had to illuminate an all-over scheme of mural painting, which, as Georges Poisson has stated, 'must have been one of the masterpieces of the art of mural painting'. Many vestiges of the original paintings survive, but all too frequently they have been 'restored' – that is to say repainted with the utmost indifference, by the architect Mimey in 1867.

If St Loup-de-Naud offers a delightful and in some ways unique example of a Romanesque church, **Rampillon** – a twenty-minute drive away to the west – provides a perfect specimen of mid-thirteenth-century Gothic. It is also one of the rare churches to have been built as a whole in one single phase of construction and not to have suffered the periodic rebuildings which are so common in a land that has known little peace. The presence of a tower more suggestive of military than of ecclesiastical architecture bears its own witness to this history of invasion and civil strife.

Rampillon is a simple and logical structure, making deliberate and effective use of the flying buttress and incorporating a belfry crowned with the four gables which are typical of this region. There is a lack of ornamentation which combines with the rough limestone masonry to create an impression which is distinctly austere.

In striking contrast to this austerity, the west front offers another miniature *portail royal* in a beautiful fine sandstone which has preserved throughout the centuries the crisp profiles of the medieval carver. This is particularly noticeable in the pleats and folds of the Apostles' vestments. The figures are no longer treated as statue-columns but are framed in an elegant, free-standing arcade which provides as it were niches for each of them.

Below is a smaller arcade containing bass reliefs depicting the labours of the seasons. Some, to the right of the door, are still clearly recognizable – harvesting, treading the grapes, beating down the acorns, killing the pig – but many have been hopelessly defaced.

Above the door, the lintel represents the Last Judgement – but it is a Judgement with no Hell. The figures, which are all represented as about the same age that Christ was at His death, present an animated and joyful scene, while over their heads in the tympanum the figure of Christ sits in majesty between His Mother and the Beloved Disciple.

The interior of Rampillon has a considerable antique charm and the unity of style is once more apparent. The walls are a warm yellow colour with traces of mural painting. In the last bay on the left of the sanctuary there are remnants of polychroming about the triforium pillars, suggesting that the original scene was extremely colourful.

There are fine old box pews and a good eighteenth-century pulpit.

There are one or two interesting wooden statues: a scalped saint, which is the usual way of depicting St Thomas à Becket, whose hostility to the King of England inevitably endeared him to the people of France; a lady holding a tower, who may be the foundress of the church, and, finest of all, a beautiful fourteenth-century Virgin and Child set in a retable of the early Renaissance.

Ten kilometres south-east of Rampillon is **Donnemarie-en-Montois**. The name – Domna Maria – dates its foundation back at least to the Carolingian epoch, before the word *domnus* was replaced by *saint*. It boasts a fine church with one of the very few cemetery cloisters to have survived in the area. It is important enough to have attracted a detailed study from the marquise de Maillé.

A walk round the outside of the church provides an excellent introduction to its history.

The south front is dominated by a tower dating from the first half of the twelfth century. Madame de Maillé argues convincingly that this was originally free-standing. There is no trace of any buildings having previously been attached to it; there are window openings on all four faces which would have required an excessively low church had one been so attached. It is probable that these towers served a defensive as well as an ecclesiastical purpose and the large surfaces of wall unpierced with windows certainly consolidate this impression. The top storey is late fifteenth-century with a richly carved Renaissance frieze immediately below the spring of the spire. Almost the only firm date for Donnemarie is the construction of this spire in 1527.

At the foot of the tower is an old well and beside the well is a small porch in which the Romanesque carvings have been re-used in a thirteenth-century building. The two angels in the tympanum have broad, bucolic faces and swing their censers with the rather awkward gestures of amateur acolytes.

The west portal has been badly vandalized. Much of this was due to the Revolution, when orders were given to an artisan named Simonnet to hammer off all the carvings. He saved what he could by covering the whole with plaster.

North of the church is the delightful **cemetery cloister** of the mid-sixteenth century. These were once common features of parochial churches, but their survival is all too rare. The one here lost its *raison d'être* as long ago as 1832 when the cemetery was disaffected.

It was almost certainly intended to complete the quadrangle with a further arcade across the east end. The spring of an arch on the north face of the church wall can imply little else. But the absence of any mark on the south wall of the Chapelle Sainte Quinette equally suggests that it was never built. The dedication of the chapel is something of a mystery, Quinette being unknown to hagiography.

To the east of the site of the cemetery is a broad archway in a rough and untutored Renaissance style. It is obviously only meant to be seen from the east. Probably the original intention was to link it by means of a covered way to the projected eastern wing of the cloister.

From this arch the walk, cut through behind the buttresses, brings us round again to the south front.

The interior of Donnemarie is thirteenth-century except for the bay in the south aisle which is taken up by the lower storey of the belfry. The church was built in two stages. From the very early thirteenth century come the choir and choir aisles. It is possible that the builder began with the design of a sexpartite vault; the piers on the north side clearly alternate *pile forte – pile faible*; but by the time he came to position the vaulting he had changed to the quadripartite formula. During a slightly later campaign which ended in about 1250 the nave was continued in a more logical manner, quadripartite vaulting being obviously assumed from the start.

On the way out of Donnemarie is the Porte de Provins, an old gateway with a tower and *poivrière*. The minor road to Provins passes the attractive little village of Thénisy on the way.

CHAPTER FIFTEEN

Vaux-le-Vicomte and the Plain of Brie

❧

Ideally one should visit **Vaux-le-Vicomte** after seeing Maisons and before going to Versailles. They form a direct sequence. Maisons was built by a *Surintendant des Finances* – almost by definition the richest subject in France. One of his successors in that post, Nicolas Fouquet, built Vaux-le-Vicomte. His extravagance led to his downfall. He was disgraced and imprisoned; and Louis XIV borrowed the whole team of artists from Vaux to undertake the creation of Versailles. Some of the features of the new Versailles – the trophies, helmets and flaming urns – are already to be seen at Maisons.

Apart from this Maisons and Vaux have little in common. Their respective architects were men of very different outlook. Mansart was a perfectionist who lost many orders by his expensive procrastination. His façades at Maisons are subtle and meticulously thought out. Le Vau was an impressionist who worked fast and sacrificed detail to theatrical effect. Vaux-le-Vicomte, which is bigger than Maisons, was completed in a third of the time.

The arrival at Vaux is one of the great architectural experiences of the Ile de France. The whole vast complex suddenly appears at the side of the road, a tumultuous compendium of buildings of different heights linked by gargantuan arcades and rows of terms; but as one moves towards the central axis offices, outbuildings and forecourts progressively assume the positions of symmetry to which they were ordained, and the château itself appears at the focal point of an artificial setting which extends over hundreds of hectares.

The whole huge context of architecture and formal garden only emphasizes the importance of the château, which is left in splendid isolation. This impression is increased by the compactness of the design, for at Vaux – as at Maisons – there are no wings enclosing the cour d'honneur. The typical French château was still built round three sides of a quadrangle. Another interesting feature of the plan is that Le Vau has put all the important rooms on the ground floor. This obviates the necessity of a Grand Staircase:

such stairs as there are at Vaux are relatively unimportant.

The *tout ensemble* has therefore much that is original. In detail it is easy to see whence Le Vau has derived his inspiration. His use of statues on the façades shows the influence of Palladio; the alternation of urns and circular dormers is clearly copied from Coulommiers; his way of placing urns above the eaves in the taller pavilions of the offices is a repetition of the Grotto of Meudon.

Le Vau's faults are only too obvious. The house itself, despite the influence of Palladio, is heavy. The low central portico of the entrance front, with its chunky Tuscan columns, has none of the elegance of the colossal order on the end pavilions. On the garden side the huge elliptical dome fails somehow to fit in with the façade. In the office blocks Le Vau has attached enormous stone arcades without any apparent thought about how these should relate to the façades nearest to them.

All these elements, some beautiful, some ponderous, some original, some second-hand, were hurriedly assembled by Le Vau and the outer shell of the buildings, begun in 1656, was completed within a single year. Eighteen thousand workmen were employed simultaneously about the house and gardens.

The interior decoration was entrusted to the painter Le Brun. He and Le Vau had collaborated before, notably at the Hôtel Lambert, but now they were to produce a new style to which Louis XIV was to give his name – a style in which painting and gilding and stucco ornament were blended into one all-embracing scheme. The style differs from the baroque in that it is never illusionist; there is always a clear distinction between the three-dimensional work of stucco and the painting which it frames.

In the entrance hall are tapestries woven from designs by Le Brun at the workshops of Maincy, the village nearest to Vaux, for, as at Fontainebleau, special manufactures had to be set up to provide for the prodigious demand. After the fall of Fouquet this workshop was transferred to Paris and became the famous Manufacture des Gobelins. The tapestries themselves were altered by Colbert. Originally they had figured the squirrel – in the patois of Anjou '*fouquet*' means a squirrel – but it also illustrated the Superintendent's device '*Quo non ascendam?*' (How high shall I not climb?) The squirrels were replaced by Colbert with his own device, the grass snake. Again this was a pun on his name, for in Latin '*colubra*' means a grass snake, which in early Christian symbolism stood for prudence. As far as Fouquet was concerned, Colbert was the snake in the grass.

In 1661 Fouquet had confidently expected to succeed Mazarin as chief minister to Louis XIV, but Louis had determined to govern himself – *'faire son métier de Roi'*. Moreover he had, at the Cardinal's instigation, taken into his service Mazarin's secretary. Colbert detested Fouquet and knew the secret of his peculation. While Fouquet walked on a carpet of flowers Colbert was preparing an abyss beneath. By August 1661 the enormous sum of 18,000,000 francs had been spent on Vaux-le-Vicomte, and Fouquet invited the Court from Fontainebleau to a dazzling fête. Everything that money, art and ingenuity could contrive was pressed into service for those fourteen hours. As the Court departed, at two in the morning, the château suddenly blazed into light with a brilliant display of fireworks, and then all was dark. Unconsciously Fouquet had pictured in his pyrotechnics his own career.

Louis was not delighted: he was indignant that any subject should so far outshine him. Nineteen days later Fouquet was arrested by d'Artagnan at Nantes. Louis and Colbert used every means to procure the death sentence, but only obtained that of exile from the Court. It was altered by the King to perpetual imprisonment and the Superintendent ended his days in the fortress of Pignerol.

The team of artists, including Le Vau, Le Brun, Le Nôtre and the sculptor Girardon, was taken over by the King for the creation of Versailles. Molière and Lully went with them. Of all the great names only Vatel the chef took another route. He went to the prince de Condé at Chantilly, where, at another entertainment of the King, he was so overcome by the failure of the fish to arrive on time that he took his own life.

In due course Fouquet's widow was allowed to return to Vaux, but in 1705 she sold it to the Maréchal de Villars. To him we owe the decoration of the Dining Room, where he has observed the ancient custom of leaving the beams uncovered and decorating them with arabesques.

In 1764 the château was purchased by the duc de Praslin, a cousin of the duc de Choiseul, and it remained in his family for over a century. In 1841 the house was carefully and rather well restored by Visconti – later to do much work at the Louvre. The future of Vaux as a noble residence seemed secure. But on 8 August 1847 an event occurred which shook the aristocracy of France. The duc de Praslin was arrested for murder. His alleged victim was his own wife, a daughter of the Maréchal Sebastiani. The trouble began with the appointment of a spirited good-looking young governess, Mlle Deluzy. The Duchess wrote in her journal: *'Mlle D. règne sans*

THE COUNTRY ROUND PARIS

partage; on n'a jamais vu position de gouvernante plus scandaleuse. Je suis aussi malheureuse que possible. Je n'ai plus ni mari ni enfants.' After an intervention by his father-in-law the Duke agreed to dismiss the governess, but he insisted on his wife's writing her a good reference. It appears to have been her reluctance to do this which led to the fatal row. After his wife's death the Duke was immediately sent to prison, where he managed to commit suicide. It must be said that the marquis de Breteuil has argued the case for the Duke's innocence, but whatever the truth of the matter it put an end to the prospects of Vaux. For the next thirty years it was allowed to go to ruin.

In 1875 the estate was bought by M. Alfred Sommier, who devoted much of his immense fortune to the restoration of Vaux. The main lines of Le Nôtre's lay-out were still discernible, but the statues had disappeared and the *pièces d'eau* dried up. The re-establishment of the former splendours of the garden took twenty years and was conducted by the famous landscape gardener Duchêne.

In the interior only two tables – the oval ones of red marble in the Grand Salon – survived from the days of Fouquet. By his death in 1908 Alfred Sommier had collected at Vaux the magnificent and wholly appropriate furniture which we see today. This, together with the original painted ceilings of Le Brun and the stucco work of Girardon and a whole team of collaborators, recreates for us, if not the exact original, at least a splendid reproduction of the style inaugurated by Fouquet.

A few kilometres east of Vaux-le-Vicomte are the imposing ruins of **Blandy-les-Tours**. It was well named. An early eighteenth-century painting shows the five towers which mark the corners of the penta-gon and the tall, square pavilion of the gatehouse, rising high above the brown roofs of the village. Two are simple stone cylinders capped with pepper-pot roofs; the other three are more complex, with smaller turrets rising above the battlements or climbing up their inner walls.

Three successive campaigns of building can be detected. There is within the compound an ancient crypt which seems to have served as a chapel. There are the fourteenth-century fortifications comprising the outer wall and towers. These in turn were rendered more habit-able by the duc de Longueville in 1508. Two hundred years later the maréchal de Villars added Blandy to his newly purchased estate of Vaux-le-Vicomte, dismantled the fortress and turned some of its buildings into a farm. A gentle decay has added to the picturesque appeal without making the buildings unrecognizable. It is still possible to mount to the top of the keep and enjoy the sweeping views over the countryside which it has always commanded and to follow the *chemin de ronde* round some of the curtain wall. It is still possible to restore many of the buildings in the mind's eye and to conjure up the historical events connected with their history.

Since the days of Robert the Pious (996–1031) the King of France was also comte de Melun. He was represented in the district by his vicomte – it is what the word Viscount means. In 1371 Charles the Wise, who provided Paris with its Bastille, ordered his vicomte – also known as the comte de Tancarville – to fortify Blandy. The danger was from Burgundy, and Blandy must be seen as an eastern outpost to the royal château of Melun.

It was at this period that the great pentagonal curtain wall was built, for the most part three metres thick, with its system of mutually defensive towers – the gatehouse, the keep, the Tour des Gardes, the Tour des Archives, the north-west tower, which contained the seigneurial lodgings, and the Tour de la Justice. This still contains the 'chambre de discipline' where those condemned to death awaited execution.

In the sixteenth century Blandy became a Protestant stronghold. Its châtelain, the marquis de Rothelin, married his daughter to the prince de Condé. It was here, in 1572, that their son, Henri de Bourbon, was married to Marie de Clèves. All the Huguenot leaders, including Coligny and the King of Navarre, later to be Henri IV, were present.

The plateau of Brie is one of the richest corn-producing areas of France and supported, in the early Middle Ages, a number of wealthy ecclesiastical establishments. Apart from the collegiate church of **St Martin**, the village of **Champeaux** (some five kilometres north-east of Blandy) would have no claim to fame. It boasts, however, a distinguished history. In the late eleventh century Guillaume de Champeaux, pupil of Anselm and teacher of Abelard, was one of the great names of Paris. It was he who founded there the Abbey of St Victor and later here the *collégiale* St Martin. This rapidly became a centre of religious studies and the nursery of religious music. Its most distinguished 'old boy' must have been Simon de Brie, who in 1281 became Pope as Martin IV. Another Canon of Champeaux, de Coulombe du Lys who died here in 1760, was the last known descendant of the family of Joan of Arc.

The present church was begun in 1160, and is therefore contemporary with Notre Dame de Paris. Since Champeaux and its six neighbouring villages formed a little enclave of the diocese of Paris in territory otherwise allocated to Sens, the resemblances between the collegiate church and Notre Dame are fairly numerous.

The solitary west tower reflects the uppermost storey of its Parisian counterpart: the large, round openings into the tribunes, now walled in, also reflect a similar feature at Notre Dame which has largely disappeared.

The remainder of the west front is part ecclesiastical and part fortress, for during the Hundred Years' War, with the Earl of Salisbury ravaging the country round about, the church often had to become quite literally the Church Militant. In the Wars of Religion, although a stronghold of Catholicism, it suffered at the hands of the Catholic *Ligue*. During the Fronde the whole place was sacked and the west portal destroyed by the troops of the prince de Condé. Finally the Revolution laid its desecrating hands upon the fabric. Champeaux was one of the few collegiate churches to be running at full strength in 1790 – its forty-two canonries and fifteen chaplaincies all being occupied. They were all evicted.

There was at that time a parish church attached to the north of the collegiate building. The parishioners, forced to agree to the demolition of the one or the other, decided, perhaps unselfishly, to sacrifice their own place of worship.

Undoubtedly the most attractive feature of Champeaux is the series of Canons' stalls – like a miniature cathedral choir – which were made in 1522, by a Parisian joiner Richard Falaise. An interesting feature, which recurs in the fretted parapet that forms the canopy to the stalls, is the five-pointed star. The misericords, which sometimes represent biblical themes, and sometimes scenes from everyday life, were regarded as in bad taste in the eighteenth century, and if Archbishop Juigné had had his way they would have been removed. Instead they were whitewashed. It was only in 1956 that this disfigurement was removed.

The sanctuary is encircled by a large and luminous ambulatory whose ample windows belong to the early Geometric period. In one of these, on the north side, is the only important survival of the original stained glass, which dates, like the stalls, from the Renaissance. Formerly there were seventy such windows, made by Nicolas Maçon and Allain Courjon of Melun. It does not require much imagination to see Champeaux in its pristine glory in the blaze of colour and light produced by this magnificent ensemble. Considering how much has been lost we must marvel that what remains manages to be so beautiful.

A little to the south-east of Champeaux is **Bombon,** a capacious château of the Louis XIII period. The main block is a little dull, partly because of the regular spacing of the windows which becomes monotonous, and partly because the roofs were rebuilt in the nineteenth century at a lower pitch which has had the effect of flattening out the whole building. The outbuildings, however, have considerable charm. The entrance is through a tall pavilion in the office block with a high pyramid roof crowned with a cupola, beyond which is the seigneurial dovecot. Since a feudal law permitted only two pigeons per hectare (2.47 acres) the extent of an estate could be estimated from the capacity of its dovecote. It thus became a status symbol which was often, as here at Bombon, given architectural prominence. Many dovecotes were destroyed by the revolutionaries, with the result that they have today a scarcity value.

Built by the Brenne family, Bombon has passed through many hands. In the First World War it belonged to the Segonzacs. It was used as the headquarters of General Foch, who was noted for the austere simplicity of his life. From here, with a skeleton staff and a minimum of protocol, he directed operations during the second battle of the Marne, and here on 23 August 1918, he received his Marshal's baton from Poincaré in the presence of Clemenceau.

Some fifteen kilometres north of Bombon, in a very attractive and secluded site just beyond Chaumes-en-Brie, are the ruins of **Le Vivier,** a hunting lodge of the Capetians largely rebuilt by Charles V. It would be most interesting to know what that prodigious constructor of castles created when he was building for his recreation and not military or dynastic purposes. We shall never know. Ornament in those days was confined to the topmost parts of the building and it is only the lower parts which survive. The ruins have been in general rather over-restored.

It was here, Georges Poisson reminds us, that the mad Charles VI was often housed. Poisson evokes the picture of Odette de Champdivers – who was employed to divert the King and who did so with such success as to bear him a daughter – inventing the new distraction known as 'playing cards'.

Just north of Le Vivier is **Fontenay-Trésigny,** whose church has a fine tower, typical of the region, with a four-gabled roof known as *un clocher en batière.* Its most distinguished feature is a staircase tower built in diaper brickwork of late fifteenth-century design. Inside it is rather dark, owing to the small number of windows filled with *grisaille* and the dark panelling and pews. There is a good eighteenth-century wrought-iron screen to the sanctuary.

Ten kilometres west of Le Vivier is **Courquetaine**, a château built in the reign of Louis XIII by the de Vigny family whose most illustrious member was the author Alfred de Vigny.

A little further west is the **Château de la Grange-le-Roy**, built at the end of the sixteenth century by Jacques le Roy who was the *Surintendant des Bâtiments de Fontainebleau* under Henri IV. Described in the mid-eighteenth century by the Abbé Lebeuf as '*l'un des plus beaux châteaux de la Brie*', La Grange was once a very considerable house, for the building that can be seen today is only one of two wings which flanked the entrance court. The main block and the other wing have been demolished.

CHAPTER SIXTEEN

Brie Française

.❦.

Just across the Marne from St Maur, on the outskirts of Paris, is the **Château d'Ormesson**, a noble house in which the best traditions of the French *vie de Château* have been nobly maintained. Few families have had a more unblemished record for integrity and public service than that of the comte d'Ormesson.

It is one of those places, not uncommon in France, which has changed its name to accommodate a new owner. It appears in the annals of the sixteenth century as Amboile. In 1609 it passed by marriage to the family of Ormesson and has been called after them ever since.

It was Olivier d'Ormesson who, as *Maître des Requêtes*, was Reporter at the trial of Fouquet. It was thanks to his strength of character – for he was subjected to considerable pressure – that Louis XIV failed to get a verdict for the death penalty. It was clear that no further promotion was likely to come the way of one who had obstructed the wishes of the King, and Olivier d'Ormesson sold his offices and retired to his estates.

One would have thought that, contrasted with the life of Versailles, this was the more attractive option but La Bruyère was unfortunately right when he wrote 'the Court does not make one happy; it merely prevents one from being happy anywhere else'. From time to time friends like Turenne would take d'Ormesson, almost by force, to Versailles and push him towards the King who gave him an icy stare and would not speak a word to him. However, when his son André was presented at Court, Louis said to him: 'try to be as honest as your father'.

But in spite of the tedium of exile, the Château of Ormesson was far from being a stagnant backwater. Most of the great names of the century – Mme de Sévigné, Racine, Boileau, Bossuet, La Fontaine and Turenne were among the visitors. But perhaps the most significant was the frequent occurrence of the name of André le Nôtre. Possibly d'Ormesson's integrity at the trial of Fouquet

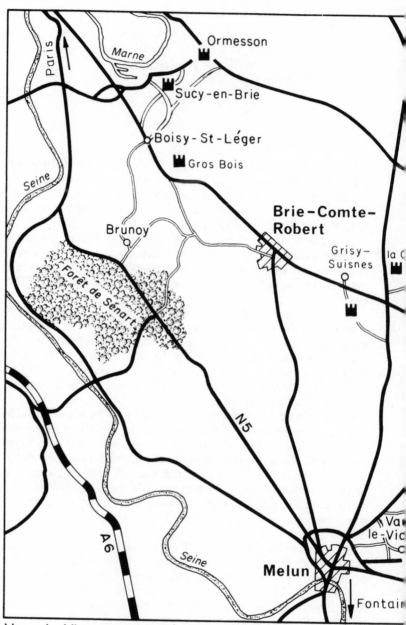

Vaux-le-Vicomte and Brie Française

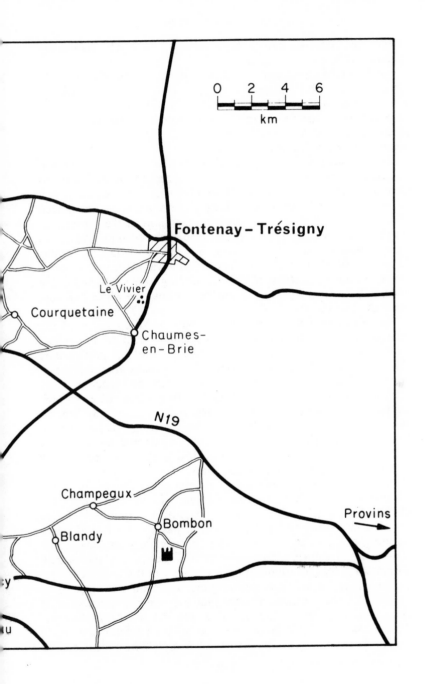

0   2   4   6
km

Fontenay – Trésigny

Le Vivier

Courquetaine

Chaumes-
en-Brie

N19

Champeaux

Bombon

Blandy

Provins

particularly endeared him to the landscape artist who had made his name at Vaux-le-Vicomte.

For Olivier d'Ormesson was a great gardener. He produced, in collaboration with President Lamoignon – the builder of Baville – a book entitled *l'Art d'orner les Jardins* which does not seem to have survived. One can imagine the pleasure that the visits of Le Nôtre must have occasioned, when the two enthusiasts could plan together the embellishment of the domain.

'The House of Narcissus', as princesse Bibesco called it, Ormesson was built towards the end of the sixteenth century by Androuet du Cerceau, standing off from the shore of a vast *miroir d'eau*. It is a building of a bold and original design; in its first state it consisted of a square block with four projecting pavilions at the corners, all capped with tall, pyramidal roofs. The two remaining pavilions were reroofed *à la Mansart* when, in 1758, a further block was added towards the east. Although no attempt was made to harmonize the styles, the proportions of the old building were continued in the new; and the same cornice, running right round the whole building, binds the two together.

The beautiful but very restrained Louis XV decorations of the main rooms make this one of the most delightful houses in France; and it has been maintained with distinction until the present day. The late comte Wladimir d'Ormesson was for many years Ambassador to the Vatican and a member of the Académie Française.

Next door to Ormesson is another distinguished château which affords a lamentable contrast. For Ormesson is beautifully kept up and lovingly cared for, but **Sucy** – once the proud domain of the Lambert de Thorigny family – is now in ruins and the blocks of flats of a building estate ironically called '*Cité Verte*' have come within eighty metres of the garden front.

At Boissy-St-Léger, only a few kilometres to the south, is the **Château de Gros Bois**. It is visible from the N19, the road from Paris to Provins. The first impression is delightful: a beautiful medley of brick and stone and slate, with high pavilion roofs and many dormers, rising at the end of a chestnut avenue with broad grass verges, neatly mown. For the estate now belongs to the Société d'Encouragement (cf Chantilly) and it is very well maintained.

The austere iron gates, whose piers are composed each of a bundle of lances, suggest at once that the essential connection of Gros Bois is with the Empire. This was the home of Maréchal Berthier, prince de Wagram. Here he held his fabulous shooting parties. On one occasion the bag numbered 5600 head of game: on another he purchased 1000 tame rabbits to remedy the deficiency of his depleted coverts.

There is a vivid picture of one of Napoleon's visits here painted by the duchesse d'Abrantès, wife of Maréchal Junot and *Dame du Palais* to the Empress Joséphine.

The life of a *Dame du Palais* was by no means easy at the best of times, but these suddenly arranged visits created all sorts of problems – '*c'était pour moi une annonce terrifiante, que ces voyages-là*'. The visit to Gros Bois was one of her most disagreeable experiences. The *Dames du Palais* were only allowed one lady's maid among four. They slept eight to a room – 'and a room in which I should not have wished to lodge one of my lower servants'. The room contained one looking glass and it was extremely cold.

Napoleon had ordered, in his usual insensitive way, that *every one should enjoy himself*. It was easier said than done. Rumours of an impending divorce were making life a misery for Joséphine and all who loved her. Berthier, who seemed to think that because he was living at Gros Bois he was living in the seventeenth century, had ordered '*les violons et la Comédie*' – but he had not taken the trouble to enquire what the comedy was about. It was about divorce. 'It would be useless,' wrote the Duchess, 'to describe the embarrassment of everyone. But as for Berthier, I can see him now, standing to the right of the stage biting his nails till the blood flowed.'

Much of the interior of Gros Bois is still as Berthier left it. His most important contribution to the decoration of the château is the **Galerie des Batailles**, designed to take eight large paintings of the battles in which Berthier had been chief of staff to Napoleon. Between the pictures are busts of the fourteen Marshals created by the Emperor, whose own bust, by Canova, presides over the whole scene from the extremity of the gallery.

Since the last private owner of the château, the princesse de la Tour d'Auvergne, was a direct descendant of Berthier's, the furniture is more or less unchanged and provides, in its homely arrangement, a better idea of life at that time than the collection at Malmaison. The **Marshal's Bedroom** and the **Salon Jaune** exemplify the love of mahogany and ormolu, with many pieces signed by the great Jacob. In the **Salon des Huissiers** there is a charming suite of children's furniture, presented by Napoleon.

In the **Salon de Passage** is a remarkable chandelier which appears to be a ring of French horns. The room itself is in late-eighteenth-century style with simple, clean lines and a minimum of low relief carving suggestive of the interiors of Montgeoffroy and Le Lude.

But we must go back to the early seventeenth century for the original decorations of the château. The Dining Room or **Chambre d'Honneur** was painted in fresco by Abraham Bosse to commemorate his second marriage. The great murals depicting the ceremony were rediscovered in 1910 beneath several layers of wallpaper. These pictures, together with the painted beams and a noble fireplace, make this room as fine a sample of its style as is to be found in the Ile de France.

During the eighteenth century Gros Bois had a succession of owners ending with the comte de Provence, the future Louis XVIII, and after the Revolution Barras, who would accept no office under Napoleon. When Fouché came to urge him Barras merely indicated the house and park and said '*voilà la seule place que je veuille désormais occuper*'.

A little digression to the south from Gros Bois leads to **Brunoy** on the fringe of the Forêt de Sénart. Its **Church of St Médard**, with a thirteenth-century choir to which a sixteenth-century nave and tower were added, retains a magnificent decoration of white and gold wood-work set up by the spendthrift marquis de Brunoy in 1772.

At the death of his father, the villagers of Brunoy witnessed a funeral the like of which had probably never been seen. Each of them was issued with six metres of black serge with which to dress in mourning. The whole château – now demolished – was draped in black and the waters of the canal before it darkened with ink. The sheep, the cows and the horses were all dyed black and the horses given a drug to blacken their urine. The church also was painted black. Fortunately this decor was superseded for the Corpus Christi celebrations on 3 July 1772. A hundred and fifty priests had been invited to take part in this procession, in which five hundred coaches were used. The route was lined with twenty-five thousand vases of flowers; and after the ceremony a banquet was served for eight hundred local peasants.

Brie-Comte-Robert, further south-east on the N19, was once the capital of Brie Française, and is now a small market town. It takes its name from Robert, comte de Dreux, the second son of Louis VI, who built the castle here in 1170. What little remains of this has become a public park to which the moat and ruins of the curtain wall provide features which are perhaps more picturesque than informative. They certainly give no idea what the building looked like.

Just to one side of the Place des Halles is an early **thirteenth-century arcade** of great elegance incorporated in what appears to

Undercroft of the Grange aux Dîmes, Provins

Provins: Tour de César

be an ordinary house. It formed part of the chapel of the original Hôtel Dieu.

But it is the **Church of St Étienne** which is the principal attraction of Brie-Comte-Robert. Seen from the south it stands up magnificently above the roofs of the town. It is a design typical of the region with a square east end, no transepts and a tower at the north-east corner. In the distance it appears to be a unity of style – a stately rhythm of large clerestory windows and flying buttresses; but a closer inspection reveals that the three western bays are different. The thirteenth-century flying buttresses stick straight out like the oars of a galleon; those of the Renaissance are slightly curved. The thirteenth-century windows are of austere simplicity; those of the sixteenth century follow a more delicate design. The older buttress piers are of rough masonry; the later ones are of excellent freestone ornamented with attached columns. It is remarkable how easily these two styles could be married. The basic formula of building is unchanged, but a new set of decorative motifs has replaced the old. The Renaissance had no alternative to offer to the gargoyle as a means of taking the water off a building and the spirit of the Middle Ages is still to be discerned in their design.

The orientation of the church reflects its dedication. On 26 December, St Stephen's Day, the sun rises distinctly north of east and the axis has been made to conform to this alignment. There is a fine view of the church from the little square on the north side. The high windows of the clerestory show the simple tracery similar to that of Amiens Cathedral. In the Renaissance part, towards the west, the date 1546 appears beneath the column on the west buttress.

Compared with these interesting and imposing façades, the interior of the church is disappointing. It is in bad condition and the leprous state of the dull grey stone creates an impression of shabbiness. This, together with the untidy clutter of indifferent pictures and poor quality statues, detracts considerably from the architecture.

The same development of style is at once visible. The choir and sanctuary are the oldest and most pure in style, showing clear affinities with Notre Dame. This is not surprising since the comte de Dreux was a vassal of the Archbishop of Paris. In particular, the cylindrical pillars of the main arcade, from which the colonettes rise to support the vaulting, recall the mother church of the Diocese. In the fourth bay these pillars give way to complex but rather shape-less piers which raise a single rounded shaft to the level of the top of the triforium, where it meets the ribs of the quadripartite vault.

The east end has been marred by a large and inappropriate retable of the Louis XVI style, but above it is the greatest glory of the whole church, the lovely rose window of the thirteenth century, which is almost a miniature of the west rose at Notre Dame. Against an overall background of a lovely blue, it shows the figure of Christ surrounded by the Apostles.

Grisy-Suisnes, some five kilometres east of Brie-Comte-Robert, is one of the great rose gardens of France. It was imperative that it should have a church with the dedication **Notre Dame des Roses**. But for sixty years the parishioners were without a place of worship. The old church had been pulled down in 1910. In 1967 a new and very modern church was built at the insistence of the Abbé Fabing.

The architect, Antoine Korady, has taken the oldest Christian symbol, the fish, for his ground plan, which might be said to resemble in outline a rather rectilinear turbot. There is something also of the streamlined elegance of the manta ray in the long, rhythmic sweep of the roof. But the simile is changed abruptly with the great spire, forty-two metres high, which suggests the lines of a sailing ship – *la barque de pierre* – another symbol of the Church. Others can see in its sharp point the thorn of the ubiquitous rose.

The interior decoration is entirely wooden and represents an extremely high standard of joinery. It provides a warm and mellow atmosphere which accords well with the text on the altar '*Aimez-vous les uns les autres*'. The theology of the Abbé Fabing is explicit. 'I thought that first of all we must raise our eyes to Heaven,' he said in a television interview; 'but secondly we had our feet on the ground and we had to think of the joy of living for all.' For this reason the church adjoins a *Centre Culturel* which provides for a variety of social activities. It was a costly undertaking; and without the Abbé's zeal the money, which came from all corners of France, would never have been raised.

The furniture of the church is also noteworthy. The font, symbolizing the living water promised to the Samaritan Woman, is in the form of an eternally overflowing spring, above which is another fish which forms the baptismal basin. The altar is a huge block of stone from Vaurion, rough-hewn in a simple oblong.

The windows, mostly triangular in shape, are by Jacques Loire and represent the stations of the Cross. The two large ones take up the themes of the organ and of the Virgin Mary, who is represented in her chapel by the only historic feature in the whole church, a lovely eighteenth-century wooden figure.

Considerable impetus was given to the cultivation of roses here

by the famous traveller and botanist, Admiral Bougainville, who
in 1800 purchased the little seventeenth-century **Château de Suisnes**.
He added the façade with the portico to this pavilion, which had
been intended only as an annexe to an older and larger building
which has now disappeared.

CHAPTER SEVENTEEN

The Lower Marne and the Grand Morin

꣠

The **Château de Champs**, a building belonging to the first decade of the eighteenth century, lies some twenty kilometres east of Paris – and a very undistinguished drive it is; suburbia, formless and faceless, has sprawled to its very gates. If one were not expecting it and looking for it, the first sight of Champs would be an overwhelming surprise, for the entrance gates, after the fashion of so many French châteaux, are on the high road, from which they are only separated by a dry moat. Behind the gates lies the forecourt and at the end of the forecourt, framed by the perspective of the symmetrical offices, is one of the most distinguished houses in France.

It is an object lesson in the dignity of simplicity. For here is no flourish of architecture, no dazzling display of fountains and statues: just the pleasing effect of beautiful stone beautifully cut; of tall windows which have retained, or regained, their multiple glazing bars; of a mansard roof alleviated by spacious dormers; of a fine frontispiece of superimposed orders to accentuate the entrance pavilion. An atmosphere of logical symmetry and quiet good taste pervades.

And this is the second surprise that Champs has in store for us, for it was the house of a parvenu and a profiteer, a lackey who became a millionaire. One might have expected a far more showy mansion from such a patron. Georges Poisson de Beauvalais was a self-made man, the son of a peasant and married to one of the village girls of Champs. He started life as the valet of the farmer-general Thévenin who once had the ill taste to remind him of the fact. He received the well-earned snub: 'that is true; but if you had been a valet of mine you would have remained one'.

There was no love lost between the old aristocracy and these 'suddenly monied men' and during the Regency – a period not conspicuous for its moral standards – it was decided to hold an inspection of accounts. Beauvalais was sent to the Bastille and his beautiful houses at Champs and the Place Vendôme – now the Ministry of Justice – were confiscated.

Champs was purchased, as Saint-Simon puts it, 'for a piece of bread' by the princesse de Conti, daughter of Louis XIV and Louise de la Vallière. She entered into the possession of what was not only one of the most beautiful, but also one of the most comfortable houses in France. And here Champs offers its third surprise. It is difficult to believe that so perfect a house should have been designed by so obscure an architect: Chamblain was only a 'second class' at the Académie.

Above all he produced, to use Le Corbusier's phrase, a *machine à habiter*. The seventeenth century had been content with a magnificent suite of rooms, each of which could be reached only by passing through the others. Chamblain, following the latest ideas of Robert de Cotte, arranged his rooms in groups, so that each bedroom had its *cabinet* and its *garderobe* and was reached by a passage. Three smaller staircases connected these apartments and facilitated the unobtrusive circulation of the domestics.

In the seventeenth century one ate where one chose. Tables were laid to order in any of the state rooms, and food was transported often considerable distances from kitchens in the outbuildings. At Champs there was a proper dining room at no great distance from the kitchens in the basement below. By the mid-eighteenth century there was certainly more than one bathroom in the house, for there is reference in the account books to 'English wallpaper' on frames for the bathrooms of Champs.

This was at a time when the château was rented by Madame de Pompadour. It was a happy chance that ordained that the final decorations should have been carried out under the orders of one whose taste was impeccable and whose slightest wish was law.

We have thus at Champs three phases of interior decoration: late Louis XIV, represented chiefly in the west half of the ground floor, of which the dining room is the only one open to the public; the two rooms painted by Huet for the duc de la Vallière, and the rest panelled and painted for Madame de Pompadour.

The two rooms by Huet offer a contrast which shows his versatility as a decorator. The **Salon d'Assemblée** is a tall and roomy apartment, lit by four windows and two enormous mirrors. The wall space is divided into a large number of small panels, probably dating from the Louis XIV period, which offered fifty-eight picture frames to the painter who filled them with light-hearted subjects – gardening, fishing, shooting – in which Chinamen, monkeys and other animals are light-heartedly engaged. There is a delightful freshness about the delicately varied colours, whose greens and pinks already seem to invite the inmate to taste the pleasures of the gardens just outside.

In a very different key is the **Boudoir** in the south-east corner. It is a cosy, intimate apartment, with a low ceiling in proportion to its reduced dimensions. Here Huet has confined himself to a close colour scheme, using only cold blues and smoky greys, to which the upholstery of the furniture is skilfully attuned.

Most of the other rooms owe their interest and their charm to the exquisite carving of the woodwork, all chiselled out of the solid oak, and in most cases painted. These represent the redecorations of Madame de Pompadour. Especially fine is the room in which she is presumed to have slept, where the peacock in full display at the top of the panel over the fireplace and the kissing doves at the bottom seem to symbolize the career of the marquise.

The colouring of these rooms is an early and wholly successful essay in restoration. For when, in 1875, the comte Louis Cahen d'Anvers acquired the property, it was in a deplorable condition. The mansard roof had been removed and replaced by a balustrade; much of the panelling, including that of the Boudoir, had been painted an ugly grey, and the formal gardens of Desgots and Garnier d'Isle had been swept away in favour of a *jardin à l'anglaise*. Cahen d'Anvers, using the plans and drawings of Mariette, restored Champs to its original and formal splendour.

In 1935 the comte Charles Cahen d'Anvers offered this splendid house, together with all the furniture which he and his father had collected, to the State. The fact that it is still used to house distinguished visitors to the President of the Republic is perhaps the highest compliment that could be paid to the creators and restorers of Champs.

Another seven kilometres east we come to **Guermantes**. To the reader of Proust, the name will immediately evoke the image of his famous Duchess. But there is no connection. The sequence of vowel sounds merely appealed to his ear, and it was not until he had finished his writing that he even came here.

This is a building of the seventeenth century – a fact which is apparent in the first glimpse from the high road, for, when the windows are aligned, it is possible to see right through the house. This betrays the single suite of rooms each opening into the next which later centuries found inconvenient.

There were here two phases of building some sixty years apart. The main block was started, together with the outhouses, in 1631; and the long wing which projects at right angles was only finished in

1710. This wing, designed by Robert de Cotte, is on our left as we approach the main entrance: it provokes some interesting reflections on the aesthetics of the style.

Nine of the windows – those of the Great Gallery – retain their original small panes and multiple glazing bars, whereas the remaining six windows of the first floor were renewed in the nineteenth century: the panes are large, the bars are few and slender. The first make a delightful façade: the second are merely dull. Notice also the contrast between the austere, municipal effect of the clock in the pediment over the main entrance and the beautiful carving in the one over the Gallery.

The two styles of Guermantes represent the two families which built it. In the first place, Claude Viole – an eminent figure in the Parlement under Louis XIII. They used to make the pun: '*le parlement n'a jamais dansé sans Viole*'. He built the main block with its high, straight roofs. It still contains a room, known as the **Chambre Viole,** decorated for the wedding of his son Pierre and Marie Vallée. The room has had an interesting history. Dismantled in 1876, it was subdivided and the panelling thrown out. In 1921 all the panels were discovered in the barns and granaries of the estate, and the whole room was carefully reinstated in its original condition. It provides a superb example of the polychroming which was a regular feature of interior decoration in the early years of the seventeenth century.

In the pavilion at the west end is another example, the **Chambre à l'Italienne,** decorated for Pierre Viole in 1645 by artists from Fontainebleau. The paintings of the ceiling, except for the central one, are identical to those by Pierre Perrier in the Galerie Dorée of the Hôtel de la Vrillière, now the Bank of France.

Pierre Viole sided with Condé in the Fronde, and during his ensuing exile was actually beheaded in effigy on the Place de Grève. But in 1659, when amnesty was granted, he returned to live at Guermantes.

In 1698 the estate was sold to the rich but unscrupulous financier Paulin Prondre, and it was for him that the sumptuous new wing was added. It contained a gallery on the first floor, thirty-one metres long, known locally as **'la Belle Inutile'.**

It must certainly have been useless in winter, for there is no fireplace in the whole vast apartment, a circumstance which makes the roof line somewhat oppressive from without from want of chimneys. But it can justly be called beautiful, and does credit to its author, Robert de Cotte. He has introduced a bold rhythm in his treatment of the piers between the windows, in which two high-set paintings alternate with one low-set mirror surmounted by a large oval portrait. These paintings were done by Mérelle and were paid for in 1709. The real richness of the room, however, derives from its ceiling, whose paintings, but not its carving and stucco work, were all renewed in 1850.

During the Regency, Prondre was involved in the financial speculations of William Law, who became, we know not how, the owner of Guermantes in 1720. His children used the large painting at the north end of the gallery for target practice. By the end of the same year Law had to leave the country: the estate was already encumbered by debts, but since Law had never paid the purchase money, it reverted to Prondre.

The last of their line, Ernestine, comtesse de Dampierre, occupied the château during the nineteenth century. She entertained lavishly, but her hospitality was somewhat offset by her taste for indiscretions. The duc de Trévise, who was a frequent member of her house parties, used to take the precaution of staying until last for fear of what might be said behind his back after he had gone.

Madame de Dampierre carried her magisterial manners into her religion. At the end of the wing occupied by the Gallery is the Chapel, also designed by Robert de Cotte, which was never deconsecrated during the Revolution. It is full of high-backed chairs, presumably for the domestic staff, for the family sat in the tribune at first-floor level. If the sermon were too long for her liking, Madame de Dampierre would cut it short with a firm: 'assez, Curé; tais-toi!'

A little north of Guermantes is Lagny, where the Church of Notre Dame des Ardents and St Pierre is one of the hidden beauties of the Ile de France. From the east it is difficult to see because of the private properties with which it is surrounded; from the west it is screened by an extremely dull façade dating from 1750 which in no way hints at the architecture behind it. To enter Lagny unforewarned is an astonishing experience.

Notre Dame des Ardents is an unusual ascription and refers to a terrible disease of the Middle Ages known variously as le feu infernal, la peste du feu or le feu ardent. The bodies of its victims became so hot that if water was poured on them it filled the room with steam 'as well as with an insupportable stench'. Death or miraculous healing were the two alternatives; and large numbers of the latter were claimed on behalf of the Virgin Mary – hence her special title 'Notre Dame des Ardents'. Modern science has suggested that the malady was a form of gangrene caused by undernourishment. Its outbreak coincided with bad harvests and it seems to have affected only the peasants.

The church has been described by M. François Salet as 'impeccable . . . we are truly in the presence of an art which has reached its apogee and the work of a man and of an epoch which had nothing to learn'. The building shows no signs of hesitation or of second thoughts; the builder knew exactly what he wanted to do and exactly how to do it.

This is high praise, but there are certain features which the practised eye will immediately detect as being discordant. The first fact to note is that the scale of the building is that of a cathedral. Only the choir and a fraction of the transepts are present, but if the transepts were completed and a nave added in proportion to the rest we should have a building some 110 metres long. There must have been prodigious financial backing before so ambitious an enterprise could even be contemplated.

But if we are thinking of a building on the scale of a cathedral we must at once be struck by the lack of height. It is only twenty-one metres from floor to keystone. The clerestory windows are absurdly small. The vaults spring from the base of the triforium so that both the triforium and the clerestory windows are contained within the arch formed by the wall ribs. On the exterior this want of height reveals itself in the lack of flying buttresses. So squat a vault is not in need of their abutment. However there is firm evidence that the church was intended to have an elevation of another five to six metres and very similar to the Cathedral of Troyes.

It remains to account both for the ambitious scale of the original intention and for its sudden abandoning. The explanation to both comes from the enthusiastic support given to Lagny by the ruling house of Champagne. This also accounts for the connection with Troyes, the capital of Champagne. But the death of count Henri III brought the male line to an end; the great fairs of Provins and Lagny were abolished and war with Flanders bled the area of what little wealth it still possessed. Lagny was left with only half its transepts, no nave and a choir that had only reached the top of the triforium. What might have been one of the most beautiful churches in France remained a fragment. Ironically, it was probably this circumstance that saved it from destruction during the Revolution.

There are some other interesting buildings in Lagny. The town hall occupies part of the old conventual buildings. In the **Place de la Fontaine** there is a row of houses with five steep gables and buttresses which are certainly medieval. The fountain from which the square takes its name is basically Renaissance, but incorporates work of several periods. It is supposed to have miraculous qualities.

South-east of Lagny is **Jossigny**, where there is a delightful little château which remained an almost perfect period piece until 1942 when it was bequeathed to the State. It is now in the most tragic state of dilapidation.

It was built in 1743 by Leconte des Graviers, a councillor of the Parlement de Paris. It stands back from the road behind a wrought-iron screen in the lightest rococo fancy – too slender, it would seem, even to support the weight of the coronet of a French count which rides proudly over the gateway. Everything about the entrance façade is subtle and exquisite and seems to reflect in miniature the more magnificent Hôtel de Biron in Paris. The façade towards the gardens is the same except for the central portion which breaks forward in a triple-faceted projection. There is a faint echo of a pagoda about the concave sweeps of the roof.

Claude-François Leconte des Graviers, the builder of Jossigny, had two sons who between them organized all the hunting for the prince de Conti. The elder brother followed Conti into exile and consumed his entire fortune in order to subsidize his master. In return, he found himself the chief beneficiary in the prince's will. Thanks to this bounty the family were able to return to Jossigny at the Restoration and the house remained in the family until the death of the baron de Roig in 1942.

A happy result of this continuity of ownership is that the interior decorations and furnishing have been preserved intact. As with the façades, the decor is in a very restrained rococo – enough to be graceful but stopping well short of the fantastic.

The **kitchen**, which answers the chapel across the cour d'honneur, is another period piece, still containing the battery of copper saucepans which was the wedding present of the prince de Conti to his godson and Master of Hounds. As the marriage took place in 1789 the present must have been one of his last acts before he went into exile.

From Jossigny we can take the minor road south-east to Ville-neuve-le-Comte and cross the N36 to Dammartin. From here it is a delightful drive to follow the Grand Morin northwards to Crécy-la-Chapelle. It is a lovely valley, peopled with poplars and backed by high wooded slopes which once were vineyards. Against this background the **Chapelle-sur-Crécy** stands out magnificently. It is immediately obvious that this is one of the most important churches in the neighbourhood, but a long detour is necessary before it can be reached. The village, however, is attractive and provides the overture to prepare us for the chapel, which is the last building on the road to Jouarre.

It is a wonderful example of early-thirteenth-century architecture in which great simplicity and unity are combined with an occasional touch of originality. It is best seen from the east, where the main road is joined by a side road from Serbonne. It depends for its effect upon the steady rhythm and deep shadow projection built up by the great piers which receive the thrust of the flying buttresses. An original feature of the apse is that the tribune windows are rectangular. The rather austere beauty of the nave and choir is delightfully offset by the more homely style of the twin aisles with their brown tiled roofs.

The trouble about Chapelle-sur-Crécy is that it was very badly sited on low ground which was liable to flooding. In the seventeenth and eighteenth centuries the floor was raised by some one and a half metres to counter this, which has considerably impaired its proportions.

This is most noticeable in the interior which looks distinctly dumpy. The raising of the floor level, having destroyed the balance of the building, did not succeed in excluding the damp; the whole place is green with it.

In the Hundred Years' War the English took Crécy and the church was badly damaged, and between 1421 and 1429 the four westernmost bays of the nave were rebuilt. One can see clearly on the pillar east of the pulpit exactly where the new work joined the old. The new bays contain some very imaginative tracery in the triforium and clerestory windows, but the capitals to the pillars which support the nave arcade were never carved, leaving the curious basin-shaped swellings of the rough-hewn state. By contrast the choir capitals are fully carved and surmounted by triple heads, grimacing grotesquely, from which rise the three colonettes which become the ribs of the vaulting.

The choir and apse exhibit a remarkable feat of vaulting. Twelve ribs all radiate out from one boss to form one of the most impressive 'spider vaults' of the district.

At the east end of the south aisle there is a statue of the Virgin over the altar in the typical pose of the fourteenth century, the weight so placed on one leg that the hip projects sufficiently to give some support to a child; it is known in French as *hanchement*. The font is also remarkable, being in the form of a double basin with light relief carving of 1531.

From here to **Coulommiers**, along the valley of the Grand Morin, is another delightful drive.

If the name of Coulommiers is known in Britain at all it is probably known for its cheeses: they have been famous for a thousand years. Charlemagne had special consignments of them sent to his palace at Aix-la-Chapelle: Philippe le Bel used to give them as New Year presents to the ladies of his court.

On the south bank of the Grand Morin and to the east of the Avenue de Strasbourg is the **Parc des Capucins**, and to the east of the park is a square garden insulated by a moat which marks the **site of the former Château de Coulommiers**.

Begun in 1613 for Catherine de Gonzague et de Clèves, duchesse de Longueville, it was still unfinished at her death in 1629; although it was sufficiently advanced, two years later, for Louis XIII and his Queen to make a special expedition to see it. Here Salomon de Brosse, architect also of the Luxembourg and of Blérancourt, placed his three symmetrical façades between four pavilions which marked the corners of a square. This he left open on the fourth side without the elaborate screen and portal which closed the courtyards of Verneuil and Montceaux. Three tiers of statues – 373 in all – adorned the façades of the courtyard.

In the eighteenth century the château passed into the hands of the Chevreuse-Luynes family. They already possessed the magnificent Château de Dampierre, together with Châteaudun and Luynes in the Loire Valley. Unwilling to take on the vast expense of its upkeep they had Coulommiers demolished.

The site today is still just worth a visit. At the end of a long avenue of poplars the alley crosses the moat to a square island which marks the emplacement of the château. Two dilapidated lodges, which were added in 1631 by François Mansart, guard the approaches. Over the door where the stonework is heavily carved is the figure of a cherub snatching away a helmet as if to invite the warrior to lay aside the rigours of the camp on entering this domain of peace and plenty. Across the space that was the cour d'honneur, two fragments of arcading, which marked the inmost corners of the building, and a very ruinous archway flanked by niches, which must have been the front door, bear melancholy witness to the style and splendour of the last great building of the house of Longueville.

Across the moat is the chapel of the Capucins, a building contemporary with the château, for the pious Catherine de Longueville built and endowed a convent on her doorstep. The château was to be the setting of her mortal life: the chapel to house her mortal remains.

For this purpose the choir was built in an unusual, two-storey design – the first floor being the choir proper and the ground floor her mausoleum – but a mausoleum of twisted columns and rococo shellwork more suited to a grotto than a religious edifice.

Having been for hundreds of years a barn, the chapel is much defaced and serves now to house a small museum of local archaeology and folklore recently established by M. Marcel Garnier.

Another architectural ensemble of interest is the **Commanderie des Templiers**, off to the right of the road to La Ferté-sous-Jouarre and overlooking the valley of the Grand Morin. Today the whole area has been built up and the old Commanderie looks strangely shabby in its brightly modern surroundings.

In 1128 Thibault II, comte de Champagne, offered the site to the Knights Templars. On 13 October 1307, Philippe le Bel had every member of the order arrested simultaneously at midnight. Thousands of harmless, unsuspecting citizens suddenly found themselves in the torture chamber. Confessions of anything from sacrilege to sodomy were extracted, and those who later retracted their confessions were, by the rules of the Inquisition, burnt alive.

The Commanderie was made over to the Hospitallers. It became a farm and from being a farm it became a ruin. In the last few years a number of local youth organizations have worked to repair the damage with the object of forming here a Museum of Paper. It is a picturesque little group of clearly articulated buildings – the Maison du Commandeur like a small *Gentilhommière* with its typical staircase tower and entrance – the chapel, late twelfth- or early thirteenth-century, with its simple alternation of buttresses and lancet windows and its very tall roof. The chief impression is one of delightful simplicity.

The works of restoration have brought to light some thirteenth-century murals, the most exciting discovery being an *Adoration of the Magi* over the west window which was hidden by a one-metre-thick wall.

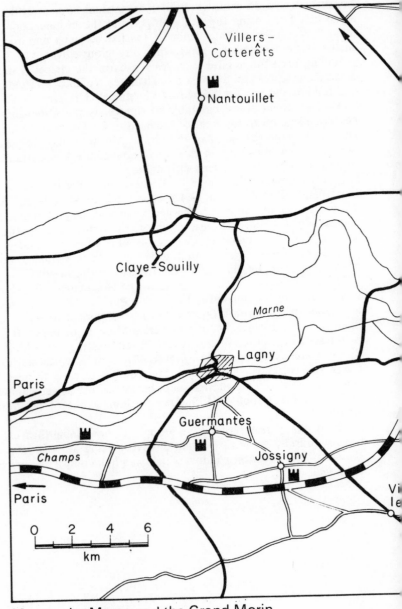

Meaux, the Marne and the Grand Morin

CHAPTER EIGHTEEN

Meaux and the Marne Valley

Thirty-five kilometres north-east of Paris in the valley of the Beuv-ronne is **Nantouillet**, a château built in the early years of François I by Antoine du Prat.

'*Jeunesse du Prince, source de belles fortunes.*' Seldom has a saying proved more true than in 1515 when the young duc d'Angoulême ascended the throne of St Louis. The men who rose to power with him were to be the great builders of the French Renaissance. The first was Guillaume Gouffier who became *Amiral de France* and built, in 1516, the immense Château de Bonnivet to the south of Chinon. At the same time Florimond Robertet, the most upright of the financiers, was building Bury on the western fringe of the Forêt de Blois. Two other financiers, Bohier and Berthelot, made the important contributions of Chenonceau and Azay-le-Rideau. François himself was building the east wing of the Château de Blois and dreaming of Chambord.

There was no doubt that François was the real ruler, but under him there was probably no one more powerful than the Chancellor, Antoine du Prat. Owing to the death of his wife, du Prat became eligible for ordination and bishoprics and wealthy abbeys could be heaped upon him. In due course he received the cardinal's hat and became papal legate.

Considering the wealth and power of du Prat and the size and magnificence of Bonnivet and Bury it is somewhat surprising that Nantouillet should be a relatively modest building. It lay well outside the Loire country and was only partially influenced by its architecture. In some ways it was unique.

The **entrance front** immediately declares the main theme: massive brick towers that owe nothing to Italy guard a gateway which is decorated in an entirely Renaissance manner while its form is still dictated by the drawbridge and wicket gate it had to accommodate.

Inside this fortified enclosure the house occupies three sides of a quadrangle open towards the entrance. The first impression it creates is one of almost austere simplicity, but a closer inspection

MEAUX AND THE MARNE VALLEY

reveals a rich and charming – if somewhat unusual – decoration.
It must be remembered also that the house has lost its original
dormer windows which would certainly have been elaborate and
used to maintain the balance between plain surfaces and almost
lace-like detail.

Du Prat was well up to date in building a straight staircase, as at
Azay and Chenonceau, but surprisingly old-fashioned in his rejec-
tion of symmetry, for the staircase is considerably to the right of
centre. The vaulted ceiling to the staircase is true to the Gothic
tradition.

In Gothic idiom also are the windows towards the end of the left
wing which clearly articulate in their shape the rise of a second
staircase; but to the left of these again is a doorway surmounted
by a hood in the form of a scallop shell which might well be one of
the overdoors of Blois.

But it is on the **garden front** that the builder has made his most
important innovation. The whole façade is divided up into compartments by a grid formed by the horizontal lines of a double string
course and the vertical lines of a series of flat pilasters without
capitals which may be regarded as residuary buttresses. Into the
compartments of this grid the windows – some large, some small –
are cut without regard for symmetry and with no relationship to
the pilasters. In this the builder shows himself quite independent of
Bury and Bonnivet where the pilasters either frame the windows or
– as in the courtyard at Bury – create a grid into which the windows
fit symmetrically.

The principal feature of the front is the projection formed by an
oratory at first-floor level in the form of an apse upheld by an arcade
which is an entirely Gothic conception.

The importance of this new ordonnance – a façade which exists
in its own right independent of the disposition of the rooms behind
it – is that it was copied at Écouen, a château some twenty-five
kilometres distant which was built soon after the death of du Prat
in 1535 by the Constable Anne de Montmorency.

Meaux is not a place to appeal to the tourist; narrow and shabby
in its older parts, modern and industrial in its outskirts, it has lost
nearly all that was picturesque except for its cathedral with its
attendant Episcopal Palace and Canons' Lodging.

The present **Cathedral** was started in 1180. The date is significant,
for in the previous year a charter had been granted by Henri le
Libéral, comte de Champagne, and Meaux had become a commune
with its own civil rights. Jean Gimpel has drawn attention, in his

fascinating book *Les Bâtisseurs des Cathédrales*, to the coincidence between the granting of charters and the building of great cathedrals.

The newly enfranchised bourgeois, proud of the rights which he had won from the feudal overlord, was inspired by a civic patriotism which sometimes knew no bounds. This local pride expressed itself in terms of ambitious ecclesiastical architecture, as at a later date it was to express itself in pompous municipal buildings. The Church was still opposed, at least in theory, to usury and profit, so that the rich bourgeois often had an uneasy conscience. He eased it by munificent donations to his local church or cathedral.

The result was that the building of a great church became, in the mid-twelfth century, what the crusade had been in previous ages – a work of piety into which Christian zeal could be channelled. With good reason the great century of cathedral building in France has been called *La Croisade des Cathédrales*.

Rebuilding at Meaux proceeded steadily from 1180 over the next forty years. Between 1200 and 1215 the choir had been vaulted and the transepts were well advanced. In the next ten years the transepts were finished and the nave completely built.

Unfortunately the stone from the neighbouring quarries of Varreddes, though extremely beautiful, is not of good quality; and in 1253 much of the work had to be done again. In particular the apse was virtually rebuilt. It was altered most significantly in the process. The tribunes were abolished and the main arcade raised to the height of the triforium. Standing today in the **crossing** one can see at once the difference, for the first three bays south of the choir have retained the tribune arches. They are in fact false tribunes, for they merely form an open-work screen between the choir and its aisles. The new apse is far more elegant, except that the eye instinctively looks for the very tall clerestory windows of Amiens or Beauvais to match the greatly increased height of the main arcade.

From the same vantage point in the middle of the crossing, the inner façades of the transepts can be appreciated. There is here a perfect unity of style. The blind tracery of the ground floor reflects the open tracery of the huge clerestory window; the triforium makes the transition between them. The work dates from the late thirteenth or early fourteenth century and was due to the *maître d'oeuvre* Gauthier de Varinfroy.

From a standpoint a little further down the **nave**, where the great piers of the crossing entirely mask the choir tribunes, the perspective is truly magnificent; the uninterrupted lines of the countless colonettes of the great piers convey an overwhelming impression of verticality.

The height is in fact only thirty-one metres – six metres less than Chartres – but the illusion of height is fostered by the narrowness of the aisles, of which the outer ones were first built much lower.

The lovely white stone is seen to its full advantage because of the absence of stained glass. Only one window – the centre light in the clerestory of the apse – has survived from the original thirteenth-century glazing.

Lack of colour is, in fact, the chief defect of St Étienne de Meaux. One has only to imagine the exquisite architecture of the apsidal chapels bathed in the reflected glory of glass such as may be seen at Reims, or to picture the huge Geometric windows of the transepts filled with the kaleidoscopic colours of Amiens or Notre Dame, to get some notion of the original effect. But whatever it was, most of it was smashed by the Huguenots when they sacked the cathedral in 1560.

For Meaux has suffered from two hundred years of recurrent violence. In 1358 it was the Jacquerie, the peasant uprising against feudal landlords. By means of accomplices within the town, the Jacquerie managed to penetrate Meaux, but the opposition mounted a successful counter-offensive; the rebels were cut to pieces, the mayor who had let them into the city was hanged and the whole place set on fire. It burned for fourteen days. The cathedral was almost the only survivor; but it had lost all its treasures in the conflict.

Thirty years later, a band of brigands terrorized the town, committing murder, rape and pillage on all sides, despoiling the churches and perpetrating 'indescribable disorders'. In 1420 it was the English who were at the gates and the Meldois were in the last extremities of a siege.

Understandably progress on the cathedral in such conditions was slow. Nevertheless the fourteenth century saw many alterations and additions to the fabric. In 1317 and 1322, thanks to donations from a wealthy bourgeois named Jean Rose and from Charles IV, two more apsidal chapels were added. In 1326, thanks again to a royal donation, it was decided to extend the nave further towards the west. Later in the century, under Bishops Jean de Drac and Jean Lhuillier, the tribunes were removed from the third and fourth bays of the nave (one always counts from the west). Finally the north tower was started and an organ loft built over the west doors. It was a bold conception, a huge semicircular arch upholding the console with blind tracery on the wall behind that is almost Perpendicular in feeling – a style which hardly ever appears outside England. The present organ case dates from 1627.

Meanwhile events were occurring which were to issue in disastrous results for the cathedral.

The Middle Ages are often called the 'Age of Faith'. It is a description which needs to be taken with some reserves. The annals of Meaux provide abundant evidence of the barbarity of the laity and the immorality of the clergy. In 1430 the Bishop, Jean de Brion, attempted to reform the latter, stating that the lives of the canons were 'so irregular at that time that an honest maiden would scarcely have dared to set foot in the Close'.

Nearly a century later the famous Bishop Briçonnet again attempted to remedy abuses. It was reckoned that there were hardly more than fourteen clergy in the whole diocese capable of exercising their office. If the Church had only managed to effect its own reforms there might have been no Reformation. It was some time before Briçonnet recognized the difference between these two alternatives. He had surrounded himself with the intellectuals of his age and it was not until it was too late that he realized that their thought was leading in the direction of Calvin and Zwingli. Meaux had become a nursery of Protestantism. A few years after his death some sixty of them were arrested at the house of one, Étienne Mangin, where they were listening to a sermon. Mangin and thirteen others were burnt alive and his house totally demolished. In 1560 the Huguenots had their revenge. The Bishop and his clergy were besieged in the palace and the cathedral systematically sacked.

With such a history of constant renovation necessitated by premature decay or deliberate vandalism, it is hardly surprising to find that the **exterior** of St Étienne de Meaux is somewhat lacking in architectural coherence. The north tower received its final form and decoration only in 1530. Apart from the over-severity of its skyline and the irritating omission of the fourth pinnacle, it is a most imposing achievement. The south tower was never completed. A makeshift arrangement of timber and slate, utterly out of keeping with the edifice as a whole, has earned it the name of *la tour noire*. If we can imagine it with its full stature, answering if not reflecting the north tower, we can see that the west front could have been one of great magnificence.

The **central and south portals** – which are considered to come from the school of Chambiges at Beauvais – have each preserved their thirteenth-century carvings in the tympanum, representing the Last Judgement in the centre and the life of the Virgin in the south porch. Above the scene of the Last Judgement are two little figures of canons, the one on the left wearing glasses and the one on the right, apparently unmoved by the momentous spectacle beneath him, sound asleep – perhaps a commentary on the Church at the time. The **north porch**, however, which can be accurately dated to 1506, is all from the same hand and depicts the story of John the Baptist. The **north and south façades** are less effective. Their interest is confined largely to the beautiful Geometric tracery and to the two thirteenth-century portals to the transepts – both of which are devoted to the patron saint of the cathedral, St Stephen. The carving in the tympanum of the south porch is a close copy of that at Notre Dame. The *Stoning of Stephen* is one of the most successful instances of dramatic rhythm in medieval carving. Unfortunately the Huguenots did considerable damage to the carvings and time, working on poor quality stone, has furthered the work of destruction. Urgent repairs had to be undertaken in the nineteenth century and the north façade was seriously over-restored.

To the north of the cathedral the Bishop's Palace and the so-called **Château du Chapitre** form a delightful group of ecclesiastical buildings which has survived, if only just. The chapter building, which formed the residence of the canons, with a cellar, Grande Salle on the first floor and bedrooms above, dates from the twelfth century.

The façade towards the palace has been very much restored and the square-cut windows of the Grande Salle are quite out of style. A nineteenth-century lithograph shows clear signs in the masonry that these were large, early Gothic windows with broad pointed arches which had been filled and re-opened with smaller windows in the Renaissance. But the most striking and original feature of the façade is the picturesque outside staircase in which the ends of the steps seem to have been carried through the containing wall to form the bold zigzag decoration of the ramp.

Across the courtyard north of the cathedral is the **Episcopal Palace**. Seen from this side it is not a particularly handsome building, though it dates for the most part from the Renaissance. Briçonnet built much of it, and being stricken with gout had ramps instead of staircases so that he could reach his chamber without dismounting from his mule. The garden front, however, is more satisfying. It was rebuilt in the early seventeenth century by Dominique Séguier. The very tall windows, supported by an open arcade, lend a great air of distinction to this front.

But although he did not leave his mark on the fabric, it is the figure of Bossuet which dominates the imagination at Meaux. It was he who laid out the garden and built the little pavilion where he often worked late, sometimes in intense cold from which he sought to protect himself by wearing a bearskin. Frequently he was driven to this sanctuary by the noisy parties given by his niece-in-law who kept house for him. She did not let up on the parties even while he was dying.

Bossuet was one of the outstanding figures of the *Grand Siècle*. When James Boswell asked Dr Johnson what he thought of 'the Bishop of Meaux', Johnson answered: 'Sir, nobody reads him.' Later, after Johnson was safely in the grave, Boswell added the footnote: 'I take leave to enter my strong protest against this judgement. Bossuet I hold to be one of the first luminaries of religion and literature.'

It is in the latter field that he is most remembered today. His *Oraisons Funèbres* – on Henriette d'Angleterre, Condé, Michel le Tellier and many other great figures of the epoch – are part of French culture today. But his greatest works were probably his religious polemics. In 1670 he was appointed by Louis XIV as tutor to the Dauphin, a task to which he devoted a zeal which was as painstaking as it was useless. The Grand Dauphin was an utterly stupid person.

Bossuet was also one of the outstanding diocesan bishops of his century. As his secretary François Ledieu records, 'he went from parish to parish, the Gospels in his hand'. He won even the admiration of the Huguenots against whom he strove with such conviction. When Louis XIV had unleashed the horrors that followed the Revocation of the Edict of Nantes, a Huguenot pastor, du Bourdieu, could write of Bossuet: 'this prelate only uses evangelical methods in his relations with us. He preaches, he writes letters and books and labours to get us to give up our beliefs by methods in keeping with his character and with the spirit of Christianity.'

Preaching was one of his great gifts, and it is sad that the pulpit which he used in the cathedral has been reconstructed. We can look on the same woodwork, but not on the pulpit which once harboured the ablest preacher in France.

A bishop's house often had to serve other purposes than the housing of a bishop. On Friday 24 June 1791 the royal family, ignominiously returning from Varennes, spent the night here. The journey, described by the duchesse de Tourzel, had been a nightmare, the intense heat being rendered even more insupportable by the great cloud of dust with which the *Berline* was enveloped – '*aussi épaisse que le plus affreux brouillard*'.

They were reasonably well looked after, but repose was difficult, for the town was upon tiptoe of excitement and every citizen had been ordered to have lights burning in all the windows. But it was here, in the intimacy of Bossuet's garden, that Marie-Antoinette made her last conquest – Barnave, one of the three Commissioners sent by the Parliament to escort the King back to Paris. From that moment Barnave became the devoted servant of the Queen.

They were not the last distinguished guests. On 15 February 1814 Napoleon slept here. On 28 March it was Blucher who slept in Bossuet's bedroom.

Between Meaux and La Ferté-sous-Jouarre to the east, the road passes through the **Forêt de Montceaux**; a little to the south of the road are the ruins of its once magnificent mansion. Built by Le Primatice for Catherine de Medici, it was bought by Henri IV for his mistress Gabrielle d'Estrées. After her death he took it back and presented it to his second wife, Marie de Medici, as a reward for giving him a Dauphin. She called in Salomon de Brosse to build the stables and chapel in the outer court. These are the only buildings which remain intact.

The **château** was ranged round three sides of a square, the fourth side, towards the east, being closed by an arcade with a monumental domed archway through which one gained access to the inner court. The greater part of this gatehouse survives, and some of the architecture of the façade behind it. The whole stood in the middle of a vast *terre-plein* surrounded on three sides by a dry moat; to the west the ground falls away sharply leaving a high terrace from which wide views can be enjoyed.

At the corners of the moat were four pavilions – of which one survives – which used to be occupied by the four secretaries of state when the Court was in residence.

The glory of Montceaux was short-lived. By the mid-seventeenth century, the château was tending rapidly to ruin. In the eighteenth century hunting parties of the prince de Conti came occasionally and kept up the buildings of the outer court for their use, while the great Renaissance ruin continued to deteriorate. The Revolution brought the *coup de grâce*.

There is nothing at first sight very arresting about **Jouarre**; a fifteenth-century church, much restored; some conventual buildings of the eighteenth century, pleasing but undistinguished; an old belfry to which is appended a nunnery church of no character. But to the east of the fifteenth-century church of St Pierre is an unassuming building which one might take for some schoolroom or library.

It contains a marvellous **Merovingian crypt** full of marvellous Merovingian tombs. It offers an entirely new experience.

For the visitor to the Ile de France becomes rapidly familiar with the thirteenth century. He will soon feel at home with sexpartite and quadripartite vaulting and will know which to expect; he will come to understand the language of the medieval carver and the aspirations of the Gothic glazier. Theirs is a world which it is still possible, thanks to their artistic activities, for us to enter. We can, on somewhat rarer occasions, step back another century or two into the age of the Romanesque. But to step back another four hundred years – back into the seventh century, back into an unfamiliar world where only the specialist historian may tread with confidence, back into the days of the Merovingian kings – strange, priestly figures with names like Dagobert, Chilperic and Theodebert who ruled not France but *Austrasie*, while their Mayors of the Palace ruled them – who prolonged the twilight of the Roman Empire and allied their civilization with the rising force of Christianity; to step back into this remote atmosphere is rare indeed.

In about the year AD 610 when St Columba was visiting Brie, he was well received by Authaire, one of the great vassals of Theodebert, King of Austrasie. Authaire had three sons named, somewhat unimaginatively, Adon, Dadon and Radon. Each was blessed by Columba and each was to found a major monastery in Brie.

It was Adon who founded Jouarre. According to the custom of St Columba it was a triple foundation – Notre Dame for the nuns, St Pierre for the monks and St Paul, built as a mortuary chapel. It was as an annexe to St Paul's that the crypts were built. For the Abbaye de Jouarre was a largely family affair. A cousin of Adon's named Theodechilde (Ste Telchilde) became the first abbess. Her brother Agilbert was Bishop of Paris. The second abbess was another cousin of Theodechilde's called Aguilberte, sister of Ebrégésile, Bishop of Meaux. The third abbess was an aunt of Theodechilde's, Ste Balde, who died almost a centenarian in 684. She had a sister in the convent known to history as la Vénérable Mode. It was as a mausoleum to this pious family that the crypt was built.

It was not, strictly speaking, a crypt. The level of the earth has risen in the course of the centuries so as to leave it half underground, but originally it formed a sort of narthex to the east end of St Paul's, so that the length of the 'crypt' lay along the width of the church. It was divided into two unequal halves, the **Crypte St Paul** corresponding with the nave and the **Crypte St Ebrégésile** with the south and only aisle.

Apart from this division the whole crypt is composed of three naves separated by two rows of columns. It is probable that these originally supported three barrel vaults, which were replaced at a later date by the present groined vaulting. On the west wall just inside the entrance can be seen some of the primitive masonry known as *opus reticulatum*, where the ends of the stone blocks, square, diamond or octagonal in section, form a decorative pattern. This is thought to derive from the wooden constructions of an earlier age.

The columns are of different coloured marble, quarried in the Pyrenees. Their capitals command attention. They are all carved with a very sure hand and show a mixture, typical of the Merovingian age, between Roman inspiration and free-ranging fantasy. Take for example the first column in the Crypte St Paul: it combines the volutes and acanthus leaves of a correctly Corinthian order with the early Christian symbols of the grass snake – representing Prudence – and the anchor – representing Hope.

In the north-east corner, tucked away in such a manner as to be scarcely visible except for one face, is the **tomb of Agilbert**, Bishop of Dorchester and later of Paris. It is entirely Irish in sentiment. In spite of its eroded condition it still proclaims loud and clear the 'sure and certain hope of resurrection'. The theme is Joy, not Judgement. There is a tremendous rhythm in the overlapping of the upraised arms of the elect which was to re-appear in the visionary drawings of William Blake.

Above the sarcophagus is placed a moulding of the headstone, which is not itself visible. It depicts Christ in Glory surrounded by the emblems of the Evangelists outward-facing to represent the mission of the Church. Here Western art has followed early Eastern tradition in portraying Christ without a beard.

The eastern wall of the crypt is lined with tombs which originally stood upon a solid dais which has been cut away to give access between them. In the centre is the **sarcophagus of Theodechilde** – '*le chef d'oeuvre de Jouarre*'. Both its sides are treated identically in a bold pattern of cockleshells – or are they the leaves of the water lily? – underlined by a Latin inscription cut in a lettering worthy of ancient Rome. It says in words what the tomb of Agilbert says in sculpture: '*EXULTAT PARADISI TRIUMPHO*' – 'she exults in the triumph of Paradise'. Unfortunately the artist had not reckoned the length of his text for the last line is cramped up and full of abbreviations which rather mar the effect. Apart from this single oversight, he has shown himself the complete master of his medium. The Irish influence in the ornament is hardly surprising in a mausoleum built by a bishop who was educated in Ireland.

Second to the right of Theodechilde is the **tomb of Aguilberte**, typical of the Celtic love of abstract ornament. In 1627 these tombs were opened by order of the Abbess Jeanne de Lorraine de Guise and the remains of the bodies transferred to reliquaries. The tombs were opened without due care and that of Aguilberte was not only broken but wrongly pieced together again.

The 'odd man out' of this series is **Sainte Ozanne**. She was an Irish princess who did not, as far as is known, belong to the family and it was not until the end of the thirteenth century that her recumbent figure was carved. She is beautiful but quite out of place in Jouarre.

The unique importance of these Merovingian remains should not distract us from the other monuments. The **Church of St Pierre** is a building of the late fifteenth and early sixteenth centuries with some original glass to either side of the apse – the windows in the north aisle are entirely modern. It contains two reliquaries of the thirteenth century and an important group of figures, coming from the workshops of Michel Colombe, representing the Entombment. The female figures belonging to it are, for no very obvious reason, housed in the Crypte St Ebrégésile.

The **Tower of Notre Dame**, which was restored at the same time as the building of St Pierre, has been turned into a little museum. The signatures of most of the Bourbon kings may be seen, together with the first edition of Bossuet's *Oraison Funèbre* on the prince de Condé, whose arms may be seen on the boss of the fine vaulted chamber of the third floor.

CHAPTER NINETEEN

The Ourcq Valley

⚜

The valley of the Ourcq, which runs north-east by north from Meaux, presents today a beautiful stretch of country with little to violate its rural peace. In 1914 it was the scene of fierce fighting, when the Germans, under von Klück, penetrated beyond Meaux, occupying, on 3 September, a line passing through Monthyon and Crécy. The English, under Lord French, were at the limits of human endurance and the situation looked desperate. But on the night of 7 September 600 Paris taxis, each making the double journey of ninety kilometres twice, brought up 6000 troops to reinforce the line. By the 9th the Germans had been pushed back to a line running from Nanteuil-le-Hardouin – Lizy-sur-Ourcq – Château-Thierry. The German advance on Paris had been halted; the battle of the Ourcq had been won.

At **May-en-Multien** some sixteen kilometres north-east of Meaux, the tall fifteenth-century church tower twice served as a look-out post for the General Headquarters of the French army. The original twelfth-century nave has become the north aisle to a new nave built on to it in the fifteenth century. The new nave must have been intended earlier, for the choir which attaches to it is thirteenth-century.

Across the river, in a charming setting of willows and poplars, can be seen the moated site of the **Château de Gesvres-le-Duc**. The feudal fortress, in conjunction with Nanteuil-le-Hardouin and Montépilloy, had formed one of the outposts of the defensive system of Louis d'Orléans, but when the seigneurie of Gesvres was raised to a dukedom the old fortress was replaced by a more habitable mansion designed by J.-H. Mansart. Gaignières shows in his water-colour a neat little château built round three sides of a courtyard and opening on the fourth into a *basse cour* flanked by two pavilions, one of which is the only portion to survive.

At **Crouy-sur-Ourcq**, north-east of Gesvres, there is a fine four-teenth-century **keep** which now stands uselessly in the corner of a farmyard and looks dangerously dilapidated. On the north side the sanitary arrangements are crudely apparent in the three '*retraits*' which project like machicolations over what was once the moat.

Attached to the keep is a slightly more residential building with a high *chemin de ronde* which becomes a little turret as it turns the corner. The architecture suggests Scotland as much as France, which is not surprising, since the 'auld alliance' resulted in a considerable influence from France on the Scottish style.

Round on the east side is the old entrance, slotted for a draw-bridge and leading straight into one of the rooms and not, as was customary, into a courtyard.

Crouy is a magnificent example of a small château to which was attached a large farm. There are traces of Renaissance doorways on the farm buildings which were in all probability the work of Robert de Sepois, Seigneur de Crouy, who was responsible for the rebuilding of the church between 1527 and 1536.

If we continue north and cross the river at Mareuil we can follow the west bank of the Ourcq by means of the little road which climbs through wooded slopes to high ground from which there are delight-ful views. A deviation to our left leads to **Autheuil**, where what was once a fine Romanesque church built in 1150 is now a barn. The west portal, nave arcades and clerestory windows may be easily identified, and beneath the eaves an extremely attractive little cornice known as '*une corniche beauvaisine*' of interlocking arches, like miniature machicolations, runs the length of the building. The church was attached to a priory and the priory to the monastery of Nanteuil. The whole ensemble was only meant to harbour one prior and three monks. It enjoyed nevertheless the rights of *haute justice* and Autheuil was once equipped with its own gallows.

From Autheuil we retrace our steps and regain the road for Mar-olles, where it crosses the Ourcq to approach **La Ferté-Milon**. High up on the right are the magnificent ruins of its château.

In 1392 the county of Valois, which comprehended in its defensive system the important fortresses of Crépy-en-Valois, Pierrefonds, Béthisy, Vez and La Ferté-Milon, was given by Charles VI to his brother, Louis d'Orléans. From then until his death fourteen years later Louis undertook a vigorous programme of rebuilding which made this chain of fortresses one of the most formidable in France, and took the art of castle building a stage further than it had reached with Vincennes.

To stand at the bottom of the dry moat of La Ferté-Milon and to look up at those mighty towers is to understand the strength of the Middle Ages. Apart from its mere size and solidity there is an overwhelming impression of technical competence. The builders knew exactly what they were doing. The design of the gatehouse towers, like those of Loches, La Roche-Guyon and Château Gaillard, is made up of two curved surfaces which meet at an obtuse but clearly defined angle. It was a device for deflecting cannon balls which required the most meticulous precision on the part of the builder. The cut of the masonry is almost unbelievably perfect. It must be admitted, however, that a certain dullness in the texture of the walls results; a ruder, more varied stonework is more pleasing to the eye. Fortresses, however, were not built for beauty.

The castles of Louis d'Orléans, nevertheless, were by no means devoid of ornament. High up over the entrance arch he had placed the Coronation of the Virgin – an exquisite tableau of sculpture in an equally exquisite frame; the lace-like intricacy of its ornament offers the most striking contrast with the smoothness of the masonry and the clean-cut simplicity of the window apertures. Four other figures in similar frames adorned the towers, representing heroic ladies – *Les Preuses* – who were to re-occur at Pierrefonds.

It is clear from the machicolations that a *chemin de ronde* ran at the same level right along the top of the walls and towers, as at the Bastille in Paris. The towers had the same superstructure that we see at Pierrefonds. This part of the building, however, was never more than an empty shell, for its eastern front was never built. But the keep at the north end, overlooking the Ourcq Valley, was certainly serviceable and during the Wars of Religion held out successfully for four years against Henri IV. When at last it yielded, he decided to render it harmless and had it 'slighted'.

Adjoining the château to the south are the remains of the once-considerable fortifications of the town with one of its four original gatehouses. Behind this is the **Church of Notre Dame**.

Of the former twelfth-century structure only the west portal remains and some of the north nave piers inside. Most of the church was rebuilt in the sixteenth century at the expense of Catherine de Medici. The tower, with its four attendant *poivrières*, has a simplicity unusual for the period. The apse, beneath which is a crypt which forms the entrance to the church, is dated 1563. It has, however, been much restored, for the building was badly damaged in 1918 when it lost much of its stained glass.

At the east end of the south aisle, however, one very fine window survives. It represents the Passion and Resurrection and is dated 1524. To the right of it are fragments of another beautiful window – *les Litanies de la Vierge*.

It was in this church that the great dramatist Jean Racine was baptized in 1640. At the age of two he lost his mother and at the age of four his father. It was the latter's mother, née Marie Desmoulins, who brought him up and it was through her that he formed his connection with Port Royal. Her house, number 14 rue de Reims, at the foot of the steep descent from Notre Dame, can still be seen as well as that of his sister, Catherine Rivière at number 5 rue Racine, also near Notre Dame.

The lower town of la Ferté-Milon is attractive without being distinguished. The Ourcq, dividing into two streams, offers an island which has been turned into an agreeable little public garden. The road to Villers-Cotterêts, rue de la Chaussée, leads to another church, St Nicholas. There is a delightful little tower which is a happy blend of Gothic and Renaissance. The buttress steps are topped with urns, the niches are framed by pilasters and pediments and the parapet is formed by a balustrade running between four little dome-capped cupolas.

Inside, the church is dull and unprepossessing, with its dirty white wooden ceiling in the form of a barrel vault with cross beams – but the eye is immediately caught by the eight windows of the apse and east ends of the transepts. The church itself was consecrated in 1491, but the glass bears the dates 1542, 1575 and 1598. The windows offer tumultuous scenes from the Bible, somewhat crudely portrayed in the most lively colours. There is an obvious change in style between the Old Testament in the north transept and the New Testament in the apse – where one, devoted to St Nicholas, is modern. The church was visited by Louis XIV on his way to his coronation at Reims and much admired by him. The windows were badly damaged in 1918 but restored in 1925 *'grâce au zèle infatigable du chanoine Devigne'*.

There is also, standing against the north wall, the most lovely rococo churchwarden's seat with a large vestment chest rather resembling a counter in front of it.

Some fifteen kilometres upstream of La Ferté-Milon is one of the most impressive of religious ruins. Longpont lies tucked away, like most Cistercian monasteries, in a little valley that had been a swamp until the monks applied themselves to its draining. Founded in 1132, it had soon outgrown its size, and in the first years of the thirteenth century it was completely rebuilt on a larger and more ambitious scale. The church was scarcely smaller than the Cathedral of Soissons, and the monks' dormitory had been found too sumptuous by the Superior of Clairvaux, who put the abbot on bread and water and ordered the rebuilding of the dormitory on lines more conformable with the Rule of Cîteaux.

Enough remains of the church to provide a splendid example of the beauty of simplicity. The steady rhythm of the great buttresses, the rich shadow-projections occasioned by their deep relief, the pleasing proportions of the windows and triforium arcade combine with the excellent quality of the stone to create, even in ruins, an impression of great and austere nobility. Such was the ideal of the Cistercian order. There was an almost complete absence of ornament, which threw into even greater relief the single statue of the Virgin which has miraculously survived. One can see the holes in the walls above, indicating an elaborate canopy beneath which she was originally housed in splendour.

In 1227 the abbey church was consecrated in the presence of the young St Louis, and it was here that he received the inspiration for his own foundation of Royaumont.

Like most religious buildings in France, Longpont has had a lengthy history of very varied fortunes. In 1325 the number of applicants was so great that the mother house at Clairvaux had to fix the limit of sixty monks and fifty lay brothers. During the Wars of Religion it reached its lowest ebb, when it was sacked by the triumphant Protestants of Soissons. In 1605 there were only three monks inhabiting the ruins. In the same year Julien Warnier was appointed prior, and thanks to his exertions Longpont recovered once more its vocation.

It was not to last. In 1724 a terrible fire destroyed two thirds of the conventual buildings. It was to repair this damage that the beautiful eighteenth-century façades of the **Abbot's Lodging** – formerly the lay brothers' dormitory – were built. They are just a shell behind which much of the thirteenth-century work can still be detected.

But the abbot's lodging was enriched at the expense of the monastery. Farms had to be sold, and the diminution of income was reflected in the decline in the number of monks. By the end of the eighteenth century only ten remained. It is to their credit that, impoverished as they were, that they managed in 1788 to bring considerable relief to the poor when the whole neighbourhood had been devastated by hailstorms.

But this notable charity did not save Longpont from the wrath of the Revolution, which destroyed it once and for all as a religious building. The church was reduced to the condition in which it remains today; the abbot's lodging was ultimately converted into a château; but many of the conventual buildings were destroyed. By a particularly happy chance the **Chauffoir** was among the portions to survive.

As a rule, there were only two chimneys to a Cistercian abbey; that of the kitchen and that of the chauffoir – these two being the only rooms in the whole vast complex to be heated. The endurance of cold was part of the ascetic life which the monks embraced, but those who were engaged on copying the manuscripts were allowed to use the chauffoir for the preparation of their ink and parchment. All were allowed to grease their boots here. There was often, as at Longpont, a room above which partook of some of the warmth and which could be used by the aged or infirm. In times of extreme cold all the monks were allowed to warm themselves from time to time.

The chauffoir at Longpont is thought to be the only survival of an internal chimney in Europe. Four pillars, surrounding a circular hearth, support the tall, slightly pyramidal, flue. The straight lintels at the base of this are fitted together by an ingenious form of stepped masonry which was apparently used only here and at Mont St Michel.

This range, together with the abbot's lodging and the ruins of the church, was purchased in 1831 by the comte de Montesquieu-Fesenzac, who was descended on the distaff side from the famous d'Artagnan. A part of the former cellars was made over for use as the parish church, which it still remains. Here is one of the most important exhibits of Longpont – the **reliquary of Jean de Montmirail**. It is in the form of a wooden coffer, bound in leather and studded with gilt-headed nails. These are so arranged as to form the circular frames to a large number of armorial badges. For the Blessed Jean de Montmirail was of noble birth. He was the friend and counsellor of Philippe-Auguste, whose life he had saved in 1193 before Gisors. But at the age of forty-five and at the height of his career he abandoned the secular life to become a monk at Longpont. At the King's Court he had been known as 'Jean Bonté': now he earned the title of 'Jean l'Humble'. He died in 1217 and many miracles were claimed for his sepulchre. The reliquary was hidden during the Revolution and was only found again in 1918 when the buildings were badly damaged in the course of a battle. It was finally restored to Longpont by the comtesse de Montesquieu.

A short distance from the abbey ruins is a fortified **gatehouse** dating from the thirteenth century, which was part of the *châtelet* built for the protection of the monastery.

South and west from Longpont stretches the great **Forêt de Retz**;

Statue columns in the
porch at St Loup-
de-Naud

Meaux: escalier du
Vieux Chapître

MIDY

Mural painting of Montceaux in the Galerie des Cerfs, Fontainebleau

'La Mancette' – Bollée's first steam coach. In the Musée du
Voiture at Compiègne

Foret de Compiègne: les Étangs de St Pierre

Château de
Pierrefonds, seen
from the east

Drawing of the
Château de Villers-
Cotterêts by
Androuet du Cerceau
(British Museum)

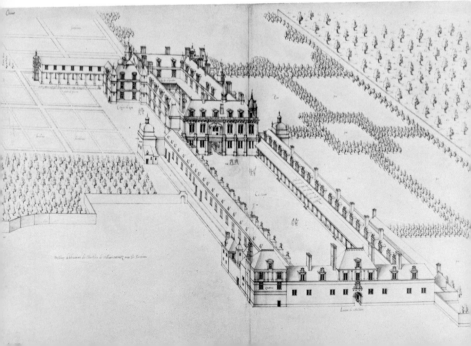

originally the property of the Seigneur de Crépy, it became, under Philippe-Auguste, a part of the royal domain. It was the scene of much fighting in the First World War and notably of a remarkable encounter between the old world and the new, when a cavalry charge, led by Lieutenant de Gironde, destroyed a squadron of German aeroplanes near the farm of Vauberon.

The hunting afforded by this immense forest attracted two royal residences, the Château de Villers-Cotterêts and the Manoir de Bourgfontaine.

The hunting lodge at **Villers-Cotterêts**, built in the thirteenth century by Charles de Valois, was greatly enlarged and embellished by François I and Henri II, the building accounts spanning the period from 1533 to 1550. The inner courtyard, which itself formed a tennis court, is surrounded by the lodgings of the royal family and preserves the pepper-pot towers of Charles de Valois' building. To this nucleus Guillaume and Jacques le Breton added a large, long outer court of office buildings.

The château of the Le Breton brothers is accurately depicted in du Cerceau's drawings now in the British Museum. At the end of the outer court was the main façade of the palace and to right and left of it were two square buildings, now destroyed, roofed with domes. They are marked on du Cerceau's plan '*Privez*', and represent the only known example of special provision for sanitation being designed and specified on the plan at this time.

The outer court has lost its covered way, which ran like a cloister round three sides of the quadrangle, but the main façade remains. It has lost the balustrade above the eaves and it has acquired a balcony of elegant eighteenth-century ironwork over the entrance arch. The façade is highly original and unlike anything else known at that date.

Inside there is one elaborately decorated room which was probably the chapel, for the ornate triumphal arch against the east wall is best interpreted as a reredos. The original barrel vault was concealed, probably in the eighteenth century, by a flat ceiling. Leading up to it are two magnificent staircases with richly wrought plaster ceilings, one featuring the salamander and capital F of François I and the other mythological scenes inspired from the *Songe de Polyphile*.

Up till the Revolution the palace belonged to the duc d'Orléans who came here occasionally for hunting. In 1808 it was turned into a *Dépôt de Mendicité* and is now an almshouse.

Villers-Cotterêts is also famous as the birth-place of the novelist **Alexandre Dumas**, and there is a small **museum** consecrated to his memory. Apart from his uniform as a member of the Académie Française, the exhibits are mostly letters and engravings. There are first editions of *Henri III et sa Cour* and *Mademoiselle de Belle-Isle* and the original manuscript of *le Comte de Montechristo*, large pages neatly covered in a well-formed hand. It was, in fact, Dumas' handwriting that secured his first job as a scribe in the household of the duc d'Orléans, later to be King Louis-Philippe.

Due south of Villers-Cotterêts, **Bourgfontaine** was built in 1315 by Charles de Valois and from an early date included a small Chartreuse. His son, Philippe VI, further enlarged the buildings. Destroyed by the Huguenots in 1567, it was rebuilt in the seventeenth century, only to be ruined again by the Revolution. It has now become a farm and presents a picturesque medley of medieval towers and seventeenth-century façades with rather unusual bell-shaped pediments to the dormers. To this building there adhere the ruins of the chapel with a tall, baroque gable at the west end.

CHAPTER TWENTY

The Automne Valley

❧

North of the Automne Valley, on the southern edge of the Forest of Compiègne, there runs a Way of great antiquity, known locally as the **Chaussée Brunehaut**. Above the village of Orrouy, this track crosses a high plateau which commands a wide view over the surrounding country. From a military point of view this plateau is of some strategic importance and from time immemorial bore the name of 'Camp de César'. It was clear that there were **Roman ruins** at **Champlieu**, but until the mid-nineteenth century no intelligent exploration of the site had been made and the raised mounds were generally assumed to be connected with fortification. It was Prosper Mérimée and Viollet-le-Duc, frequent guests of Napoleon III at Compiègne, who first realized that this raised hemicycle might conceal a Roman theatre; the State undertook the expense of excavation and in due course the arena was triumphantly revealed.

It is probably of second-century date and was capable of housing an audience of four thousand. Behind it are the foundations of thermal baths complete with atrium, surrounded by a portico of twelve columns, frigidarium, tepidarium and sudatorium – the sweating room – together with the necessary hypocausts.

Opposite the theatre are the remains of a temple which, it may be inferred from the ruins, was of a refined architecture and a high standard of sculpture. Some of the figures recovered in the dig – representing Ceres, Apollo, Prometheus and Leda among others – appear to have been originally painted in a mixture of dull red and yellow ochre.

From the importance of the theatre and the excellence of the temple it may be inferred that there was here a *Castra Stativa* – a permanent wintering place for the Roman legions.

There is a charming little road from Champlieu to Crépy-en-Valois. It passes by **Glaignes** where there is a splendid specimen of *le style Rothschild* visible from the road, a massive château that sits superbly against the richly wooded slopes which in autumn display every gradation from almost scarlet to the palest of yellow ochres. For

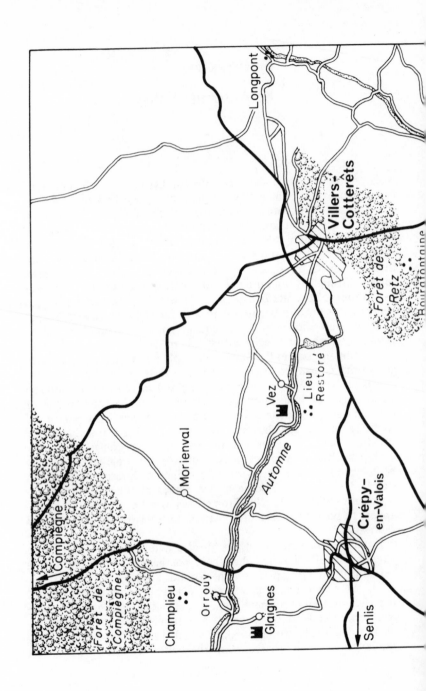

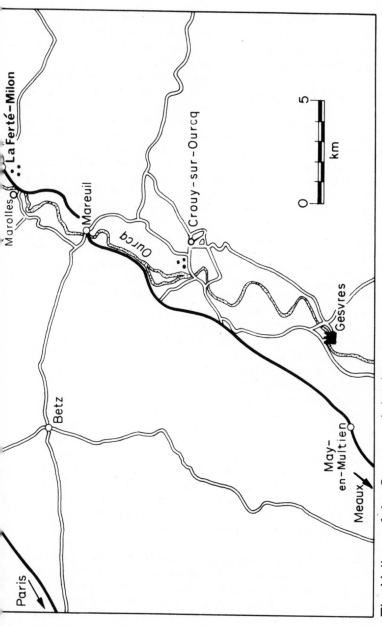

The Valleys of the Ourcq and the Automne

the last kilometre or two the road runs through typical poplar plantations until it suddenly emerges before the cliff-like walls of a medieval city, surmounted by the tall roof and spire of a solitary church. **Crépy** was the ancient capital of Valois, the county which gave its name to a dynasty of kings. To appreciate its strength the visitor should drive through the town and descend into the rue des Fossés and pass beneath these outer ramparts of the castle. It is today a pretty road, but seen in terms of fortification the armour plating of the almost vertical slopes affords slender hope of escalading.

Nevertheless, after a terrible siege in 1344, the English troops under the Duke of Bedford effected an entry and Crépy was systematically destroyed. Fifteen hundred houses were razed to the ground, the château burnt out and much of the curtain wall dismantled. Charles d'Orléans, the comte de Valois at the time, was taken prisoner to England.

On his return, twenty-five years later, he set about the restoration of Crépy, but it never regained its original importance. In 1728 it suffered another blow of a very different nature. It was by-passed. The main road from Soissons to Paris, which used to pass through Crépy, was moved to the south-west – the present N2 – and with it went most of the city's trade.

The oldest quarter of the town, the north-west corner, which contains the ruined abbey of St Arnould, the church of St Denis and the remains of the château, has retained a considerable charm, and a walk among its narrow twisting streets is rewarding. At **number 19 rue Jeanne d'Arc**, above a printer's shop, are some massive machicolations and an inscription relating to the saint. In 1429 she came to Crépy with the newly-crowned Charles VII and their reception was tremendous. '*Voici un bon peuple!*' she exclaimed to Dunois; 'I have not as yet seen any rejoice so wholeheartedly at the King's coming. I would to God I could end my days here.'

On the corner of the rue de la Tour and the rue Alphonse Cardin is a delightful house, the **Maison St Joseph**, built in 1650 by Pierre de la Grange, the King's Attorney in Crépy. The L-shaped façade, adorned with niches, busts and roundels, rises imposingly behind a noble archway framed between pilasters and overhung with Virginia creeper.

At the end of the rue Alphonse Cardin is the **Church of St Denis,** which offers the contrast between a small and very simple nave and a large and lightsome chancel which still manages to create an impression of spaciousness. This duality is the result of the destruction, in 1434, of much of the original building by the English.

During the Revolution it was put up for sale, and would have suffered a second demolition had it not been bought by certain well-meaning individuals who restored it, in 1803, to its proper use.

Immediately opposite to St Denis can be seen the remains of the **Abbey of St Arnould**. In its day it was one of the finest churches in the district – whose twin towers, mounted like those of Morienval as sentinels to the apse, added a distinctive element to the skyline of Crépy. Two of its abbots, Girard and Hughes, were canonized and the relics of Arnould himself made the place a centre of pilgrimage. In 1790, however, there were only six monks to be evicted; the buildings were sold for their materials and largely destroyed.

There survives, however, an immense vaulted undercroft of the twelfth century which is in process of restoration, and some fine eleventh-century capitals to the pillars of what was the crypt.

To the south of St Arnould is the **Old Château**, a somewhat formless remnant of venerable masonry. The fenestration is clearly not original and most of the distinctive features have disappeared except for a magnificent but weather-beaten Renaissance doorway which is, nevertheless, somehow more suggestive of a grotto than a fortress. It is worth noticing the nails on the entrance door: their heads are embossed with the letters H and M, standing for Henri IV and his wife Marguérite de Valois.

Inside there is the lovely little **Chapelle Saint-Aubin**. It shows how charming the bare bones of early Gothic architecture can be. The three lancets at the north end are devoid of ornament and the whole effect depends upon the pattern of the vault ribs and the nice cut of the masonry between them. Only in the rather unusual *culs-de-lampe* is the enrichment of a little sculpture permitted.

Beneath these the walls are lined, inappropriately enough, with eighteenth-century panels which are very good of their sort and come from the choir stalls of St Arnould.

The rest of the château is occupied by a museum of archery. Even those who have no interest in this sport are advised to enter if only to see the **Grande Salle** on the top floor, with a wonderful open-timbered roof, and another room adjoining from which there is an excellent view on to the only other important remnant, the **Tour de Valois**.

Further to the east are the ruins of the fine **Church of St Thomas**, also a victim of the Revolution. We can still read the inscription above one of the doors: 'The People of France recognize the Supreme Being and the Immortality of the Soul', which was placed there in 1794. Three years later, as if this insult was too much for the old church, the building collapsed and all except the western façade was cleared away.

The dedication to St Thomas is interesting. In 1165 Thomas à Becket fled to France and stayed at Crépy with the comte de Valois, who was at the time building this large church just to the east of the city fortifications. He took the exiled archbishop to see the works and Thomas asked to whom it was to be dedicated. 'To the first martyr,' answered the count, thinking of Stephen. 'Do you mean the first who was or the first who is to be?' asked Becket, thinking of himself.

Shortly after the murder, the comte de Valois made a pilgrimage to Becket's tomb and decided to dedicate his church at Crépy to the new martyr. He sent a French sculptor to make a statue of Thomas. The result was very fine and said to be an excellent likeness, but unfortunately it did not survive the Revolution.

If there was ever a charming name for a charming place it is surely **Morienval**. One theory is that it means 'the valley of the Morini', a tribe referred to by Caesar, some of whom may have been left behind, in the course of their migrations, in this peaceful place.

But whatever its origins, Morienval emerges from the mists of history in the late ninth century as one of those rare and slightly dubious institutions – a double monastery. That is to say a single church shared between two religious communities, one male and one female, both under the rule of a single abbess. As an organization it may have contained the seeds of its own destruction, for it did not last long; the monks found their way increasingly into the ranks of the secular clergy and the ladies were left to their convent.

In the eleventh century the **abbey church** was rebuilt and provides, apart from one Gothic extension to the north transept, a delightful example of the Romanesque style, all too rare in this region.

Seen from the south-east, from the *Butte de Fossement*, it stands out well in front of the gathered roofs and gables of the village, its three towers just clearing the skyline. The western tower, which marks the original entrance, is a larger, lower structure than the two eastern ones, which stand to north and south of the apse and raise their airy belfries – a double arch upon a double arch upon a double arch – high above the rooftops of the nave and transepts. The apse, with its five little round-arched windows, seems to have pushed its way through between them and flowed out into the ampler space beyond. Beneath these little windows a further fan-shaped roof projects to enclose a narrow ambulatory which is the earliest addition to the building. For the original apse was built on sloping ground and a shifting of the subsoil caused its walls to slip. The ambulatory was added in 1125 by way of abutment. It disputes with May-en-Multien the distinction of containing the earliest cross-ribbed vault in existence.

Since the *raison d'être* of the ambulatory was structural necessity, we need not be too surprised to find it so narrow that it scarcely fulfils its function as a passageway behind the choir. It is quite useless liturgically. The aesthetic effect, however, is architecturally exciting. Each column that receives the narrow arch across the ambulatory is flanked by three more slender columns to either side; the columns therefore appear in groups of seven, whose capitals thus form a continuous band of sculpture between the windows.

The effect is nowhere more apparent than from the middle of the nave, for one of the columns of the ambulatory is exactly central to the perspective, and the procession of arches to right and left creates the most beautiful play of light and shade behind the high altar.

The main arcades of the nave are clearly the original Romanesque, but the quadripartite vaulting is as late as 1625. In the early seventeenth century three successive abbesses, each of the noble house of Foucauld and each named Anne, were appointed by the Crown: for three generations the benefice of Morienval passed from aunt to niece. Under their rule Morienval experienced a renaissance. It was the second Abbess Anne who conducted the considerable programme of reconstruction of the church, mostly at her own expense, in 1625.

It was she who extended the side aisles so that their western façades were level with that of the tower: it was she who adorned the entrance with pillars and pediment in a style so foreign to the church. It was she, unfortunately, who was responsible for the fact that the upper windows of the apse were enlarged in size and decreased in number.

A further restoration, carried out in 1878 by the architect Selmersheim, reconstructed the original appearance of these windows. They are deeply recessed into the thickness of the wall in such a manner that each has, as it were, a miniature stone staircase leading up to its embrasure.

With the death of the last Anne de Foucauld, the fortunes of Morienval declined. In 1742 Louis XV, advised by the Bishop of Soissons, decided to close the abbey down. The nuns refused to go. The King then, advised by the Bishop of Soissons, appointed the prioress to be abbess of le Parc-aux-Dames at Crépy, and with her went the will to resist. In 1745 the religious community of Morienval ceased to be.

The question then arose as to which church should serve the parish – the disaffected abbey or the original parish church of St Denis. It is the sort of episcopal problem in which, whatever move the bishop may make, he cannot win. But if the parishioners were indignant at the loss of St Denis, posterity at least can be grateful to Mgr de Fitz-James for the preservation of the abbey church.

Although there were only fourteen nuns, the end of the abbey was the end also of the village. Its epitaph was written by the curé at the time: 'the existence of this Abbey used to maintain a commerce in the Parish on which it flourished. Now it is depopulated and deserted and its remaining inhabitants reduced to misery.' How often was that to be said of the destructions of the Revolution!

Closely connected with Crépy-en-Valois is the **Château de Vez** (pronounced as it was originally spelt: Vé). There had been from time immemorial a fortified place on this site which was the capital of Valois long before Crépy. But of the buildings which survive today none is of earlier date than those of Raoul d'Estrées. His name, rendered famous by his descendant Gabrielle, who was mistress to Henri IV, has a curious history. Originally known as Raoul Duchemin, he was ennobled by Philippe-Auguste for his bravery at Bouvines. He translated his name into Latin – de Stratis – and then transliterated it back into French as d'Estrées. As no title could be conferred in those days without land, the King granted him the fortress of Vez and its dependencies in support of his new nobility. Between 1214 and his death in 1222 he built the *logis* of the château, which is now in ruins. We can see his arms, with angel side-supporters, over the chimney-pieces which still adhere to the walls.

The fortifications of Raoul d'Estrées were found to be insufficient when the English Edward III made his triumphant march from Calais to Reims. The lord of the château appealed to the local inhabitants, whose lands were being ravaged, and by a communal effort the defences of Vez were augmented and strengthened. Those who could afford to do so gave money; those who could not contributed their labour, and the present system of walls and moats was evolved. In 1360 the first stone was laid for the great *donjon*.

Some thirty years later Vez, together with Pierrefonds, La Ferté-Milon and Béthisy, was made over by Charles VI to his brother Louis d'Orléans who became comte and later duc de Valois. He greatly increased the strength of his chain of fortresses, and it is very probable that the donjon at Vez was built by the same master mason who was responsible for Pierrefonds.

If so, it shows his versatility, for there is little resemblance between the two buildings. Vez is a square block whose angle towers are little more than the rounding off of the corners. A single turret carries the staircase up to the platform of roof and then becomes a look-out tower with its own smaller staircase turret capped with a pepper-pot cone. Nothing could be less like the great ring of towers which is the essence of Pierrefonds.

To walk round the donjon, craning one's neck at the machicolations and gargoyles high overhead, is to form some idea of its strength. Above the south front, where the curtain wall runs out from a facet of the keep, is a projecting flue of masonry which contained the *retraits*, the sanitary provision for the garrison.

The curtain wall is equipped at strategic intervals with an embattled projection, one of which is called the Tour Jeanne d'Arc. It was in the spring of 1430, just before her capture at Compiègne, that she spent some two months at Crépy 'prowling round the city' as Hanotaux has put it, 'like a wakeful watchdog gathering his flock together'. She was often at Vez, and tradition relates that she spent long hours on the ramparts overlooking the valley and its approaches.

Vez itself was spared the fate of Pierrefonds and La Ferté-Milon only to fall into dilapidation from want of use and upkeep. It was restored to its present condition by M. Léon Dru who purchased the domain in 1890. Dru was an engineer who had worked with Lesseps and spent much of his time in Russia. It is in Russian costume that the sculptor Frémiet has portrayed him on his tomb in the chapel – the part of the château which has received the most extensive restoration. It has now been turned into a museum filled with objects dug up at Champlieu and other places in the neighbourhood.

Down in the valley at the foot of the slope dominated by the castle are the picturesque remains of a small Premonstratensian abbey known as **Lieu Restoré**: it is a title which has been twice earned. Founded in 1131, it was ruined in the course of the Hundred Years' War and for a long time lay desolate. In 1540 it was rebuilt. In the round-arched windows of the conventual buildings the influence of the Renaissance is already apparent, but the church is a late and exquisite flowering of the Flamboyant Gothic. The west door is surmounted by three little niches of an astonishing delicacy of workmanship, while the gable above contains the most beautiful rose window in France – intricate as a snow flake and almost miraculously intact.

But the Wars of Religion made this renaissance short lived and the system of commendation – the appointment of non-residentiary abbots by the Crown – ensured its continued uselessness. Lieu Restoré became a barn and a barn it would in all probability have remained if it had not been for a schoolboy's dream.

In March 1964 Pierre Pottier, whose childhood ambition had been to see these crumbling ruins rescued, arrived on the site with his wife Pierrette, his three-month-old child, a pickaxe and a bucket. His act of faith bore fruit. Friends came to lend a hand; a contractor lent him the use of a lorry; the landowner, M. Souillac, advanced 6000 francs for the propping up of one of the vaults. In due course the State decided to come in on this courageous effort. Lieu Restoré is being restored again.

CHAPTER TWENTY-ONE

Compiègne

✤

There is little about **Compiègne** today to suggest a strategic site of military importance. The remains of a tower known as the Tour Jeanne d'Arc, a little to the west of the bridge, and the Porte Chapelle to the east are the most significant remains of the old fortifications. But we only have to go to the famous **Clairière de l'Armistice** at Rethondes to see what is in fact a replica of the railway carriage in which the First World War came to an end, or take the road to Royallieu where the Nazis established one of their infamous concentration camps, from which 48,000 French men and women were deported, to be reminded of the recent part that Compiègne has played in military history. The fine buildings south of the bridge, combining a sense of traditional grandeur with a more modern approach to architecture, represent at its best the post-war reconstruction.

Although no fewer than 600 houses were destroyed in the last war, none of the chief monuments of the town was among them. Compiègne is a place of considerable interest to the tourist.

'My great delight in Compiègne,' wrote Robert Louis Stevenson in his *Inland Voyage*, 'was the **Town Hall**.' The building was also singled out by Viollet-le-Duc as the most beautiful piece of civil architecture in the north of France. 'It is a monument of Gothic insecurity,' continues Stevenson, 'all turreted and gargoyled and slashed and bedizened with a half a score of architectural fancies. Some of the niches are gilt and painted; and in a great square panel in the centre, in black relief on a gilt ground, Louis XII rides upon a pacing horse, with hand on hip and head thrown back. There is royal arrogance in every line of him; the stirruped foot projects insolently from the frame; the eye is hard and proud; the very horse seems to be treading with gratification over prostrate serfs, and to have the breath of the trumpet in his nostrils.' Stevenson has read a great deal more into the statue than it warrants and was obviously ignorant of the true character of that unassuming monarch.

The presence of Louis XII gives the date of the Town Hall,

which was built between 1499 and 1509 by one Pierre Navier from Meaux. The stone came from St Leu d'Esserent and is the finest in France.

The famous belfry contains the original bell dating from 1303. It has the name 'Bankloque' and was used as the tocsin. The chime is achieved by three automatons dating from the early sixteenth century called *Picantins*. They are described by Stevenson: 'as the quarter approaches they turn their heads and look knowingly one to the other; and then kling go the three hammers on three little bells below. The hour follows, deep and sonorous from the interior of the tower; and the three gilded gentlemen rest from their labours with contentment.'

Adjacent to the Town Hall is the **Musée de la Figurine Historique**, containing 85,000 tin soldiers illustrating military costume throughout the ages.

Near the Tour Jeanne d'Arc, or, more properly, Tour de Beauregard, at the end of the rue du Harlay, is the **Musée Vivenel**. A man of humble origins, Antoine Vivenel became an architect and a contractor and amassed a large fortune. He was self-educated; and the wide range of his interests, as well as the discernment of his taste, is well illustrated in his collection.

Vivenel was one of the first to perceive the essential connection between the progress of civilization and the development of the art of ceramics, and his specimens afford material for a complete study of that development. In his acquisitions from Egypt, Greece and Rome he illustrates three main themes in human thought. From Egypt, the idea of the survival of the soul. From Greece, the basic humanist assumption 'Man the measure of all things', while from Rome comes the cult of the individual – in other words, the rise of portraiture.

To this collection representing antiquity, the administrators of the museum had added a range of exhibits of more recent local historical interest. It was begun in 1965 with a competition which had the possibly misleading title 'Become Detectives', aimed at the youth of the district. It produced some four hundred and fifty items illustrating local costume, household utensils, instruments of agriculture and forestry, and the tools of the craftsman as well as objects connected with birth, marriage and death, local customs and fêtes, children's games and sports.

Not far from the Musée Vivenel is the **Church of St Antoine**, an excellent building which is basically thirteenth-century – as the transepts and adjacent bays of the nave bear witness – but which owes its most exciting features to the sixteenth century. There is a very good west front in a crisply ornate Flamboyant style with each storey typically isolated from the one above by a rather fanciful balustrade. The twin arches frame heavy, deeply carved Renaissance doors.

But it is the choir that constitutes the especial glory of St Antoine. It stands high above the rest of the church, exquisite but not over-decorated. The flying buttresses – great slices of stone with lightly embossed blind tracery and arches pierced and fretted into a delicate open-work tracery – support the weight of the vaults with a minimum of masonry.

The interior of the church is somewhat marred by the use of a rather dirty white stone. The nineteenth-century windows tell the story of Joan of Arc. For it was here at Compiègne that Joan, fighting a rearguard action at the city gate, found that the draw-bridge was already rising before she could re-enter the town and a Burgundian soldier pulled her off her horse and made her prisoner.

It is, however, not with St Antoine but with the other big church of St Jacques that Joan of Arc is known to have been connected. She made her Communion here on 23 May 1340, a few days before her capture.

The **Church of St Jacques** is not so distinguished as that of St Antoine, but it has some interesting features, not the least being the flying buttresses which are carried on to piers which project like chimneys through the aisle roof.

It was started in 1235 and from this period dates the choir with its glazed triforium, known in French as a *claire-voie*. Later in the thirteenth century the nave and aisles were added, with wooden ceilings rather than stone vaults; but progress was slow. The Hundred Years' War was not a propitious time for the building of churches in this area and it was not until the mid-fifteenth century that work was again contemplated, in the form of the lofty tower on the west front. However this was never finished. It is clear from the way the masonry ends in open dovetails or *pierres d'attente* that at least a new portal was intended if not another tower to match the existing one. The Wars of Religion prevented the realization of this dream.

The interior was affected by the history of the château which is within the parish. It was Louis XV who made the old 'Logis du Roi' into a palace, and he spent a little money at the same time on the church. The effect was not altogether happy. The pillars of the nave were encircled with dark wooden panelling which creates a rather absurd 'puss-in-boots' appearance. In 1750 the choir was adorned with marble and its medieval screen removed and replaced by an elegant wrought-iron screen. At a later date the balustrade from Louis XVI's bedroom was brought here to serve as the altar rail in the chapelle de la Vierge.

Not very far from the church of St Jacques is the **palace** itself.

'*Je suis logé à Versailles en Roi, à Fontainebleau en Prince et à Compiègne en paysan.*' With these words, Louis XIV tells us most of what we need to know of the previous château – an irregular compendium of buildings grouped around the nucleus of Charles V's medieval castle. In spite of the inadequate accommodation, Louis came here no fewer than seventy-five times.

The château of Compiègne is the third royal palace of France – and there were only three capable of housing the whole Court. But it is the 'poor relation' of the other two. Volumes have been written on Versailles and Fontainebleau, but Compiègne has not so far attracted any major study.

Its history is relatively short. The present building dates from Louis XV, but it was not finished at his death. Louis XVI undertook the completion, and much of the decoration of the palace dates from his reign. It was his favourite residence and his expenses here furnished one of the subjects of complaint by the *Assemblée des Notables* on the eve of the Revolution.

In 1810 Napoleon decided to add Compiègne to his official residences – a move connected with his second marriage to the Archduchess Marie-Louise of Austria – and he undertook some important redecoration.

In 1852 his nephew, now the Emperor Napoleon III, spent ten days here, and for the next eighteen years he made it his autumn residence. Undoubtedly this marked the most brilliant period in the history of the château. Since the collapse of the Second Empire only desultory use has been made of it, the occasional visit of some foreign royalty or the establishment of some military headquarters punctuating the long periods of oblivion.

When, in 1751, Ange-Jacques Gabriel was invited by Louis XV to draw up plans for the rebuilding of Compiègne, he was presented with a somewhat difficult problem. In using the original site of Charles V's castle he was obliged to build on a roughly triangular plot and to contend with a rise in the ground level sufficient to demand a building of three storeys towards the town and of two towards the park. One cannot but admire the way in which he turned these difficulties into assets. For Compiègne was conceived as a summer palace; its rooms are light and airy, and since the state apartments, which are on the first floor towards the cour d'honneur, are on the ground floor towards the park, all of them communicated directly with the gardens.

From the point of view of comfort and convenience Gabriel could hardly have done better, but aesthetically the result was not wholly satisfactory. It is impossible not to regard the garden front, with its endless rows of windows, as dull, its decorations banal and its skyline deplorable. By contrast, his façade towards the town is wholly successful if not entirely palatial. Somehow it suggests an unusually grand municipal building rather than the house of a king.

The difference in floor level enabled Gabriel to provide an impressive entrance – the **Galerie des Colonnes,** from which a monumental staircase rose to the equally impressive Salle des Gardes. In the Galerie des Colonnes are exhibited some of the magnificent tapestries which Louis XV ordered for the château – a series of dramatic scenes in which the life of Esther is depicted by Audran in an architectural setting which bears a suspicious resemblance to the Grand Trianon. At the end of the **Salle des Gardes** is the **Ante Room** which, by means of coupled doorways set to left and right of the apse, gave access to the apartments of the King and the Queen respectively.

The mixture of the Louis XVI and Empire styles at Compiègne affords an interesting comparison. The **Salon de Jeu de Marie-Antoinette** is by far the best example of the former. It is a lovely room, cool and spacious; the decorations are rich without being oppressive, for the tall rectangular panels are left blank. The silk hangings and curtains, recently re-woven at Lyons from a faded remnant, import the freshness of a rose garden, pink and green and slightly out of focus, and even when the curtains are drawn the room retains a delightful luminosity.

In the **Dining Room** – again a deliciously cool apartment – the mixture of styles begins. It was Napoleon who had the walls painted to resemble marble of a glowing oyster satin colour, which accords well with the admirable paintings in *trompe l'oeil*, done by Sauvage in the previous reign. The overdoors by Sauvage are in fact among the most distinctive features of the palace.

But it is in the **Library,** at the other end of the suite, that the *style Empire* first comes into its own. The bold ormolu decorations against the sombre mahogany woodwork blend harmoniously with the gilt and calf bindings of the books. One of these – Newton's treatise on mathematics – received the impact of a cannon ball in 1814, and stood up to it extremely well. Beyond this room is the apartment

C.G.I.F. 241 Q

The Palace of Compiègne

1 Salle à Manger
2 Galerie des Tableaux
3 Salon Bleu
4 Salon des Fleurs
5 Grand Salon
6 Boudoir
7 Chambre à Coucher
8 Premier Salon
9 Bibliothèque

10 Chambre de Napoléon 1
11 Chambre du Conseil
12 Salon de Réception
13 Salon des Cartes
14 Salle à Manger
15 Antichambre
16 Salon de Jeu
17 Antichambre

N

3
4
1
5
2
6
7
8
9
10
11
12
13
14
15
16
17

Galerie
des Cerfs

Musée de
la Voiture

Salle
de
Bal

Chapelle

Salle des
Gardes

Musée du 2nd
Empire

COUR
D'HONNEUR

originally prepared for the Empress Marie-Louise.

It was for reasons of diplomacy that the marriage with the Archduchess of Austria had been arranged. It was a prospect which only her own impeccable sense of duty could have enabled her to tolerate: as the baron de Meneval puts it 'she regarded herself almost as a victim sacrificed to the Minotaur'.

She was just seventeen, *'très simple, très naïve et d'une intelligence ordinaire'*. Her journey from Vienna was a prodigious undertaking, and she arrived at Chalons 'more tired than it would be possible to express'.

Napoleon meanwhile, having inspected minutely the newly decorated rooms destined for his bride, was waiting at Compiègne with an impatience which he could hardly master. Elaborate arrangements had been made for the first meeting in a series of magnificent tents in the neighbourhood of Soissons: everyone knew to the nearest centimetre where he or she was to stand. But on the day before the Emperor suddenly decided to anticipate the ceremony. At ten minutes' notice he took Murat and one valet in a carriage with no livery and, 'chuckling like a little boy' at the thought of the escapade, vanished in the direction of Soissons. At the Relai de Courcelles, in pouring rain, they met the first outriders of the royal equipage, and in a few moments the carriage came into view. No sooner had it stopped than Napoleon, opening the door himself, jumped in and greeted his astonished bride with a kiss. His gesture had the desired effect. When Marie-Louise had sufficiently recovered her composure she said, simply and naïvely, 'Sire, your portrait did not flatter you.'

It was for Marie-Louise that the avenue leading from the centre of the main façade was prolonged *à perte de vue* as far as the Beaux Monts, some five kilometres from the palace. It was intended to remind her of Schönbrunn.

In the Empress's suite the confusion of styles becomes more complicated. Louis XVI's rooms, redecorated and refurnished under Napoleon I, regained under Napoleon III some Louis XVI furniture, which had once again become the fashion. In the **Premier Salon de l'Impératrice** there is a large suite in this style. A sharp eye may detect the originals – for some of the pieces were replicas – by the slightly more square appearance of the little gilded pineapples which form the finials to the chair backs. In the **Bedroom,** amid some rather heavy specimens of Napoleonic furniture, is a delightful commode by Daguerre from Marie-Antoinette's rooms at St Cloud.

Compiègne's **Musée de la Voiture** has an extremely interesting collection covering a fairly wide field. First are the horse-drawn vehicles, for which the French have the delightful adjective '*hippomobiles*'! The earliest is from the eighteenth century, there being no survivals in France of any coach of earlier date. The cumbersome *Berline* was, in spite of its name, created in Paris, but later in the eighteenth century the French looked towards England for a succession of lighter and therefore faster carriages. To the ornate structures of the Regency succeeded the more functional – and for that reason more beautiful – designs of the age of McAdam.

Their names are often picturesque. There is, for example, a particularly charming *Désobligeante* – so-called because it offered accommodation for one person only. Its painted panels reveal that it was used for following the chase. There is another *Désobligeante* here which Queen Victoria used for her visits to the south of France.

The sledges provide, perhaps naturally, the greatest opportunity for fantasy in design, some resembling dragons with lights inside the head which shone out through the eyes. In France such a vehicle was a playful luxury. In the last hard winter before the Revolution, many of the courtiers at Versailles had extravagant sledges built. For Louis XVI the intense cold provided an opportunity rather of bringing personal relief to the poor. He is said to have described his charitable activities with the phrase '*voici mon traineau*'.

The history of the bicycle can be followed here also, starting with the *Draisienne*, propelled by the feet, to the *Velocipède* in which pedals first appeared. This led to the disproportionate enlargement of the pedal wheel resulting in the Penny Farthing or *Grand Bi*. Finally the introduction of the chain produced, in 1890, what we recognize as a bicycle.

Power-driven vehicles range from Bollée's first steam coach, known as *la Mancette*, and the comte de Dion's steam car, to the first internal combustion engines. All the great names are here – de Dion Bouton, Renault, Delahaye, Georges Richard and Guynemer – the last named being an inhabitant of Compiègne.

Locomotives are not included, but there is, in the Cour des Cuisines, the *wagon salon* of Napoleon III which gives some idea of the luxury of travel in those days. It was specially designed for him by Viollet-le-Duc and executed with the same minute attention to detail that would have been observed in the construction of a piece of furniture for one of the imperial palaces.

The fact that Compiègne had been a residence favoured by Napoleon I is perhaps sufficient reason that it should have appealed also to his nephew, Napoleon III – but there is more to it than that.

For it was here that he fell in love with Eugénie de Montijo.

Eugénie had eighteen triumphant years of reign at Compiègne, but towards the end of her life she made what was probably the mistake of returning incognito to the scene of her happiness. She was not recognized by the guide who took her round the palace, but when she came to the **Salon des Fleurs** – a room named from the beautiful panels painted in 1810 by Dubois – she turned instinctively to the architrave on the right of the door leading from the **Grand Salon**. There, pencilled on the woodwork, was a line such as is made in nurseries to mark the height of a child, with the inscription 'Louis – dix ans'. The poor woman burst into tears, and only then did the guide recognize his former mistress. Her only son, the Prince Imperial, had been killed in the Zulu wars.

Behind the state apartments and forming the acute angle of the triangular plan of the château runs another wing in which the most important of the reception rooms is situated – the **Ballroom** – thirty-nine metres long by thirteen wide. It is essentially a shallow coved ceiling, painted to represent the major victories of Napoleon, supported by a double colonnade of Corinthian columns and lit by fifteen enormous chandeliers. It was used for the official balls of the Court under Marie-Louise, but under Eugénie it served as a dining room.

For in the days of the Second Empire, the château became the scene of special and privileged house parties known as the *Séries de Compiègne*. All sorts of people were asked. Alongside some of the great names of the French aristocracy or of European diplomacy figured those of Pasteur, Verdi, Gounod, Flaubert, Dumas and Alfred de Vigny and many others who were to make the century great by their contributions to science, music and literature. One can imagine amateur theatricals performed by such a cast, produced by Prosper Mérimée, with scenery by Viollet-le-Duc.

The guests came, of course, on a special train. Fourteen first-class coaches for the servants and six *wagons salons* for the guests. Each guest was expected to bring his personal domestic, and this was known to cause embarrassment to those who kept none. There were even stories of young men bringing their personal friends disguised as *valets de chambre*,

One who did precisely this, and has left an account of the experience, was Paul d'Hormoys. He tells how the sculptor Caristides received one day a letter: '*Par ordre de l'Empereur*,' it ran, '*le Grand Chambellan a l'honneur de prévenir M. Caristides qu'il est invité à passer six jours au palais de Compiègne, du 14 au 21 novembre.*

Réponse s'il vous plaît: signé – Duc de Bassano.'

His first anxiety about the expense involved was allayed by the painter Boulenger, who had been on a previous *Séries*; and the problem of the *valet de chambre* was solved by d'Hormoys volunteering.

Six large *chars-à-bancs*, each drawn by four horses, awaited the guests at the station and conveyed them to the château. In the Vestibule Caristides was met by a footman and conducted, down endless corridors, to a room hung with grey chintz and furnished with a bed 'as large as that of Louis XIV at Versailles'. In the capacious hearth there burnt a fire large enough to roast an ox, while outside the window the Forêt de Compiègne, still glorious in the dying autumn, extended its golden perspectives as far as the eye could see.

Tea was served in his room, and at seven o'clock the footman reappeared to conduct him to the Cabinet des Cartes – the room next to the Dining Room where the huge maps of the forest lined the walls. Here the guests formed a double rank, the men on one side and the ladies on the other. Louis-Napoleon and Eugénie now made their entry, and newcomers were introduced, the gentlemen by the *Grand Chambellan* and the ladies by the *Dame d'Honneur*. It was not a formidable ordeal, for both the Emperor and the Empress had a gift for putting people at their ease. Artists were astonished and delighted to hear their latest exhibit appraised; ladies were impressed and flattered to be asked solicitously about the health of some ailing relative. It was clear, but not too transparently obvious, that their Imperial Highnesses had done their homework.

Large dinners were held in the Ballroom, where covers could be laid for a hundred guests, and the great surtout de table ordered from Sèvres in 1859, a replica of that used by Louis XV, setting out all the stages of a stag hunt, could be displayed. Only those destined to sit next to the Emperor or Empress had places allocated to them, the others being free to sit where they chose, and an atmosphere of princely informality was maintained.

After dinner there was some form of entertainment. Sometimes it was amateur theatricals, sometimes dancing to a pianola. Sometimes it took a more serious form, such as a lecture by Pasteur on the circulation of the blood.

If the weather was fine, excursions were made to places of interest in the neighbourhood. The **Forêt de Compiègne** is, in fact, one of the most beautiful in France, largely because the natural contours of the ground form a series of hills which give a depth of perspective to the views. The timber, some of which is truly magnificent, is

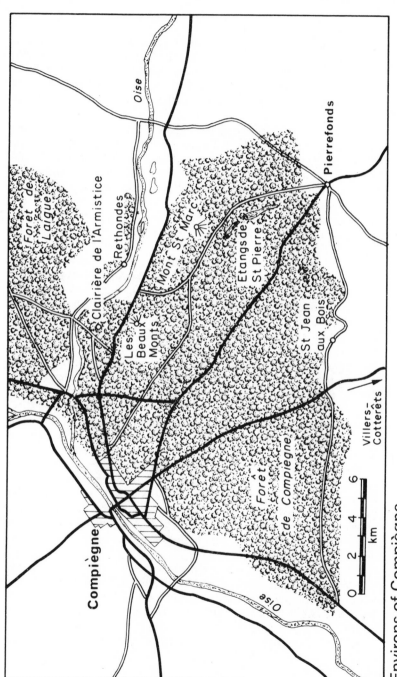

Environs of Compiègne

largely beech and the most attractive time to visit is in late October. Of the hills the most conspicuous are the **Beaux Monts** in the north, from which one may command a view right down the avenue to the château, but perhaps the loveliest of all are the **Monts St Marc** from which the prospects over the Aisne Valley are as beautiful as they are extensive.

Between the hills are the valleys, peopled with poplars and sometimes, as at the **Étangs de St Pierre**, opening into a series of lakes. Here and there a clearance in the forest reveals some charming house or hamlet which in times past harboured a religious community. Such is **St Jean-aux-Bois**, a delightful hamlet where the houses, reached through an archway flanked by pepper-pot turrets, are grouped like a miniature cathedral close round the stately but simple structure of the abbey church.

It is, in fact, a somewhat unusual building. On entering, one is struck by the surprising height obtained by the raised arches, considering that it is what one might call a 'single-storey' church, with no triforium and no clerestory. It is this height that confers its peculiar distinction upon St Jean-aux-Bois, together with its splendid luminosity which brings out the full quality of the cream-coloured stone. But we must remember that many of the windows would have contained stained glass of a rich and sombre colouring. Only one remains – in the central lancet of the east window, but four of the original thirteenth-century *grisailles* windows can be seen as well. To the south the sole survivor of the conventual buildings is the chapter house, now a chapel, where the stones are green with moisture.

More often than not the imperial house parties were taken to **Pierrefonds**, on the eastern edge of the forest; and one can imagine the cortège jingling along with Viollet-le-Duc as Cicerone. On one of these visits, Mme de Metternich informs us, the comtesse de Castiglione, who took her beauty with a deadly seriousness, contrived to have a fall among the ruins in such a way as to exhibit *'les plus belles jambes du monde'*. Nobody took any notice, *'persuadés que la chute était volontaire et faisait partie du programme'*. She had, in fact, broken several bones, and her gesture, if it was a gesture, was an expensive one.

For nearly three and a half centuries the massive ruins of Louis d'Orléans's fortress had overhung the little town. Too often associated with rebellion against the Crown, it had been blown up by order of Richelieu. At the time of the Revolution it was sold off cheaply, and bought by Napoleon.

By 1857 the taste for things medieval was in full favour and

Louis-Napoleon conceived the idea of restoring either Pierrefonds or Coucy to its pristine glory. Perhaps the greater proximity of the former to Compiègne decided him in its favour and he naturally confided the task of reconstruction to Viollet-le-Duc.

It was at first intended only to rebuild the keep and two north-eastern towers, known as the Tour Godefroi de Bouillon and the Tour Hector. This was the least-affected portion of the ruin; explosives had not been used on this side owing to the proximity of houses.

The reconstruction was extremely accurate, for enough survived of the original building to furnish most of the information needed. A detailed drawing made before the work began shows the Tour Hector with the machicolation of the *chemin de ronde* almost intact. The level at which the roof of the *chemin de ronde* met the inner drum is also indicated; and, against the wall of the square look-out tower which backed the Tour Hector, a single battlement bears sufficient evidence that there was a second crenellated parapet at the base of the conical roof. One can state with confidence that these two towers appear today almost exactly as they appeared at the end of the fourteenth century when they were built.

Whatever our views on the value of pastiche, it must be admitted that Viollet-le-Duc made an extremely competent job of it. Some of the work in the courtyard and all of the work on the interior, how-ever, owes more to his imagination than to the Middle Ages; but his was a well-trained imagination. He was a most considerable scholar and, as he stated himself, there are only too many ruins in France.

Now, as one drives in from Villers-Cotterêts, the first sight of the towers and *poivrières* rising out of the valley below is really exciting; and as the road winds down into Pierrefonds one gets more magnificent glimpses. It is well worth the visitor's while to make an intelligent exploration of the back streets from which many of the best views may be obtained.

In the castle's **Grande Salle** Viollet-le-Duc has clearly enjoyed himself. The monumental chimney-piece with the nine statues of Heroic Ladies – *Les Preuses* – is borrowed from Coucy, but he has availed himself of the opportunity of depicting Eugénie and her Maids of Honour. The row of figures would make an interesting comparison with the famous Winterhalter of the same group in the château at Compiègne.

Pierrefonds is not the perfect restoration which might enable us to recapture the atmosphere of the feudal age. Rather it is a fascinating document in which we can study the nineteenth-century conception of that age. Viollet-le-Duc did not hesitate to 'correct the errors' of his medieval authors; and he sometimes produces a perfection which was not theirs. Perhaps the last word is with André Maurois: *'je préfère plutôt des fautes vivantes que la perfection morte'*. Architecturally the 'faults' of the medieval builders were often their most endearing qualities.

CHAPTER TWENTY-TWO

Senlis and the Halatte Forest

❧

Senlis has a history as long as the Christian era, the medieval city having been superimposed upon the foundations of its Roman predecessor Augustomagus, the royal château upon the site of the praetorium or governor's palace, the Hôtel de Ville upon that of the forum and the cathedral of Notre Dame upon that of the temple of Jupiter.

An aerial view of Senlis shows clearly its historical construction. There are two concentric rings of fortification – the inner, marked by the roofs of the houses built against the Gallo-Roman wall, many of whose towers are still embedded in their structure – and the outer dating from the early thirteenth century, revealed by the trees which were planted when the ramparts were turned into boulevards. Most of the outer wall has disappeared, but at the south-east angle, near the Collège St Vincent, a massive bastion remains.

In spite of the many hazards of history, not the least of which was a serious threat by the Germans in 1914 to burn the whole place down, Senlis has preserved, perhaps more than any other town in the Ile de France, its character of an old cathedral city, insulated and introspective. It is as if its ramparts had somehow protected it from contact with the world beyond. Its crooked, cobbled streets have preserved much of the charm and most of the hygienic defects of their medieval past.

Senlis has not accommodated itself to the automobile: it is a place to be visited on foot. Although the main approach today is by the rue de la République, made in 1752 to facilitate the passage of the Court to Compiègne, the more interesting approach for the visitor is along the original **rue Vieille de Paris** from the south. One must imagine the appearance of the old medieval town, with its walls and towers rising above the waters of the Nonette, as it first appeared to anyone coming from the capital.

Immediately to the right of the Porte de Paris was a Carmelite nunnery, formerly occupied by the Cordeliers. Its beautiful Flamboyant gateway now stands in the Place Gérard de Nerval. The buildings themselves have been used as a barracks for long enough to retain little of their aspect of a thirteenth-century nunnery.

From Les Carmes the rue Vieille de Paris mounts steeply towards the cathedral. This street has grim associations. During the uprising of the serfs known as the *Jacquerie*, Senlis opened its gates to the insurgents. But the feudal lords soon united to avenge the atrocities of their tenants, and in June 1358 a troop of them entered the town. As they advanced up the main street the insurgents suddenly launched a succession of heavily loaded carts down the hill, which took the noble army so completely by surprise that it was forced to beat a retreat.

A little to the right, between Les Carmes and the Town Hall, is a parallel street called the **rue du Haubergier** containing a **museum** of the same name. An elegant Renaissance house of brick and stone with an octagonal staircase tower, it is devoted to the archaeology and history of the region: on the ground floor to the Gallo-Roman period, with interesting remains of the old Augustomagus and a treasure trove from the Forêt d'Halatte; on the first floor to the medieval period, which offers an extremely fine head of a Prophet from the west door of the cathedral, and on the second floor to documents and charters relating to the history of Senlis.

Apart from its many old and beautiful houses, Senlis is a city of disaffected churches. Many, such as St Rieul, have disappeared completely. Others have been degraded. St Aignan has become a cinema; St Frambourg, whose gable end and huge rose window, now filled in and pierced with a triple lancet, can be seen from the square in front of the cathedral, has become a garage. Finest of all is **St Pierre**, east of the cathedral, once the centre of the largest and richest parish in the town: it is now a covered market place. The fifteenth-century nave, set at an odd angle to the thirteenth-century choir, was never vaulted, but always had a wooden ceiling. On the north side, a Romanesque tower is crowned with a spire built in 1432, while on the south side a large belfry, added at the time of the Renaissance, seems dull without the golden ball that was designed to surmount it. But the rich and somewhat unusual decoration to the west front is still more or less intact. It bears the date 1516, and may well have been designed by Martin Chambiges while he was working on the cathedral.

To the west of the cathedral is the important ensemble of the royal castle or **Chastel du Roi**. The former conventual buildings, rebuilt in the eighteenth century, now house the **Musée de la Vénerie** – a collection of considerable interest to enthusiasts for the chase. But even those who are not interested in the sport of kings are well advised to pay their entrance fee merely to gain access to this picturesque and historic group of buildings.

In the Dark Ages the Château of Senlis was one of the principal residences of the Merovingian and Carolingian monarchy. It was here, in 987, that Hugh Capet was elected king. In 1120 Louis VI ('the Fat') founded a chapel dedicated to St Denis and proceeded to a considerable reconstruction of the château. At the end of the twelfth century Philippe-Auguste was often here, and it is to him that the outer fortifications of the town are due.

In 1375 the château became the official residence of the children of Charles V ('the Wise') who also made important additions to the building. Here was celebrated, in 1420, the marriage between Henry V of England and Catherine of France. The last king to stay at the château was Henri II, when still Dauphin. Henri IV came several times, but he put up in a house in the town. It was from here on 21 March 1594 that he set out for Paris to win his kingdom and to become the first Bourbon on the throne of France. The fact was commemorated by the last of the Bourbons, Charles X, returning from the last coronation to be held at Reims. On his orders a bust of the *Vert Galant* was placed with an inscription over the door of the Town Hall.

The eighteenth century saw a steady decline in the condition of the château; and finally, on 16 October 1793 – the very day of the execution of Marie-Antoinette – the buildings were sold to a private owner, which was the prelude to their destruction.

The Revolution left the château a ruin, but enough remains to be of interest. On the north side of the enclosure, against the city wall, can be seen the foundations of the donjon, which incorporate some of the original tower of the praetorium.

Beyond the donjon are the kitchens, approached through a double Gothic archway supported upon a single Roman column. On the wall above can be seen some of the decorative arcading of the Salle des Maréchaux, and behind it one of the best preserved of the towers of the ancient city wall. Last in this range is the high gable of the Chambre du Roi (the window towards the courtyard is modern) with its attendant tower in which St Louis made his oratory. There are still traces of his earlier work upon the eighteenth-century façade, and this is typical of Senlis as a whole; its particular atmosphere of continuity with the past depends largely upon the way in which older buildings are so often incorporated in later ones.

But the greatest attraction of the whole group of ruins, buildings and gardens of the Chastel du Roi is the magnificent view which it commands of the **Cathedral of Notre Dame**.

The one event of cardinal importance in the history of the cathedral is the disastrous fire which broke out in June 1504, when the roof was struck by lightning and its timbers set alight. It burned fiercely for two days until the gutters of the town became rivulets of molten lead. Although the bells melted in the intense heat, the west end of the cathedral miraculously survived, but the whole of the roof and clerestory had to be rebuilt. This explains the superimposition of so much Flamboyant work upon a twelfth-century base.

Begun in 1155, the original nave and choir had some of the severity of Noyon, which still appears in the **west front**; and this sets off to the greatest advantage the richly carved doorway, in which we can see a close relation to the Portail Royal of Chartres. Over the door a representation in full relief of the *Falling Asleep of the Virgin Mary* is one of the earliest examples of the way in which the Mother of Our Lord came to dominate the imagination of the thirteenth-century sculptors.

Unfortunately it is not usually possible to enter the cathedral through this door: it would be the perfect point at which to begin a tour of the interior. From the top of the steps which lead down into the **nave** the whole magnificent perspective may be taken in at a glance. It is one of the great successes of the Gothic style.

The regular alternation of massive piers and single columns – *pile forte – pile faible* – was interrupted in the mid-thirteenth century when the transepts were added. These were placed so as to make the nave rather short and the choir rather long.

The clerestory, demolished by the fire, was rebuilt some six metres taller – one can still see where the original vault sprang against the wall by the organ. This increased height of the nave has the effect of making the aisles seem almost squat by contrast. They give the impression, as they curl round into the ambulatory, of a low, vaulted corridor which encircles the choir, rather than that of an airy forest of pillars which is the glory of the later Gothic cathedrals. There is some good modern glass by Barillet in the ambulatory which greatly enhances the general effect. The previous windows were blown out in the course of a bombardment in 1940.

The High Altar was brought here in 1791 from Chaâlis. Behind it are four charming absidal chapels which, together with the west front, escaped the ravages of the fire. They seem to mark the moment of transition between the Romanesque and Gothic styles.

The **Chapter House**, dating from the late fourteenth century, was built by Pierre l'Orfèvre, whose arms can be seen upon the bosses. It is divided into two sections, the smaller of which served as the chapter library and the larger as the chapter house proper. The vaulting springs from a central column with a remarkable capital depicting *la danse des fous*. The stained-glass windows, also dating from the fourteenth century, are the best in the cathedral.

There is some fancy vaulting to some of the side chapels, especially the **Chapel of St Denis** to the east of the south door, with its elaborate system of free-standing ribs and pendants. These date, of course, from the reconstructions after the fire.

François I, appealed to by the canons, made a handsome contribution, and we can see his salamander over the north porch and also the capital F, which was his badge, in the windows of the north clerestory. Martin Chambiges was called in and the half-ruined cathedral was raised again, taller, as might be expected of the architect of so much of the work at Beauvais, and clothed in an elaborate lacework of Flamboyant tracery and open carving. The rose window in the south transept is almost identical with that of Beauvais.

The south transept overlooks the Place Notre Dame, from which one of the finest views of the cathedral is to be obtained; but to see the whole we must walk right round it, and a very delightful walk it is. From the rue aux Flagearts the *abside* rises magnificently from its scaffolding of flying buttresses above the brown roofs and old grey walls of what was once the bishop's palace. Senlis, in fact, ceased to be a diocese in the days of the Revolution and the building now serves as the *Tribunal Civil*, but from this side it has not lost anything of its atmosphere. One would not be surprised to see a figure in an episcopal *soutane*, breviary in hand, pacing up and down the trim little garden before the palace. The houses around, charming and irregular, are typical of the architecture of a close. It is here more than anywhere else that Senlis throws back the echoes of the past.

Over the whole scene presides the imposing spire of the **southwest tower**. This, like the transepts, was an addition of the mid-thirteenth century – a cluster of slender columns and tapering pinnacles sixty-five metres high, which commands a wide sweep of country: the valleys of the Thève, the Nonette and the Aunette, and the great forests of Chantilly, Ermenonville and Halatte.

The **Halatte Forest** lies to the north of Senlis, a vast expanse of woodland in some ways more beautiful than that of Chantilly, perhaps because the contours are more varied. It contains a number of minor architectural treasures which provide enough points of interest along a pretty road to form a most agreeable excursion.

The road to the north rises to a high point at Fleurines, and then dips down to the river Oise at **Pont Sainte-Maxence**. The bridge from which one half of the name derives was built in 1774 by Jean Perrouet with a surprisingly modern use of flat, elliptical arches; unfortunately it was destroyed in 1914, but the town has retained many old houses of interest and beauty. The church, dedicated to the Irish martyr Maxence, from whom the other half of the name is taken, is large and unusual and would be extremely beautiful if it were not built in a cold grey stone which does not set off its architecture to advantage.

In plan it is almost a miniature cathedral: a central nave with fine lierne and tierceron vaulting is accompanied by two aisles of nearly the same height, each bay of which has a Flamboyant vault of different design. Unfortunately the glass is in a poor condition, and the ambulatory, which is little more than a succession of enormous niches, is dark and ill-lit.

But the real glory of Ste-Maxence is the Renaissance porch to the south aisle. It is quite out of scale with the rest of the church, and suggests that they were beginning to rebuild on altogether more grandiose lines. Doubtless the Wars of Religion interrupted the rebuilding, which was never completed. Like many others of its sort it appears to have been a Gothic structure in Renaissance clothing, rather than a building conceived and planned throughout in accordance with Italian ideas. There are some interesting tombstones which were brought here from the Abbey of Moncel.

Moncel, nearly two kilometres east from Pont Ste-Maxence, is another conventual building which has survived while its church has disappeared – in this case, completely. But Moncel is a building of the seventeenth century, and the seventeenth century was an age of real religious zeal. How different is the architecture here from the palatial, or semi-palatial, façades of Chaâlis, La Victoire or St-Christophe. Moncel was inspired by an ideal of austerity not far removed from that of the thirteenth century, and it has as the result some of the beauty which often derives from simplicity.

Standing in the courtyard, with one's back to the space left by the demolished church, one is immediately struck by the fact that there are no chimneys. The only two original ones are on the east front. The huge mass of brown roof is uninterrupted except for one or two tiny dormers. The windows are small and unadorned and set fairly widely apart. The only architectural contrivance is the somewhat rough-hewn arcading of the one surviving range of the cloister.

Morienval: choir and apse

Morienval seen from the Butte de Fossement

Behind the cloister there are older buildings which date from the foundation by Philippe le Bel in 1309, of which the old refectory, now the Chapel, is worthy of note. Beneath the great brown roof is the original *charpente* of timbers which is one of the finest surviving examples in France. Philippe le Bel had a residence a hundred metres to the east called Fécamp, of which the turreted gatehouse, now sadly dilapidated, alone remains.

Continuing eastwards, we come to **Pontpoint**, one of the most attractive, and attractively situated, churches of the district. In spite of the disadvantage of standing in an unusually overcrowded and unprepossessing necropolis, it sits magnificently on the high ground overlooking the valley of the Oise – a happy mixture of grey stone and brown tile.

In a countryside adorned by innumerable fine churches, Pontpoint stands out by reason of its originality. One senses immediately that there is something different about it. One of the unusual features is that the windows are placed directly above the pillars and not in the interstices between them. It is also lop-sided, having two transepts to the south and none to the north.

The interior is of a beautiful white stone which, on a sunny day, is bathed in colour from the stained-glass windows. A solid Romanesque nave, dimly lit by small, round-arched windows, opens into a Gothic chancel and apse which are flooded with light. To the right, the double transept forms a complex of quadripartite vaulting that gives a wonderful impression of airy spaciousness, despite the cluttering effect of enormous and wholly indifferent oil paintings with which it is encumbered. Without these, and without the two large and ugly side altars, Pontpoint would offer one of the most satisfying of architectural experiences.

If Pontpoint has any rival in the land it is the neighbouring **Church of Rhuis**, a little further upstream, near Verberie. Rhuis *is* what Pontpoint *was* – before its Gothic additions. Compare, for instance, their square-based bell towers, each with its high stone pyramid of roof; each is of three tiers of round-arched apertures, but at Rhuis the topmost storey is awkwardly superimposed. Its openings are larger and seem to gape, and the whole storey stands on a sort of platform which disconnects it from the lower part of the tower. At Pontpoint the three storeys form a single unity, each being separate from, and yet at the same time linked to the other by an identical string course, which forms as it were the eyebrows to the arcade.

Inside, one's first impression is of the almost rude simplicity of the building. Traces of mural painting and of polychroming in the fumbling attempt at a ribbed vault in the south aisle suggest that its original appearance was utterly different. There is a curious effect caused by the fact that in each of the nave arches the abacus projects only towards the interior of the arch, creating a flat, sliced appearance towards the nave and aisles. Near the font there is an interesting funeral stone, lightly etched as if on brass, to Jehan Bohion, dated 1637.

On the way back from Rhuis to Senlis or Chantilly, we can pick our way by the use of a map to **Raray**; it is a splendid note on which to end the day.

The approach is unexciting, across the typical wide fields of endless agriculture towards the *massif* of woodland which forms the constant background to this sort of country. We reach the woods and suddenly a clearing on the right reveals a distant glimpse of château – a tall roof, two high pavilions with slender chimney stacks and façades of a beautiful pale stone at the end of a grassy drive. It is only a glimpse: the trees close in again and we come to a tiny village. Our attention is diverted by the remarkable fortified farm – a pleasant medley of brick and stone and plaster with mullioned windows framed between two little turrets built out on corbels and a roof pierced by two handsome Renaissance dormers; to the left the massive drum of a pigeon house capped with a huge conical roof completes the picture.

The **château** is reached by a small gateway between the cour d'honneur and the office buildings. It reserves its greatest surprise for those who persevere in this unpromising approach. For the cour d'honneur is enclosed on either side by a magnificent arcade. It is an affair of the greatest audacity and originality; one of the most astonishing achievements of the French seventeenth century. Above each of the eighteen arches, raised upon a pedestal supported by scrolls, is the figure of a hound, each in a different pose, so placed that they all converge upon the central archway of the arcade, over which are mounted the figures of a wild boar (on the south arcade) and a stag (on the north).

There is something that suggests Thurber about the attitudes and expressions of the dogs, and where the tail is erect and (one feels) wagging, the sculptor, with a fine disregard for finesse, has inserted an iron pothook. Nobody knows who was the author of this impressive decor.

The dating of Raray is a nice problem for the architectural historian. The rounded pediments of the two pavilions suggest the days of Henri IV. The square-cut frontispiece, with its swags and trophies, suggests a much later date. The fact that the windows to the left of the frontispiece are regularly spaced while those to the right are not also suggests an earlier building which has been skilfully 'modernized' under Louis XIV or even Louis XV.

But whatever the history, the result is entirely satisfying; this is one of the most beautiful as well as one of the most interesting of the châteaux of the Ile de France. Alas, the main block is no longer furnished, let alone inhabited. The comte de la Bedoyère lives in the west wing and offices. But the visitor is allowed to wander freely round the exterior and to penetrate eastwards into the woods as far as the 'Porte Rouge' – the gateway to the forest. This ornate doorway is obviously connected with the arcading of the forecourt. Within the complex pediment Diana sits between two handsome hounds, while over her head a unicorn looks in elegant reproach at two more hounds who seem to be guilty of the vulgar error of mistaking him for a stag.

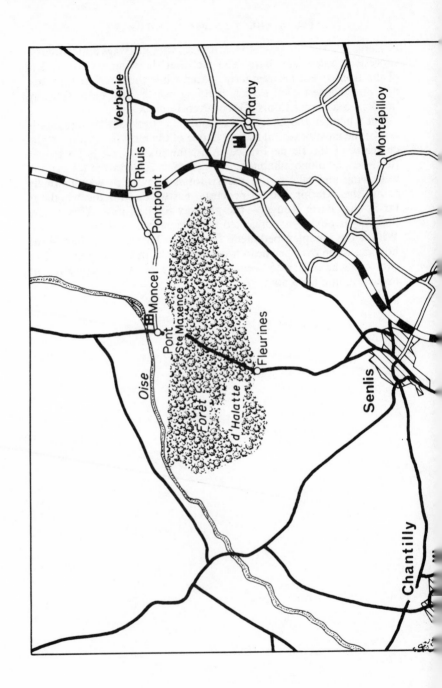

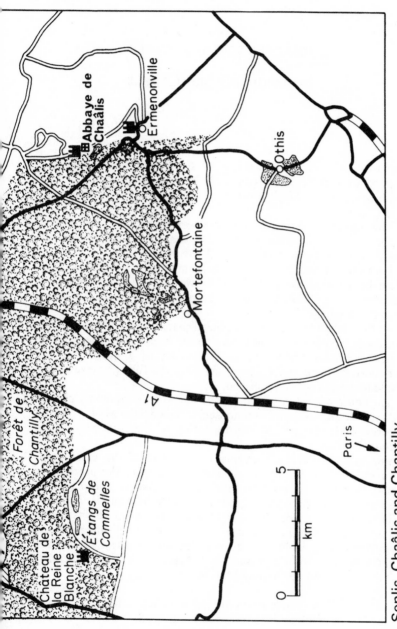

Senlis, Chaâlis and Chantilly

Abbaye de Chaâlis

Ermenonville

Othis

Mortefontaine

Forêt de Chantilly

A1

Paris

Château de la Reine Blanche

Étangs de Commelles

0   km   5

CHAPTER TWENTY-THREE

Ermenonville and Chaâlis

❧

For those who enjoy the writings of Gérard de Nerval, the whole area south of Senlis is of exceptional interest. *Sylvie* would be ideal reading during a leisurely visit to Ermenonville, Mortefontaine and Chaâlis.

The **gardens** of **Ermenonville** have been described as the greatest work of art of the French eighteenth century, and they were the creation of one man – the marquis René de Girardin.

Girardin formed his taste in the course of a visit to England. Here he admired the gardens of Stowe and Blenheim, but most particularly he admired those of the poet Shenstone at Leasowes, near Birmingham.

At Ermenonville he found a medieval château that had been largely remodelled in the seventeenth and eighteenth centuries. The beautiful classical façades which enclose three sides of a quadrangle are contained between four towers which were carefully preserved when the feudal castle was demolished.

The house was set in a dismal landscape – 'a sort of dreary plateau with no features'. Girardin set himself to remodel the whole area into a series of landscape pictures according to the principles of his mentor Rousseau.

For Girardin was a wholehearted disciple of the great Jean-Jacques. He brought up his children according to the precepts of *Émile*, he based his political views on the *Contrat Social* and he designed his gardens on the lines suggested by the *Nouvelle Héloïse*.

In creating his garden, Girardin knew exactly what he was doing. To him beauty was use and use beauty. The embellishment of the countryside went hand in hand with the improvement of farming and the bettering of the peasants' lot. Armed with these principles, he set out to emulate the English lord

> whose ample lawns are not ashamed to feed
> The milky heifer and deserving steed.

Happy peasants and replete livestock were part of the *tableau vivant*, the animated landscape picture which was his ideal.

It must have been the greatest day in Girardin's life when, in 1777, Rousseau accepted his offer of hospitality and came to Ermenonville. Here Rousseau lived, and here in July of the following year, he died, thereby giving Girardin his supreme opportunity to crown his creation with a mausoleum to the genius who had inspired it. The artist Hubert Robert was called in, and in due course the design had been agreed on. An island in the middle of the lake to the south of the château was planted with poplars; embowered by these, the philosopher's tomb, in the form of an antique altar, was inscribed on one side with the legend *'Ici repose l'homme de la Nature et de la Vérité'* and upon the other *'Vitam impendere vero'* – 'Consecrate your life to Truth'.

Like most idealists, Girardin welcomed the Revolution as a liberation from servitude, and he joined in the debates with speeches conspicuous for their noble sentiments and generous ideals. Like most idealists he recoiled in disgust from the atrocity and contempt for justice which marked the reign of Robespierre and retreated in disillusionment to Ermenonville. He was pursued, denounced and imprisoned in his own château. From this impotent and humiliating position he saw the gardens which he had created laid waste by vandals and the mortal remains of Rousseau snatched from the Ile des Peupliers to be reinstated in the Pantheon in Paris by a people who honoured the philosopher with their lips but betrayed his principles in their every action. Broken-hearted, Girardin ended his days at Vernouillet.

Ermenonville has lost today much of its former atmosphere. The château is now a restaurant and the park a caravan site. But the broad outlines of the gardens, with their lakes and groves and grottos, are still much the same. The **Autel à la Rêverie**, where Rousseau loved to meditate, may still be seen, but the *'calme enchanteur'* which used to reign there is less easily recaptured. The north gardens have lost, among other features, the Tour de la belle Gabrielle, which figured so conspicuously in contemporary engravings, but the **Maison du Vigneron** has survived. The view from beyond the lake, with the **Ile des Peupliers** in the foreground and the château peeping through the foliage of the trees behind, has retained most of its charm.

The Temple of Philosophy was left deliberately unfinished to emphasize the imperfection of human thought. The columns that were erected were put up in honour of the greatest thinkers of the world, culminating, of course, in Rousseau. It was intended that others should be erected as they came to be merited.

Mortefontaine, south-west of Ermenonville, is still a charming village, but the château at which Joseph Bonaparte gave his brilliant receptions, and where his daughters Caroline and Pauline were married to Murat and to the Prince Borghese, is now a school. Its park, once a rival to that of Ermenonville and made famous by Corot, now belongs to the **Château de Vallière**, a typical example of *le style Rothschild* that reminds one of Waddesdon in Berkshire. It is the seat of the duc de Grammont and is strictly private.

At **Othis**, a little to the south of Ermenonville, the **Church of the Nativity** alone commands our attention. It is a little jewel. Its lovely Renaissance façade to the south aisle, dating from the second half of the sixteenth century, is as unusual as it is attractive – a charming little composition of niches and roundels. Note the peculiar scroll tracery to the rose window and the way in which the buttress presents its narrow front in the guise of a fluted pilaster.

The interior, dating from the fourteenth century, is also delightful. The spiral sweep of the steps up to the pulpit, the strong ribbed vaulting to the apse and the fine monuments on the eastern walls of both aisles all blend together in one pleasing harmony.

The **Cistercian Abbey of Chaâlis** was founded in 1136 by Louis VI in memory of his brother Charles, Count of Flanders, who had been murdered in Bruges. It is from the Latin *Caroli Locus* (Charles' Place) that the name Chaâlis derives.

The new abbey was soon a thriving religious community, and as numbers increased it became necessary to rebuild the old priory church on more spacious lines. In 1219 the new building was ready for consecration. It was designed on a plan similar to that of Noyon Cathedral, with its transepts rounded off by a series of absidal chapels.

The surviving ruins of the north transept, at the point at which it communicated with the monks' dorter, show an architecture of typically Cistercian simplicity – the slightly elevated arches springing from single cylindrical pillars, no triforium, and tall lancets providing ample daylight to the clerestory.

The former abbot's lodging had been to the east of the church, where the private **chapel**, much restored in 1875, still stands – in all essentials a building of the late thirteenth century on the lines of the Sainte Chapelle in Paris. The paintings on the vaulted ceiling, often ascribed to Le Primatice, who did so much work at Fontaine-bleau, are more probably by his pupil Nicolo dell' Abbate. In the nineteenth century Gérard de Nerval objected to them on other grounds: 'all these angels and all these saints created the impression, rather, of nymphs and cupids with their naked bosoms and thighs'.

These paintings, which were largely restored in the nineteenth century by Paul Balze, a pupil of Ingres, were ordered by one of the abbots of the Renaissance, Hippolyte d'Este, Cardinal of Ferrare, the builder of the Villa d'Este at Tivoli. A faint echo of that famous ensemble still lingers at Chaâlis in the walled rose garden, with its high battlements ranged like a row of tombstones on either side of a heavy renaissance archway above which the Cardinal placed his coat of arms. Already family pride was beginning to replace religious zeal in the architecture of the community.

Oddly enough it was the monument to religious zeal and not the monument to family pride which the Revolution destroyed, leaving only a portion of the north side of the church and cloisters. Mme de Vatry demolished more of the cloisters to open up more largely the views from the south windows of her house. She also pulled down the wings of Aubert's building which had formerly enclosed the court. If the entrance front today strikes the eye as being a little monotonous, we must remember that its proportions are not those intended by the architect.

The last occupant of Chaâlis was Mme Jacquemart-André, the wife of a wealthy financier, who purchased the domain in 1902 and installed in it her interesting, if somewhat miscellaneous, collection of pictures, furniture and objets d'art, and re-created on the ground floor a series of interiors in the late Louis XIV style, the furniture of which is truly magnificent. It is only to be regretted that she did so at a time when it was believed that all panelling of that epoch was painted grey, and that the 'gris Trianon' which has been so carefully and so happily removed from the walls of Versailles should reign supreme at Chaâlis. It is a slight defect; Louis Gillet, one of the most distinguished of its Conservateurs, has described Chaâlis as 'un des plus beaux tableaux qui nous présente, dans si peu d'espace, toute la suite de notre passé'.

At her death Mme Jacquemart-André bequeathed the château and its collection to the Institut de France to be preserved for ever 'un lieu de beauté et de repos'.

When the abbey church of Chaâlis was pulled down the High Altar was transferred to the Cathedral of Senlis. Much of the magnificent eighteenth-century panelling from the choir, carved by the Slotz brothers, was moved to the parish church of **Baron**, a few kilometres north-east of Chaâlis. It is a large building dating from the twelfth and thirteenth centuries, with a stone spire added in the fifteenth. It has retained many of its old box pews and is not un-worthy of the distinction conferred upon it by the arrival of the panelling. Its high apse, a feature typical of the region, seems almost made to contain the elaborate niche surmounted by a *Gloire* – a tumultuous arrangement of clouds and cupids (or are they angels?) and radiating shafts of rather solid light.

Joan of Arc received Communion here on the eve of the Battle of Montépilloy. It was in August 1429. Senlis was at that time in the hands of the English, and its inhabitants had appealed to Charles VII to deliver them. On 15 August he came, together with Joan, from La Ferté-Milon, and on the following day he attacked the Duke of Bedford and the English forces. The result was indecisive, but it enabled Charles a few days later to re-enter Senlis.

The **Château de Montépilloy**, originally a twelfth-century fortress of the Bouteillers, formed part of the defensive system of Louis d'Orléans, and it had been reinforced by his masons. Most of the gatehouse and some of the *donjon* survives together with a tall column of jagged masonry which has somehow resisted the forces of destruction and, being visible for miles around, continues to bear witness to the significance of the name '*Mons Speculatorum*'. This tower was certainly the look-out post.

CHAPTER TWENTY-FOUR

Chantilly

ঔ

The Chantilly Forest has not the same beauty as that of Compiègne; the contours are less varied. To the south, however, the river Thève carves its valley through the outskirts of the forest, forming a series of beautiful lakes – **les Étangs de Commelle** – culminating in a pretty little hunting lodge, the **Pavillon de la Reine Blanche** – the only building added by the Condé family after the Revolution. It has no connection with *la Reine Blanche*, the mother of St Louis, but was an old mill to which the architect Dubois gave, in 1825, the appearance of a miniature château in the newly popular 'troubadour' style.

There is still a stag hunt in Chantilly, the *Pique Avant Nivernais* of the marquis de Roualle, and when the mists of autumn rise from the Étangs de Commelle, one can hear the beautiful *sonnerie de chasse*, like an echo from the past, informing those who can understand its language of the movements of the quarry; or one can penetrate deep into the forest and listen to the roar of the rutting stags.

For many people the chief interest of Chantilly will be its **racecourse** and its attendant colony of racing stables which contain today nearly three and a half thousand horses. For Chantilly has become the seat of the *Société d'Encouragement pour l'Amélioration et le Perfectionnement des Races de Chevaux en France* or '*Société d'Encouragement*' for short, which administers the vast Terrain des Aigles to the west of the main road to Paris, and the rapidly expanding training grounds of Lamorlaye and Gouvieux to the east. The French equivalents to the Derby – the Prix du Jockey Club – and to the Oaks – the Prix de Diane – take place annually at Chantilly.

It all began on an autumn morning in 1833. 'Prince Labanoff,' writes the princesse Thérèse de Caraman-Chimay, 'who had arrived from Russia to hunt the stag, was returning to the stables with a group of friends, when they started across the meadow where the racecourse is at present. There was a touch of frost in the air and the horses were spirited. The broad expanse of springy turf, too, had an irresistible appeal and someone suggested a race. No sooner said than done, and the thundering hooves that morning heralded what was going to become one of the most famous racecourses in the world.' The next year the event was repeated, and Lord Henry Seymour became the first president of the committee.

That Chantilly should have become one of the most famous of racecourses owes something to the fact that it is one of the most beautiful, and this in turn it owes to the incomparable background formed by the château and its enormous stables.

One of the best approaches to the château is to walk across the **Pelouse** from the racecourse, leaving the stables '*ridiculement belles*' on our left for a future visit. The château now lies before us, an exciting complex of grey roofs and honey-coloured walls which, on a windless day, is perfectly reflected in the waters of the capacious moat.

Seen from this angle it is at once apparent that there are two almost entirely separate buildings. In front the **Petit Château**, or **Capitainerie**, and behind it the high roofs, domes and cupolas of the **Grand Château**. But whereas the Petit Château is, externally, much as Jean Bullant designed it in 1560, the Grand Château has been rebuilt at least four times.

Montmorency, Condé and Aumâle are the great names in the history of Chantilly. The Constable Anne de Montmorency was one of the most redoubtable figures of the French Renaissance. He combined in a manner typical of his age the role of a ruthless man of war with that of an enlightened connoisseur of art. Chantilly reflected this duality. In its external architecture the Grand Château, designed for him by Pierre Chambiges, retained a stern and military aspect. But within the safer precincts of its court, or in its sumptuous apartments, it was a palace and not a fortress. The year 1560 saw the addition of the Petit Château, a most unmilitary piece of mannerist architecture.

In 1632 Henri de Montmorency was unwise enough to join Gaston d'Orléans, the factious younger brother of Louis XIII, in a rebellion against the all-powerful Cardinal de Richelieu. The rebellion failed and Henri was executed at Toulouse. His estates were confiscated by the Crown. In due course they were returned to his sister, the princesse de Condé, whose husband had won, at the age of twenty-two, the victory of Rocroi.

When the Grand Condé retired from his dazzling career as a general he devoted his energies to the improvement of his domain. '*Chantilly,*' wrote Saint-Simon, '*était ses délices.*' He describes how the great commander would review his gardens, followed by a bevy of secretaries armed with pen and paper to take down on the spot the ideas which occurred to him for the elaboration of the design. The ideas were turned into realities by the landscape gardener, Le Nôtre.

All the great names of the century occur in the annals of Chantilly, for Condé understood men of letters. Bishop Burnet declared that 'there was not in France a better judge of wit and knowledge'. Mme de Sévigné, Boileau, Mlle de la Fayette, la Bruyère, Racine, Molière, Fénelon – all were here at some time.

The Grand Condé died in 1686. It is probable that Chantilly was at this moment more beautiful than it has ever been since. The great work of Le Nôtre in the gardens, with their Gargantuan stone steps and their glittering expanses of water, was largely accomplished. But in this sumptuous setting there still stood the picturesque group of buildings of Anne de Montmorency encompassed by seven great cylinders of stone, its skyline animated by the gables, pinnacles and pointed roofs which cast their intricate reflection in the lake.

It was not to last. The latest visit of Louis XIV had underlined the inadequacy of the accommodation. Condé commissioned Mansart to rebuild the Grand Château, and by 1691 the work was completed. The new building was simply deplorable. Even contemporary eulogists could find no more exciting praise than to call it *regular*. This must have been the dullest set of façades ever designed by Mansart.

In the eighteenth century Versailles ceased to exercise the monopoly which it had enjoyed under Louis XIV, and Chantilly became the scene of ever more numerous and ever more brilliant receptions.

The duc de Bourbon, Condé's grandson, who never took the title of Condé, had greatly increased his already ample fortune by the financial system of William Law. He was fantastically rich, and the fantastic **stables** of Chantilly were the direct result of his extravagance. It is also said that he believed in reincarnation and expected to return to this earth as a horse. Whatever the truth of this may be, the new stables were his pride and joy. They were built, by the architect Jean Aubert, on an exact alignment with the window of his Grand Cabinet in the Capitainerie. When the doors at each end were open he could see from his window right through the enfilade of the stables. Two hundred and forty horses could be accommodated in this equine palace, with a staff of eighty-nine personnel to maintain them. There were sixty-nine vehicles and three packs of hounds, one for red deer, one for roe deer and one for wild boar.

The duc de Bourbon also redecorated the Capitainerie. His is the earliest interior work at Chantilly to survive. The rooms on the first floor are a blaze of white and gold in the intricate and elegant style of the Regency.

The rooms are chiefly remarkable for the paintings of Christophe Huet. In the **Chambre de Monsieur le Prince** he has left a series of canvasses in which the animals are traditional enough but the frequent occurrence of palm trees and pagodas in the background declares his taste for *chinoiserie* – a taste which is even more evident in the **Salon des Singes**, so named after the painted panels in which the chief interests of the prince – war, hunting, alchemy and architecture – are depicted with monkeys taking the place of men. This exotic decorative ensemble is known as the **Grande Singerie** to distinguish it from the **Petite Singerie**, a tiny and exquisite variation upon the same theme in the room below which is only shown to visitors who are accorded the privilege of a private tour.

Beyond the Salon des Singes the **Galerie des Batailles** renders homage, in a series of paintings by Lecomte, to the military achievements of the Grand Condé. Not all his achievements, however, were to his credit as a member of the royal family. During the uprising known as the Fronde he had taken arms against the young Louis XIV. This subject is delicately handled in a large canvas by Michel Corneille which is known as *Le Repentir*. Condé is seen declining the fanfares of Fame, while at his feet Clio, the muse of history, tears out the offending pages from her register. Before such a picture the descendants of Condé could receive their sovereigns with equanimity.

And so they did. In 1722 Louis XV stayed here on his return from his coronation at Reims. Every night the whole place was illuminated. After the hunt the *curée*, the ceremonial throwing to the hounds of the entrails and other remains of the stag, was performed by torchlight in the courtyard of the château to the accompaniment of 'very harmonious fanfares' on the hunting horns. Later at night there were fireworks, of which the most astonishing feature was a 'golden rain' which projected a vault of fire right across the main perspective of the gardens. The vast pelouse before the stables was floodlit for the soldiers and peasants to dance on. Sixty thousand bottles of wine and fifty-five thousand pounds of meat were consumed in the course of the festivities. Some of these scenes are depicted on a Sèvres vase in one of the windows of the Galerie des Batailles.

In addition to the royal family, Mansart's château could accommodate eighty guests of distinction. They were mostly lodged in the attics. 'I was astonished,' wrote the duc de Croy, 'to arrive at my rooms by way of the window. The next day I walked, full of admiration, right round the attics inside the balustrade. It is the most beautiful thing I know, and the most unusual.'

Even this accommodation, however, was considered inadequate, and later in the century the prince Louis-Joseph added the **Château d'Enghien**, a plain but pleasing row of buildings, on the opposite side of the terrace to the main entrance. It was built by the architect Le Roi in the space of four months and was 'gallantly furnished'. The duc d'Enghien, for whom these rooms were added, was kidnapped by order of Napoleon and judicially murdered in the dry moat of Vincennes on 21 March 1804.

It was a year fatal to the fortunes of Chantilly. Immediately after the fall of the Bastille the family had fled to Germany, where the prince de Condé soon found himself the rallying point of the émigrés. It is perhaps not surprising that his domain of Chantilly should have been singled out by the revolutionaries for destruction. Having served as a prison and as a barracks it was ultimately sold to speculators who realized what they could from the sale of the materials. By 1804 the whole of the Grand Château had been taken down to basement level and most of the garden pavilions had disappeared. Only the **Hameau**, a collection of seven rustic buildings designed by Le Roy in 1774, has survived intact. It was the prototype to the more famous Hameau of Marie-Antoinette at Trianon. It was amusing to the cultivated and privileged members of the Court of Chantilly to play at country life, but the sumptuous classical interior of the grange shows that they could by no means dispense with the grandeur and luxury to which they were accustomed.

It remained for Chateaubriant to write the epitaph to Chantilly. 'This Château, these gardens, these fountains "which were never silent by day or by night" – what is left of them? A few mutilated statues . . . a few carved armorial trophies upon walls that are crumbling; a few coats of arms on which the fleurs de lys have been effaced; the foundations of towers that have been pulled down; some marble horses above the empty stables which no longer resound to the neighing of the Charger of Rocroi;[1] near the Riding School, a tall gateway that was never finished. This is all that remains of a race of heroes; a testament sealed with a noose has placed their heritage in new hands.'

His last remark refers to the death of the last of the Condés, Louis-Henri-Joseph, who was found hanging from his window in the Château de Saint-Leu. He had bequeathed his vast but forlorn

[1] They never could have!

estates to an eight-year-old boy, Henri d'Orléans, duc d'Aumâle.

Had Henri d'Orléans lived at a time in which royalty was not proscribed in France, he would have been a soldier all his life. Described by the brothers Goncourt as 'the typical cavalry officer of the old school', he had won his spurs by capture of the Smalah of Abd el Kader and was well launched on a glorious military career when his father, Louis-Philippe, was turned off the throne of France and he was obliged to retire with him into exile.

Denied by his country the career to which his talent entitled him, he was also dogged by a pitiless fate in his family life, as one by one his children died before him. The death of their eldest son, the prince de Condé, so broke the Duchess's heart that she followed him to a premature grave.

The duc d'Aumâle was made of sterner stuff. Widowed, bereaved and exiled, he rose superior to his misfortunes and found the one remaining consolation open to him in his interest in books and paintings.

At Orleans House in Twickenham, and in his remote Worcestershire Manor of Woodnorton, he began to amass the collection which is now at Chantilly. In the auction rooms of Colnaghi's and Christie's and at every important sale in Europe, the Duke's agents were to be seen. When the hammer fell and the lot was adjudicated to 'His Royal Highness the duc d'Aumâle' there was often a round of applause.

By the time of his death in 1897 the duc d'Aumâle had spent seven and a half million *francs d'or* on his collections – a figure which needs to be multiplied by about forty to obtain its equivalent in modern francs. He had amassed a gallery of masterpieces which defies description. Only a visit – a long and leisurely visit – to the **Musée Condé** can reveal the amazing quality and diversity of the collection. For the serious student there is also the **Library** – 12,500 books, each one remarkable for its rarity, its origin or its binding, and 1493 manuscripts.

Outstanding among the latter are the famous **Très Riches Heures du duc de Berry**, begun in the early fifteenth century by the brothers Limbourg and completed seventy years later by Jean Colombe. It is perhaps the most fabulous of medieval illuminations, offering, in addition to its own exquisite perfection, a priceless document on the architecture and the costumes of the period. The duc d'Aumâle regarded the *Très Riches Heures* as one of the most precious gems in his collection, and when he took his guests to see the wonders of his library he would make this the *pièce de résistance*, always

272

handling the book and turning the pages himself, and wearing a special pair of white gloves for the purpose.

Hardly less important in quality are the forty miniatures from the **Book of Hours of Étienne Chevalier** by Jean Fouquet. This book was undoubtedly Fouquet's masterpiece. In all his paintings, Paul Wescher has observed, 'two traits are conspicuous: his pleasure in dramatic action and his joy in everyday life. They are like variations on a great theme: God in France, the ever present Christ and the Saints seen under a French sky, standing resolutely on French soil.' As such they would naturally have appealed to a patriot and a Catholic such as the duc d'Aumâle.

Another remarkable feature of the collection is the series of drawings by Jean and François Clouet. Often the drawing was to serve as a sketch for some larger painting, as Clouet's notes on the colouring suggest, and the artist, knowing that he might never get another sitting, concentrated his attention upon the face, combining an astonishing power of observation with a penetrating understanding of human nature. So successful were these studies in conveying the personality as well as the physiognomy of the sitter that they were sometimes ordered as actual portraits. 'It will suffice that it should be done in pencil,' wrote Catherine de Medici, ordering portraits of her family to take with her on her travels, 'in order to have it sooner.'

Catherine de Medici collected Clouets on a large scale and her private rooms were almost papered with them. In 1736 the greater part of the collection was purchased by Lord Carlisle and they adorned one of the rooms at Castle Howard until 1889, when they were bought by the duc d'Aumâle.

It had long been the dream of the duc d'Aumâle to resurrect the Grand Château upon its old foundations. On his return in 1871 he took up the project once more, but by now his needs were different. With the death of his younger son, the duc de Guise, 'it had pleased God,' as he puts it, 'to extinguish the last light of my domestic hearth.' The new building was to house his collection and not his family. He sought a new architect to create his museum, and he found the man after his own heart in Honoré Daumet.

Daumet produced a pastiche which delighted at least his own contemporaries. It has something of the monumental grandeur of Mansart's building while avoiding its monotony; it recaptures the more picturesque, indented skyline of the Montmorency château while harmonizing better with the Capitainerie.

In the interior Daumet has achieved two brilliant successes –

the elegant sweep of the **Grand Staircase** with its magnificent handrail of copper, brass and galvanized iron, and the **Chapel**. This last is basically a copy of the Chapel at Écouen, for it was built to contain the sixteenth-century woodwork and windows as well as the altar – a masterpiece of Renaissance carving from the chisel of Jean Goujon – all of which had originally stood there.

On 25 October 1886 the whole magnificent ensemble of Chantilly, the château with its immense and opulent domain and its priceless collections, was made over by the duc d'Aumâle to the Institut de France. It is worthy of remembrance that this noble act of generosity and patriotism was his response to the pettiness and ingratitude of a Republic which had just, for the second time, driven him into exile.

CHAPTER TWENTY-FIVE

The Forests of Montmorency and L'Isle-Adam

✣

In 1227 the young St Louis was present at the consecration of the abbey church at Longpont, the finest Cistercian monastery in all his kingdom. This, together with a bequest from his father, inspired him to found his own abbey at Cuimont which he now named **Royaumont**. The site fulfilled the requirements of the Order, being remote from all human habitation and abundantly supplied with water.

Although the first of these conditions no longer applies, there is still at Royaumont an atmosphere of retreat from the world – an oasis of peace in a busy and built-up area – and it still stands among rivulets of clear water which delight both eye and ear and contribute greatly to the sense of physical and spiritual refreshment the place imparts. For Royaumont, though no longer used for religious purposes, has become a *Cercle Culturel* – a centre of music and learning and art – which is at least not out of harmony with its original character. Some of the nooks and corners of its buildings are suggestive of a life of pensive erudition, only to be compared with some Fellows' Garden at Oxford or Cambridge in the old days. One can imagine the great thirteenth-century scholar Vincent de Beauvais pacing up and down here as he pondered on his vast encyclopedia, the *Speculum Majus*.

The first building the visitor comes upon, with the workshops below and the latrines above, is divided down the middle by one of the many rivulets; this served the dual function of turning a water wheel, which activated the machinery in the workshops, and of flushing the latrines.

It was in the north gallery of the cloisters that the monks assembled every Saturday after Vespers for the 'Maundy' when they washed each other's feet. St Louis was known to assist at this ceremony and in many ways to share in the life of the monks while he was in residence at Royaumont. His earliest biographer portrays him on his knees feeding a leper in the infirmary. He had his own meals in the refectory and took his turn at serving the others at table.

The **refectory** at Royaumont is one of the most satisfying achievements of the Gothic age. It was indeed fortunate that the Cistercian rule of austerity in architecture should have coincided with a style in which the beauty is almost wholly structural and only in a few details, such as capitals, ornamental. Although the Gothic was still in its early days, the builder is quite sure of his technique and has dared to rest his quadripartite vaulting upon extremely slender columns.

What the rule did not forbid was spaciousness. A hundred monks – the maximum at Royaumont – could have sat down to eat in a considerably smaller apartment. They ate in silence with one of their number reading aloud from the charming ambo contrived in the west wall. In order not to encroach upon the open spaces of the refectory, this ambo is built out and forms a projection on the west front. The kitchen, which is naturally next door, has been very much restored.

Of the **church** there are few significant remains. The foundations are marked out on the ground. The south wall abutting the cloister shows that the south aisle was lit by a row of oculi. Being a royal foundation, Royaumont had a rather greater luxuriance of decoration than was usual, including stained-glass windows which were specifically forbidden by St Bernard who 'deemed as dung' anything which attracted the eyes or delighted the senses. Within the lifetime of St Louis the General Chapter at Cîteaux condemned this deviation from austerity in the royal abbey.

It was no easy task demolishing a building of such solid workmanship; the use of explosives might have rendered the stone unfit for further use, so the pillars of the nave were sawn through as if they had been trees, chains were attached and a team of oxen used to bring down the whole edifice, except for a single pile of masonry – the staircase turret at the eastern corner of the north transept. It is enough to show both the style and the proportions of the whole church.

In 1645 Cardinal Mazarin became Abbot of Royaumont, but six years later, wishing to recompense the House of Lorraine for military services, he made prince Alphonse, a boy of twelve, abbot in his place. The boy's father, prince Henri de Lorraine, Grand Écuyer of France, took full charge of the estates. The abbatial lodgings became 'sa maison de plaisance'; the gardens were laid out with walks and alleys like a miniature Versailles. When Prince Henri died his son commissioned Coysevox to erect the magnificent monument in the part of the church that every monk had to pass on his way from the dormitory to the choir.

Already the gap between the abbey and the abbot's lodging was beginning to widen. The process was completed when, in 1781, the abbot, Le Cornut de la Balivière, pulled down the old buildings and erected a splendid new house, designed by Le Masson, which is an interesting specimen of its style but wholly inappropriate to its context. La Balivière was Royal Almoner and an assiduous courtier of the duchesse de Polignac. They were among the first to emigrate in 1789, and six years later the last Abbot of Royaumont died in destitution in Vienna having never so much as seen his abbatial palace.

In 1923 the two properties were finally separated. The conventual buildings were turned by M. Henry Gouin into the *Cercle Culturel* and the abbatial palace became the home of the Baron Fould Springer.

The little town of **Luzarches,** south-east of Royaumont, has been by-passed by the N16 and has therefore retained something of the atmosphere of its past. The oldest building of interest is probably the timbered market place or *Halle*. It was Jean de Beaumont, Seigneur de Luzarches in the early eleventh century, who brought back from Rome the relics of St Côme and St Damien. They were the patron saints of surgery, and right up to the Revolution the members of the Confrérie des Barbiers-Chirurgiens were under obligation to attend the Mass of St Côme here at Luzarches and to offer free treatment to all who presented themselves.

The church is dedicated to the two surgeon martyrs. Some of it is very old, the choir and its apse dating from the eleventh century. The lower storey of the tower is twelfth-century with a Renaissance top storey which is too big for it. The west front was built in 1551 by the architect Nicholas de Saint Michel.

Inside, the nave is of nineteenth-century rebuilding in vaguely Renaissance style, but the old choir has been beautifully restored since the war. The three apses, which offer such a quaint façade towards the cemetery, represent in their form the early twelfth century, the late twelfth century, with Romanesque vaulting, and on the south the thirteenth century.

Another three kilometres south on the N16 at Épinay is the magnificent **Château de Champlatreux.** In 1757 the President Molé, who had married a daughter of the wealthy banker Samuel Bernard, wanted a residence commensurate with his wife's fortune. He employed the architect Jean-Michel Chevotet, who designed what is usually considered to be his masterpiece.

It must be admitted, however, that Chevotet's façades are distinctly heavy. The huge mass of the imperial dome and the almost vertical lines of the mansar roofs contribute to an impression of heaviness. The garden front, with its oval projection in the centre, is more successful. It overlooks the vast perspective across the park and the bas reliefs of the three pediments tell of hunting and fishing and the pleasures of country life. The house is not open to the public.

There is nothing about the remote view of **Belloy-en-France**, a little to the west of Champlatreux, to suggest that it is worth a visit. But from nearer to it becomes apparent that the west front has unusually fine Renaissance decoration.

There has been much learned and inconclusive speculation as to who might be the architect behind the design, in which the name of Jean Bullant is mentioned without any solid backing of fact. It would be far more interesting to discover the identity of the craftsman, for it is in the execution rather than the design that its virtue resides. All of the carving is good and some of it exquisite. There is no reason why a master carver, using some book of designs such as the *Raison d'Architecture* of Diego di Sagredo, should not have produced the ensemble himself.

It is a design in which imagination, not to say fantasy, plays a greater part than classical scholarship. The author does not hesitate to invert the correct sequence of the three orders, putting the Corinthian at the bottom and the Doric at the top, where it forms a balustrade, and he has shown himself a true child of the Gothic age in the two gargoyles which leer across at each other from the opposite corners of the pediment. Although in style it belongs to the Second Renaissance, it must be previous to 1547, for the capital F and the salamander of François I are to be seen in the spandrels of the arch.

Le Mesnil-Aubry, further south on the N16, has a Renaissance church, but built in two separate campaigns. The north aisle is the oldest part of the building and bears its own date of 1531. The vaulting is complex and different in each bay.

We know, from a date in the choir, that the building was in progress in 1582. This new campaign, which was carried right through with no change of style discernible, was of the most solid and excellent workmanship. It may have been the direct result of the land having come, in 1554, into the possession of Constable Anne de Montmorency. His portrait and his escutcheon both appear in the stained-glass windows, and it is highly probable that he paid for the reconstruction of the church. The windows are very fine and can be dated between 1554 and 1562 when the boy Gabriel de Montmorency died. They resemble the windows of Écouen, now in the chapel at Chantilly. The use of blue enamel was now applied to stained glass and plays a conspicuous part in the colour scheme.

The star vaulting of the nave roof springs from the Doric pillars of the main arcade. It is a severely correct Doric except in its proportions. The builder has not hesitated to make the half columns which carry the main vaults twice the height of the others.

The family of Montmorency was one of the oldest in France – 'race héroïque et antique' of Ronsard's eulogy, they traced their ancestry at least to 950. By the sixteenth century they claimed the title of First Baron in Christendom. Anne de Montmorency had been a childhood friend of François I, under whom he rose to be Constable of France. His arrogant rudeness made him many enemies and in 1541 these procured his disgrace. But under Henri II he returned to full power and was made a duke. Among the qualifications for ducal rank the title deed mentions that he built 'deux des plus belles maisons . . . de notre royaume'. One was Chantilly and the other Écouen, now a museum of the Renaissance.

In the absence of documents, the château of Écouen is not easy to date, but the presence of the salamander among the decorative details, together with the date 1544 on the chapel, set the south and west wings within the reign of François I. The crescents on the north wing likewise attach it to the reign of Henri II, for the crescent was the emblem of Diana and so of Diane de Poitiers.

The big porticos or frontispieces are of self-evidently later workmanship. They do not tie in properly with their façades and they are top-heavy. Beneath their massive arches and colonnades the little entrance doorways look absurdly out of scale. The portico on the south side of the courtyard has the importance of being the first known use of the colossal order in France.

These frontispieces, together with the outward face of the north wing, are attributed to Jean Bullant, who was in Montmorency's service from 1556 and lived at Écouen.

The dividing up of the façades into a large grid by means of flat pilasters, with no capitals, crossed by string courses between each storey, seems to have been copied from Nantouillet. But the most striking innovation is the use of square pavilions at the corners. This is almost certainly derived from the Villa Poggio-Reale at Naples. But what is most important about Écouen is its extreme simplicity. The west front could even be called severe. The great windows are cut into the stonework with no ornament; the panels of the façade that have no windows are left plain; the bands between the double string courses are devoid of roundels. Only the dormer windows and chimneys are allowed any decoration and these are obviously copied from originals in the Loire Valley.

More important than the architecture was the sculpture. Two statues of *Prisoners in Chains* by Michelangelo occupied the niches under the south portico. They ultimately found their way to the Château de Richelieu. The chapel boasted an altar by Jean Goujon – now at Chantilly – and a *Pietà* by Rosso – now at the Louvre. The chimney-piece of the Salle d'Honneur enframed a *Winged Victory* by Jean Goujon which is still in place.

The **Salle d'Honneur** is a magnificent room which has fortunately preserved much of its original character. The floor is paved with porcelain tiles from Rouen; the fireplace is a mosaic of coloured marbles; the window recesses retain vestiges of painting. One can conjure up an image of rich and varied colouring which the room must have presented.

A few other mantelpieces, with their paintings, have survived; but most of the château was drastically altered by Napoleon to become a school for the daughters of the Légion d'Honneur. Madame Campan, the sister of one of Marie-Antoinette's ladies in waiting who wrote invaluable memoirs of the period, became the *Directrice*. She gives a delightful account of an unexpected visit by Napoleon on 3 March 1809. The outriders of the Imperial equipage were already on the gravel before anyone knew that the Emperor was coming. Two orders from the *Directrice* were all that were needed: '*En classe et les Dames à leur poste!*' A few minutes later the carriages rolled into the courtyard and the visitation began.

Napoleon was at his best on these occasions. He was not looking for faults but seeking to give encouragement. He picked out girls not distinguished by their looks and asked them questions so simple that they were certain to have the pleasure of giving him the right answers. Finally he asked what the fare was in the refectory on feast days. He was informed that tarts or creams were served to mark the occasion. '*Eh bien!*' he concluded; '*dimanche, en réjouissance de ma visite, faites-leur donner des tartes et des crêmes!*'

After the fall of the Empire Écouen reverted to the Condé family and thence to the duc d'Aumâle. He took most of the ornaments of the chapel for his new building of Chantilly.

The **Chapel** at Écouen was built in the 1540s. It is nevertheless true to Gothic methods of construction, with a rather complex ribbed vaulting. But it has been observed that the profiles of the ribs are those of a classical architrave. The vault is richly painted, chiefly with the armorials of the family in which we can read the motto ἀπλανος (*aplanos*). This could mean anything from 'unerring', 'immovable' to 'straightforward'.

The town of **Montmorency** is chiefly famous for having housed Rousseau while he was writing *La Nouvelle Héloïse, Émile* and the *Contrat Social.* In 1756 Mme d'Épinay had done up a small garden building in her park which she called the Hermitage. '*Mon ours,*' she said to him; '*voilà votre asile!*' On 9 April he took up residence. It was just the moment at which the countryside began to come alive; the violets and primroses were already peeping through the snow; '*la nuit même de mon arrivée fut marquée par le premier chant du rossignol*'. The open country enchanted, intoxicated him; '*je comptais bien que la forêt de Montmorency serait désormais mon cabinet de travail*'. By the end of the following year he had broken with Mme d'Épinay. He installed himself not far off in a house called Le Montlouis in what is now the rue Jean-Jacques Rousseau – for while the Hermitage was wantonly destroyed, **Montlouis** survives and has been turned into an excellent little museum. His bedroom still preserves the form which he gave to it; the kitchen is as it was when Thérèse Levasseur and her mother worked in it; the table on which the great philosopher wrote is there and the candlesticks in glass funnels which he used when he worked in the open air. At the end of the terrace is the little garden house which he called the '*donjon*' where he delighted to work, sometimes having, as he put it, 'no fire but the fire in my heart'.

Another interesting building is the **Auberge du Cheval Blanc** in the rue de Pontoise, which was a popular meeting place in the eighteenth and nineteenth centuries. It still has its sign, painted by Isabey on one side and by Gérard on the other by way of settlement of their bill.

The most interesting building at Montmorency is the church, or rather the **Collégiale St Martin,** for it was not built to serve as a parish church but as a mausoleum – 'the St Denis of the Montmorency family'.

The late Flamboyant was not the happiest of styles. From outside one can see at a glance, from the huge, unbroken slope of roof, that there are no clerestory windows and that the nave must needs be dark from want of them. From the inside this lack of clerestory makes the nave not only dark but heavy, the complex lierne and tierceron vaulting being too low over our heads.

During the Revolution a commission arrived to accomplish the 'suppression of marks of feudalism'. It resulted in the removal of enough armorial brasses and bronze for the casting of two cannons.

In the late nineteenth century the church needed much restoration. The architect Lucien Magne gave it an entirely new west façade. He also built the tower, which is elegant and matches well with the rest. He has delicately re-introduced the 'marks of feudalism' in the ducal coronet beneath the cross on the topmost pinnacle.

The family tombs were removed during the Revolution, and the recumbent figures of Anne in full armour and his wife Madeleine can be seen in the Louvre. It was, however, essentially in the stained-glass windows that the family was commemorated, and fortunately these have survived.

With the exception of the east window, which is allowed to be purely religious in its imagery, the subject matter is the Montmorency family and its collaterals, cousins and sisters and aunts together with their husbands and such characters from Scripture and hagiography as shared their Christian names.

The twelve windows of the choir and apse were made between 1524 and 1545 and conform in general to the medieval concept of stained glass. One of the principles of translucence is that if a piece of glass is surrounded with a dark frame, such as the leads provide, it yields its full colour and luminosity; if it is juxtaposed with white or colourless glass, the surrounding light takes away from the colour and the luminosity. This principle was still observed in the early Renaissance, as in the choir at Montmorency. But the two windows which face each other at the beginning of the nave – representing the Constable and his wife and dated 1563 – already depart from it. In the latter the leads almost form a grid with little or no relation to the shapes of the composition.

This change of style was the result of the increasing use of enamel. This procedure virtually amounts to painting the colours on to a plain glass. As several colours can be laid on to the same piece it is no longer necessary to separate them by a lead.

With this new technique came a tendency to be fully pictorial, with architectural perspectives and distant landscapes. It is a matter of taste, but it can be strongly argued that a window fulfils its function best as part of the decoration of the church when its subject matter is confined to one plane. In pursuit of their pictorial effect Renaissance glaziers often ignored the mullions of the tracery and spread their composition right across the window.

Among the earlier windows of the choir the one presented by Charles Villiers de l'Isle-Adam is of outstanding quality. He was

Bishop of Beauvais and was naturally led to employing Engrand Leprince, whose beautiful windows at Beauvais, Rouen and Gisors have earned him a just reputation as the greatest of glaziers of the French Renaissance.

A little to the east of Montmorency is **Groslay**. Although it is only thirteen kilometres from the Boulevard Périférique, it has retained much of the character of a country village. It is the centre of a large fruit growing area and should be visited in blossom time. The church of St Martin is one more of the whole series of churches built or enlarged by Anne de Montmorency. To a twelfth-century structure which had been much restored in 1460 the Constable added a new choir and north aisle. This latter bears the date 1532 on one of the buttresses. As usual his additions included a set of stained windows, of which the legend of Ste Barbe and the Tree of Jesse are outstanding.

At **Taverny**, on the western margin of the Montmorency Forest, is yet another church of the Montmorency family, who once possessed here yet another château. The church is of early thirteenth-century date and stands up magnificently against the high wooded slopes behind. It creates first and foremost an impression of sturdy solidity. In spite of this, it needed much restoration in the nineteenth century particularly to the south and west fronts. But the north façade of the nave is original and very fine. The old aisle roof is of brown tiles, which need a fairly steep slope to throw off the water, which in turn entails a tall triforium on the inside. The east end also has escaped the heavy hand of the restorer.

The interior is a fine example of the early Gothic executed in a lovely stone. Although the clerestory windows are of obviously Flamboyant design, they harmonize well with the earlier parts. There is a certain robustness about their tracery which accords well with the prevailing atmosphere of strength and simplicity. An attractive feature is formed by the little chapels on the east wall of the transepts, each one exactly in line with its corresponding nave aisle so as to form an admirable climax to its perspective.

The apse, magnificently framed by the great piers of the crossing, is closed by a Renaissance screen which partially obscures the windows. Since the stained glass is without merit this does not detract from the beauty of the building. The screen itself, which was erected by order of the Constable Anne in the reign of Henri II, is very good of its sort. The figure of the Virgin is modern and the statues in the niches either side of the altar are importations, but the four Evangelists are original. The altar frontal is also remarkable;

it is decorated with embroidery studded with pearls dating from the reign of Louis XIII.

The church has some interesting furniture. Among the tombstones there is a fine one to Mathieu de Montmorency who died in 1360. The organ case is a splendid piece of Renaissance work incorporating thirteen carved panels depicting the life and death of St Bartholomew. The series apparently overflows on to the churchwarden's seat, where the fourteenth scene can be admired at closer range.

From Taverny we can travel north via Villiers-Adam on an attractive *route forestière* to **L'Isle-Adam**. The town takes its name from Adam de Villiers who built here in 1014 a fortress on the second island commanding the important waterway of the river Oise. It was replaced in the eighteenth century by a new mansion for the prince de Conti. Louis-François de Bourbon-Conti was one of the more attractive figures of the age. Described by Rousseau as 'a great prince of much learning and wit' he refused to pay court to Madame de Pompadour. Louis XV ordered him to say *something* to her, so he sat on her bed and exclaimed '*tiens, vous avez un bien bon lit pour une femme comme vous!*' His expulsion from Versailles was predictably immediate and he set up his own court at L'Isle-Adam.

Madame de Genlis records how every lady invited had a carriage and horses placed at her disposal and liberty to invite her own circle of friends to dine privately in her own apartments. The most enlightened of men, the prince de Conti liked to pretend to be a despot. Once, when a poacher was brought before him he decreed in a loud voice 'one hundred strokes with the cane and three months' solitary confinement!' But when Mme de Genlis enquired of the steward how the wretched man was faring, she learnt that his real sentence had been three months' banishment from the estate, during which the prince saw to it that his family was well provided for.

The Conti château, confined to its narrow emplacement, had length and height but little depth. The painting of it by Olivier at Versailles shows the *bat l'eau* – a stag being driven into the water, immediately in front of the rather gaunt-looking building. Nothing is left of it but some of the balustrading round the island.

The **church** at L'Isle-Adam, like so many of the Montmorency churches, is dedicated to St Martin. The west front, attributed without proof to Jean Bullant, is an excellent example of a Gothic *portail* translated into Renaissance terms. The archivolt over the main door contains a half circle of carved figures representing the

Virtues and Vices. The porch was damaged during a bombardment in 1940 and most of the figures are modern.

Inside, the same style prevails. The nave pillars are simple cylinders with capitals which are in fact cornices, with triglyphs and rosettes forming a ring round each. Owing to the very high and ridiculously small clerestory windows, the nave is rather dark – a defect not uncommon in Renaissance churches. The quadripartite vaulting of the nave gives place to complex lierne and tierceron in the chancel and sanctuary, which bears the date 1499 – when the church was consecrated – and the arms of Montmorency.

The furnishings of the church amount almost to a collection; the sixteenth-century stalls, with their misericords representing the everyday professions – the baker and the barber, together with a sow and Aristotle – come from Bordeaux. The pulpit, which is dated 1560, is of German origin. It is an elaborate structure of wood, mostly inlaid but sometimes painted to resemble inlay, brightly gilded. The pillar behind it is covered with Spanish leather.

A little to the north, on the road to Beaumont, is the pagoda or *Pavillon Chinois* of **Cassan**. In 1778 the domain was bought by a M. Bergeret, who went, a few years later, to Italy with Fragonard. It was from Fragonard's design that the pagoda was built. The estate of Cassan is mentioned by Balzac in *La Physiologie du Mariage*. He stayed here with his friend Villiers La Faye, to whom he exclaimed '*L'Isle-Adam est mon paradis terrestre*'.

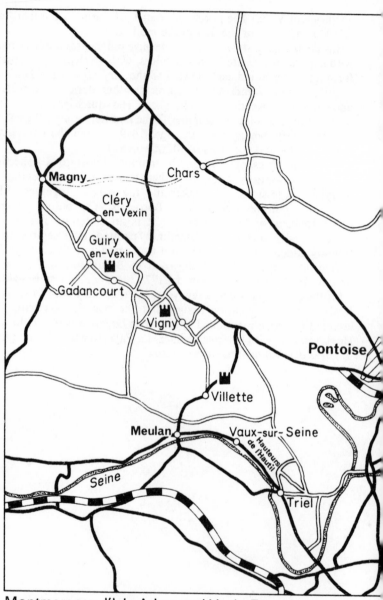

Montmorency, l'Isle Adam and Vexin Français

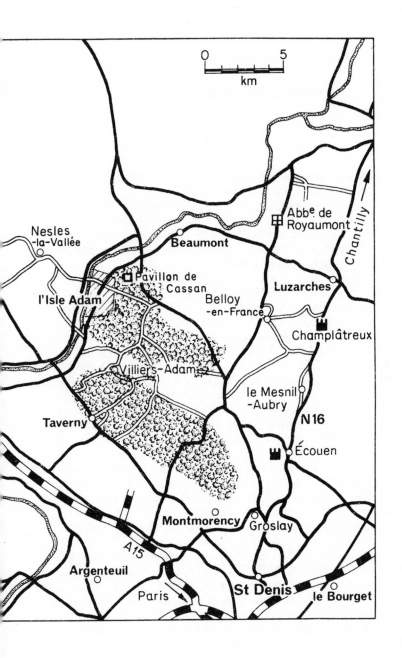

0   5
km

Nesles
-la-Vallée

Beaumont

Abbé de
Royaumont

Pavillon de
Cassan

l'Isle Adam

Belloy
-en-France

Luzarches

Chantilly

Champlâtreux

Villiers-Adam

le Mesnil
-Aubry

Taverny

N 16

Écouen

Montmorency

Groslay

A 15

Argenteuil

Paris

St Denis

le Bourget

CHAPTER TWENTY-SIX

Pontoise and the Vexin Français

❧

Pontoise was once a stronghold of considerable importance guarding
the approaches to Paris from Vexin Français. A seventeenth-
century engraving by Chastillon shows a walled city dominated by a
high escarpment which supports a large and formidable castle.
The latter has disappeared completely, but Pontoise retains from the
days of its importance two spacious churches and a museum in
what was once an episcopal palace.

The church of Notre Dame, at the foot of the hill, is of little
interest, but the **Church of St Maclou**, up in an attractive old square,
the Place du Grand Martroy, is a magnificent building which has
only since 1966 been accorded the dignity of a cathedral.

It is worth having the successive campaigns of construction
clearly in mind before beginning to inspect. The primitive church
was started in 1140, just late enough for its builders to have profited
from the experience of those at St Denis. The apse, with its radiating
chapels, and portions of the transept survive from this period.

In 1435 it was decided to enlarge the church. The west front was
pushed out some twelve metres and two more bays added to the
nave and aisles. The centre of the west front and the second bay
on the north side of the nave are all that remain today.

In 1525 the north aisle was pulled down and replaced by a double
aisle in early Renaissance idiom.

In 1560 Lemercier took down the twelfth-century nave and south
aisle, replacing them with the buildings which we see today. St
Maclou, therefore, is a composite structure of early Gothic, Flamboyant, early and late Renaissance work.

With this in mind it is easy to make sense of the main west front.
The central portion, with the tower and gable, represents the
Flamboyant. Left of this there now projects the west end of the
second north aisle with pilasters reminiscent of Chambord and a
delightful little niche cut into the corner, while to the right the
original west end of the south aisle has been rebuilt in the more
classical style of the late Renaissance.

Château de Villarceaux: the Tour de Ninon

Notre-Dame de Mantes

Inside one is immediately impressed by the mere size of the building, though it has to be said that the clerestory windows are disproportionately small compared with the massive solidity of the nave arcade, which could easily have supported a far loftier structure. The double north aisle is a tremendous achievement, the sturdy cylindrical pillars with their highly fanciful capitals producing an effect not unlike the thirteenth-century formula of Notre Dame. The south side of the church, as we would expect from its later date, adheres more correctly to the classical orders. The south aisle opens into a series of ever-wider chapels to correct the oblique angle at which the south wall was built – presumably because of a site restriction necessitated by the road. The object was clearly to try to balance the double aisles on the north.

The old transepts have been largely swallowed up in these new buildings, but the crossing forms the most dramatic juxtaposition of styles in the whole building. The two western piers are immense drums with the largest Corinthian capitals that would be possible in such a space. The woodwork here is on a monumental scale also, including two curious balustraded tribunes upheld by massive consoles. All this serves to build up the strongest contrast with the perfectly lovely Gothic arch to the east of the crossing. The oldest part of the church, this arch looks as if it had been built yesterday; and its chaste and elegant architecture frames the view into the primitive sanctuary. Between the old and the new arch is a fine canopy of lierne and tierceron vaulting.

This ancient sanctuary is brought into sparkling life by the brilliant colours of Max Ingrand's modern glass, which provides a striking and obviously deliberate contrast with the dirty colours of the *grisaille* in the lower windows.

Besides its architecture, the church of St Maclou has many furnishings of distinction. Most of the woodwork is good – the organ loft (1716), the pulpit (1653) and the churchwarden's seat with panels of Renaissance sculpture. There is some good eighteenth-century glass in some of the north aisle windows and more in the Chapelle de la Passion at the west end next to the tower. Here is a magnificent Holy Sepulchre. The figures of the Entombment date from 1550, but the wooden group above, representing the Resurrection, is of eighteenth-century workmanship.

East and a little north of St Maclou is the **Musée Tavet-Delacour**, housed in the delightful **Hôtel d'Estouteville**, built in 1477 by Cardinal Guillaume d'Estouteville, Archbishop of Rouen, who had also left his mark on the Château de Gaillon. It contains some rare manuscripts and some letters from Voltaire as well as the jawbone of Dagobert and one of Catherine de Medici's legs.

Some fifteen kilometres north-east of Pontoise we come to **Nesles-la-Vallée**.

The first and most obvious feature of the church at Nesles is its tower. There is internal evidence that the tower was once free-standing and that therefore the present church was built on to it. It is an unusual position in which to site a single tower. Twin towers to either side of the choir were more common.

The tower can be dated from its style in the early twelfth century; the rest of the church from the end of the twelfth and beginning of the thirteenth centuries. It was just the time when the great cathedrals of Laon and Notre Dame were making their influence felt throughout the region and little villages, which during the Romanesque period had developed their own style distinct from that of the cathedrals, began to reproduce on a small scale an architecture which was evolved to cover vast areas.

The first feature which a perceptive eye will notice at Nesles is that whereas it has sexpartite vaulting, it is not built *pile forte – pile faible*. There simply would not be room for the intermediary column, the *pile faible*; the church is too small for this formula. Instead, the intermediary vault comes to the platform of the triforium immediately above the point of each of the nave arches. Since there was already abundant precedent for covering areas of this size and greater with a quadripartite vault, there is no justification for this arrangement. The builder is obviously trying to copy Laon or Notre Dame.

An even more perceptive eye will detect the existence of a sexpartite vault from outside by the alternation of thick and thin buttresses on the exterior wall. These buttresses were not really adequate. One might regard Nesles as an illustration of the problem which led to the development of the flying buttress. The builder has done his best to balance the thrusts, but the nave vaults are ominously flattened and the iron tie rods which had to be inserted are probably the chief reason why this roof has not collapsed.

The pews are very attractive, with their neat little balustrades behind, and at the end of each row is a *strapontin* which pulls out to provide one more seat in case of need.

A steep and winding minor road takes us west from Nesles to the main Pontoise-Gisors road and **Chars**, where the **Church of Saint-Sulpice** is one of the most important in the area. Of the original early twelfth-century structure there survives the west front, the nave and its aisles. There was at first, as so often, only a wooden ceiling and it was not until 1160 that the nave received its vault. The nave, with tiny clerestory windows, no tribune and no triforium, is very dark, a defect which is not much helped by the set of modern *grisaille* glass.

Unfortunately the centre part of the church collapsed and had to be rebuilt in the sixteenth century, with the result that the symmetry has been upset. But the choir with its apse is still almost exactly as it was at the end of the twelfth century.

It is one of the greatest architectural successes in the region, dramatically conceived and boldly executed. The master builder was clearly determined to achieve a maximum impression of height. The narrowness of the nave gave him an initial advantage, for narrowness adds to the illusion of height, but he has missed no opportunity of increasing it. At every level he has introduced some means of superelevation. In the main arcade he has placed his pillars very close to each other and raised slender, heightened arches above them, almost prefiguring the proportions of Beauvais Cathedral. The round arches of the triforium, large in themselves, are placed within a taller containing arch pierced with an oculus. Above, in order to raise the wall even higher, he has set a row of cusped roundels. His façade has already doubled the height of the main arcade before it reaches the clerestory windows. Through these successive storeys of decoration, the clustered shafts rise steadily to the topmost cornice, where each receives the thrust of its corresponding vault rib. It is astonishing to find, in so insignificant a little place, such an important architectural achievement and a builder sufficiently 'at home' in the new style to carry off this *tour de force*.

From outside the church it is possible to infer something of these interior dispositions from the extra height of the choir roof and the sturdy flying buttresses needed to uphold it. After the collapse of the original tower, a new and stronger one was built between 1562 and 1576. Like so much work of this sort in the region, it is attributed to Nicolas Lemercier.

The entrance to the original walled town of **Magny-en-Vexin**, due west of Chars, is marked by two Gargantuan gate piers which mark the site of the former Porte de Paris. By following the boulevards right and left one would be able to retrace the original line of fortification.

Magny is chiefly famous for its church, the château of the Villeroy family having disappeared long ago. The English burnt the church in 1436 and it was not until 1500 that the present building was started. Only the old west gable and the belfry were incorporated in the new church.

It seems that Gisors was the architectural centre of Vexin at this period. The first architect in charge of the reconstruction, Guillaume le Maître, came from Gisors; so did his successor the more famous Jean Grappin, to whom the south façade is due. The south porch is dated 1548. It still follows the medieval schema, having statues right round the archivolt. The statues have disappeared, but their little stands remain.

The interior is not in itself remarkable except for the tall, slender round-arched windows of the apse which have great dignity and charm. But some of the furnishings are important.

In the south transept are three marble statues of Nicolas III de Neufville, his son, also Nicolas, and the latter's wife, Madeleine d'Aubespine. A typical daughter of the Renaissance, Madeleine was the author of a book of poems and a translation of Ovid. Before the Revolution these statues were all housed in a special mausoleum.

But the most important feature of St Martin de Magny is the baptistery with its domed canopy upheld by a circular arcade – like an ornate Renaissance gazebo. Each pillar bears three statuettes, each standing beneath a delicate little canopy. It was built in 1534 but was completely dismantled in the Revolution to preserve it from vandalism. In 1808 it was re-erected. The altar was rebuilt from the remains of the mausoleum and on it stands an alabaster figure of the Virgin and Child dating from the fourteenth century and originating from St Denis.

On the road back to Pontoise from Magny is the little village of **Cléry-en-Vexin**, with a church which owes its origin to the pious foundation of seventeen religious edifices by the Crusader Galeran, comte de Meulan. There is, however, no vestige of a church of that date above ground. The choir and transepts are early thirteenth-century and the nave and aisles sixteenth-century – in other words the last period of the Gothic into which some of the ornaments of the Renaissance have already been incorporated.

The west porch above all commands attention. The builders of the Flamboyant period were more interested in decoration than in construction, and all the ornament of this little village church is concentrated on its porch.

At **Guiry**, south of Cléry, there is a handsome château of late-seventeenth-century date. It is persistently attributed to J.-H. Mansart but in no way resembles his other buildings. The central attic storey with three windows divided by niches with statues, all contained beneath a large segmental pediment, is a most unusual feature. To either side of this the dormer windows, each framed between little Ionic pilasters and carrying a triangular pediment, seem to reflect the late Renaissance. Beneath the mansard roof the façades are extremely simple, the balance being maintained by the survival – or restoration – of the original multiple glazing bars.

The **Church of St Nicolas** is a solid piece of early-sixteenth-century work with some survivals of the older fourteenth-century church in the north transept. The greater part of the building was carried out between 1519 and 1558. The west portal, deeply recessed beneath a round containing arch, is attributed to Jean Grappin.

There was a Gallo-Roman villa at Guiry, the discovery of which stimulated an enlightened mayor to devote part of the *mairie* to a **museum**, which is very well arranged and would provide a good starting point for a study of the archaeology of the region.

A pretty road leads south-east to the village of **Gadancourt**, attractively situated on a wooded slope with all its approach roads shaded by avenues. The church belonged originally to a priory founded by Agnès de Montfort and built in the mid-twelfth century. It is a sturdy little building with a squat Romanesque tower supporting a stone spire. The château, a plain structure of the mid-seventeenth century, replaces an earlier *manoir*.

The **Château de Vigny** was built by the Cardinal Georges d'Amboise, who was in many respects for France what Wolsey was for England, but unlike Wolsey he came from a noble family. They were great builders, whose main seat was Chaumont on the Loire. At the beginning of the sixteenth century Charles d'Amboise started Meillant in Berry. At the same time Georges d'Amboise se to work on his archiepiscopal palace at Gaillon and here at Vigny.

The building cannot have been begun earlier than 1504 when he purchased the estate. It may be conjectured that it was substantially finished by 1508, for it was at this date that Georges d'Amboise started 'italianizing' at Gaillon. There is no italianizing at Vigny so it is reasonable to suppose that it was finished too early for the new craze to have affected it. Vigny thus stands in the main tradition of the châteaux of the Loire before the Renaissance began to influence the style.

An unusual feature of the entrance front is the exact symmetry of the gatehouse. This was usually upset by the inclusion of a small wicket gate alongside the main archway. It is noticeable also that the towers are treated in a different manner from the façades. In the latter the topmost windows cut through the eaves and rise to half the height of the roof, thus having the decorative effect of dormers. It is a device which does much to alleviate the façades. In the same way the severe lines of the pepper-pot roof were often broken at this period by chimneys and dormers, which greatly added to the picturesque effect. If the towers at Vigny look like candles with their extinguishers still crammed down on top, it is because the architect has not applied to them the same aesthetic principles which he has used so happily in the intervening wall spaces.

The chapel to the right of the entrance front is a nineteenth-century addition, for when the comte Vitali bought the estate in 1867 he undertook a large work of restoration and made several additions to the structure.

On the other side of the building the alterations are more obvious and fundamental. Vitali has thrown open the courtyard and built a new *donjon* in the style of François I. It is difficult not to believe that some of the decoration of the upper storeys is not the fanciful addition of an over-romantic imagination.

From Vigny the valley of the Aubette runs south to join the Seine at Meulan. Although so close to Paris it is still deep in the country. In place of the littered outbuildings of suburbia there are compact villages that form entities distinct from the fields around. New buildings are mostly of high quality and seem to belong to some coherent plan.

In one of the most attractive parts of the valley is one of the most delightful of the châteaux of Vexin Français – the **Château de Villette**. Its entrance lodges are right on the little road to the east of the valley, and framed between the gate piers, which are linked overhead with an elegant canopy of wrought iron, is the entrance front, a smaller, simpler version of Champs that is all charm and no ostentation.

Built in 1667 for the comte d'Auffay, it was remodelled in 1696, in all probability by J.-H. Mansart, and soon acquired the name of 'Petit Marly'. To appreciate this courtesy title one needs to take a little track which doubles back up the hillside opposite the entrance gates. Here, where a broken balustrade marks what seem to have been the architectural extremities of the lay-out, one can look down on to the château and see the broad avenue that stretched up behind it on the contrary slope to an obelisk which marks the opposite extremity. Where this slope comes down into the gardens, there is an elaborate cascade which reflects the general dispositions of Mansart's *Rivière* at Marly. The garden front breaks forward into a large, triple-faceted projection which affords to the windows of the Salon all-round views of the parterres and fountains.

Just before the Revolution this was the home of Sophie de Grouchy, sister of the Maréchal de Grouchy and wife of the marquis de Condorcet – a man ennobled by Voltaire with the title of '*l'homme le plus nécessaire à la France*'.

For a few years Villette represented at its best all that the ideal of the country house has ever stood for. André Chénier, Beaumarchais, Benjamin Franklin, Madame de Staël, Turgot and d'Alembert were frequent visitors and in the delightful alleys of the garden would talk of liberty and equality and the rights of man. The ugly turn which the Revolution was to take was never foreseen. The gilded youth of France 'walked on a carpet of flowers which covered an abyss'. Condorcet, fiercely critical of the September Massacres, had to take poison to escape the guillotine, and when the fall of Robespierre brought relative security, his widow sadly reunited at Villette the survivors of the shipwreck.

The present owner, M. Robert Gérard, has magnificently restored the château and gardens to their pristine shape and splendour.

At **Vaux-sur-Seine** there is a château which occupies a superb position with extensive views over the Seine Valley. Built in the reign of Louis XI by Olivier le Daim, it has been so heavily restored as to have lost almost all its original character. Its chief interest is that it was the home of the duc de Saint-Simon's father.

The **Church of St Pierre-ès-Liens** (St Peter ad vincula) has a certain rugged, almost rough-hewn grandeur about it. The choir and transepts, together with the rather squat tower, date from the twelfth century, but the tall windows of the apse are later, probably fourteenth-century, insertions. Embedded in the south wall are the pillars of the nave arcade, showing that there was once here a side aisle. The whole building was heavily restored and modified in the sixteenth century.

There is some colourful and effective modern glass in the central windows of the apse, dated 1961 and signed by J.-J. Borghet. In the centre, illustrating the dedication of the church, is St Peter being delivered from his chains and on his right is Ste Barbe, whose modern function is the protective care of miners.

From Vaux a charming little road climbs the hillside to join the N322 along the **Hauteurs d'Hautil**, from which a turning right descends again to **Triel**, where there is one of the most unusual churches in the district.

The original building of the thirteenth century consisted only of a nave of four bays with side aisles, two rather narrow transepts and a further two bays of choir. In the fifteenth century a large chapel was added to the north of the choir. In 1550 the accommodation was still deemed insufficient and a new choir was added of far more generous proportions. As the route d'Hautil crossed in front of the old east end, the new choir had to bridge the road. The extra elevation thus acquired left room for a crypt beneath.

The shape of the new choir is somewhat peculiar – a polygonal ambulatory set in a square east end, leaving curious triangular chapels at the corners. This choir contains a remarkable series of windows dating from 1520–57, attributed from their excellence to Jean Leprince. One of them represents the story of the Cock of Santo Domingo. The legend is worth relating.

A pilgrim to Compostela attracted the amorous interest of a young lady. Unable to obtain any satisfaction from him, she hid money in his boots, accused him of theft and had him hanged. Some time later his father recognized the body on the gallows, which then proceeded to explain to him the circumstances of his conviction. The father related the improbable story to the notary, who was eating a roast fowl at the time. The notary declared that he would not believe the tale unless his roast bird came to life. No sooner had he spoken the words when his cock sprouted feathers and leapt from the table.

CHAPTER TWENTY-SEVEN

The Epte Valley

꙳

The valley of the Epte is a countryside of unsensational charm. Sometimes the high wooded slopes on the Normandy bank almost overhang the river, as at **Baudemont**, opposite Bray-Lû. Further upstream towards Gisors the hills draw back from the river and the country becomes more open, leaving a broad strath through which the river meanders, the lines of pollard willows alternating with great *massifs* of poplar which provide shelter and shade for the cattle. Pretty villages with delightful churches punctuate the roads on either side. The unhurried labours of the farm accentuate the note of rural peace. Here and there the remains of a castle raise their silhouette against the sky, but their ancient, crumbling walls have long been assimilated into the peace of the countryside. It is difficult to remember that this was once the most bloodstained frontier of France.

The names of the villages were then the titles of the men of war, Osmond de Chaumont, Gilbert de Boury, Enguerrand de Trie and Baudoin de Bray, who fortified their seigneuries against the Norman invader, for since 911 the Treaty of St Clair, a verbal agreement between Charles le Simple of France and Rollon of Normandy, decreed that this valley should divide their dynasties.

On the Norman side there is Baudemont, a somewhat formless ruin which commands, as so often a fortress did command, a magnificent view. Then, a little further upstream is **Château-sur-Epte** – and it is well worth the slight detour from the main road up to the castle. It consists of a large, roughly circular *enceinte*, now entirely occupied by rather ramshackle farm buildings. Among them is a fine cylindrical dovecot. To the right of the entrance is the keep on its mound, sitting astride the curtain wall. It is thought to be the first circular keep in France and is known to have been built by Robert de Bellême for William Rufus in 1087. It is remarkable that the curtain wall has no towers to protect it; the art of fortification was still in infancy.

At **Dangu** the château continued to play an important role during the Hundred Years' War, but was demolished in 1560. The church, with its tall slate spire, is a striking and in many ways interesting edifice. The west door still boasts some beautiful Flamboyant decoration which is very deeply undercut – what the French call *'fouillé'* – the whole protected by a later porch in the Doric order. The Renaissance features to this otherwise Gothic church are due to the widespread influence of Anne de Montmorency, the portrait of one of whose sons is to be seen in the *grisaille* window in the family chapel.

A little north of Dangu is **Neaufles**, another round keep on the top of an artificial mound which is probably later than Château-sur-Epte for its walls are thirty centimetres thicker. A study of the stone keeps built during the eleventh century shows a steady increase in the thickness of the walls. This led to the replacement of ladders by stone staircases contrived within the thickness of the wall. Communications between floors were complex in order to baffle the invader.

But the most important of all the Norman castles on the Epte is fortunately the best preserved – the **Château de Gisors**. In 1097, according to Orderic Vital, William Rufus ordered the construction of a fortress here. Chaumont, Trie-Château and Boury-en-Vexin formed an offensive concentration to which Neaufles was an inadequate answer. The King was on his way to the Holy Land and left the choice of site and the design of the fabric to Robert de Bellême – *'ingeniosus artifex'*.

Robert de Bellême constructed a mound some eighteen metres high with a circular curtain wall round the summit in which his keep was placed eccentrically to the north. As at Château-sur-Epte there were no towers – the staircase tower is a fourteenth-century addition. In the construction of his walls he follows Vitruvius by embedding a number of heavy wooden beams into the rubble by way of reinforcement. He was interested only in the passive strength of the walls and the difficulty of access to the keep. This he achieved by a narrow vaulted passage, at the junction of the keep and the curtain wall, which formed a death trap into which the attackers might well have been reluctant to penetrate one at a time.

In 1223 Henry I added to this an outer bailey with a radius of about a hundred metres. It had three gates, two towards the town and one, the Porte des Champs, towards the north, and it was set about with square towers open on the inside. This was an important new idea. The chronicler Robert de Torigny claims that Henry 'rendered it impregnable by lofty towers [*turribus excelsis inexpugnabile reddidit*]'. François Gébelin takes the term *'excelsis'* as meaning a tower that rose high above the curtain wall and covered it with its fire.

To this basic design Henry II made a number of significant improvements. An inspection of the keep will reveal that the lower part of the walls is of rough masonry but the upper parts of well-cut freestone. The latter represents Henry II's additions – and the increased height necessitated the support of buttresses. He also reorientated the keep, making the main entrance through a large archway on the south side. Within the curtain wall he built, in penitent mood, a chapel dedicated to St Thomas à Becket. He also increased the effectiveness of the outer curtain wall, building a round tower, the Tour du Diable, to protect the Porte des Champs, and altering the square towers of the west wall so they were either rounded or triangular in shape. This was more likely to deflect the projectiles that were fired against them. Another chronicler records how Philippe-Auguste, at the age of twelve, took part in a colloquy with Henry II and how his companions were lost in admiration of the new look at Gisors.

Philippe-Auguste in his turn, profiting by the imprisonment of Richard Coeur de Lion in Dürnstein, possessed himself of Gisors and made the last important additions – certain improvements to the south gate known as the Tour du Gouverneur, and the building of the massive round keep known as the Tour du Prisonnier. The graffiti on the walls of the lowest chamber fully justify the name of the tower. It is a design of great clarity and simplicity and strategically placed at the point where the town wall joined that of the château. Like all towers built by Philippe-Auguste it is of excellent masonry, with stone vaults to the chambers which could only be approached from the outside at third-floor level.

A last addition was made in the sixteenth century when the progress in artillery made further precautions essential. The lower part of the outer wall, from the Porte de Ville to the Porte des Champs, was protected by an outer earthwork behind which was a gallery, pierced with frequent arrow slits which formed a *chemin de ronde* at ground level.

The Château of Gisors continued to play a role in the defence of Vexin Français until the reign of Henry IV, since when it has been abandoned.

The **Church of St Gervais and St Protais** at Gisors is of almost unique interest. Not only does the fabric include excellent examples of most of the styles between the thirteenth and sixteenth centuries, but it is also unusually well documented. It is possible to put accurate dates to most of its members and to state the names of the chief workmen concerned. It is worth summarizing the main phases of building.

The choir and aisles, built by Blanche de Castille, were dedicated in 1249. From 1487–1507 the choir and aisles were surrounded on three sides by new chapels. Robert Jumel, Pierre Gosse and Guillaume le Maître were named as *maîtres d'oeuvre*.

In 1515 the transepts were built, starting with the south porch, carved by Robert Grappin, and ending with the north porch in 1523. In 1521 Grappin took over as *Maître Maçon*.

In 1528 experts were assembled from Beauvais and Les Andelys to advise on the reconstruction of the nave and north tower. The latter was completed in 1536, the nave five years later.

In 1537 Jean Grappin, son of Robert, took over and began the central west façade in early Renaissance style.

In 1551 he was replaced by Pierre de Monteroult who built the south tower. In 1591 work was abandoned owing to faulty sub-soil.

All this can be detected in the fabric itself. The west front dates from left to right. It shows the transition from the Flamboyant, in the north tower, by way of the early Renaissance, in the exuberant decoration of the central façade, to the more severely classical conception of the south tower. One may assume, since the lowest order is Doric and the one above it Ionic, that the third was to have been correctly Corinthian.

The south front is Flamboyant, with the most impressive gargoyles. The stone, from the quarries at Vernonnet which supplied the Sainte Chapelle, is so pock-marked by the weather as to produce naturally the effect obtained artificially by 'rustication'.

The north front also is riotously Flamboyant, with stags' heads added to the tracery and the most delicate fretwork in the decoration of the flying buttresses. The sculptors have been busy everywhere so that the rare interstices of plain stone come almost as a relief.

Entering by the south porch, the visitor is immediately confronted by a forest of pillars – there are forty-two free standing – some twisted, some fluted, some faceted, some plain and some as elaborately carved as an Egyptian obelisk. The first pillar in the south aisle is hexagonal in section and adorned with bas reliefs representing the various labours of the Tannery, presided over by the figure of St Claude. The carving is the work of Nicolas Coulle and was paid for in 1526 by the Corporation of Tanners.

Not only do the pillars of the nave exhibit a great diversity in their form and in their decoration, but the ceiling which they uphold contains almost every possible variety of vaulting. The arrangement appears to be deliberate. The main vault is lierne and tierceron throughout; the inner aisles are plain quadripartite throughout; it is only in the outer aisles and the ceilings of the chapels that the proliferation begins. Here it seems that the builders have given free range to their fantasy.

It is quite a surprise to find embedded in this bizarre construction a choir of simple thirteenth-century Gothic. As was often the custom in the Ile de France, the east end was rectangular, but it was opened in the late fifteenth century by a spacious archway to reveal the newly constructed chapels behind it.

In the last war the whole church was nearly destroyed, for in June 1940 it burned for three days. The sixteenth-century organ, the roofs and the belfry were burnt out and the bells were found on the ground cracked and half melted. As the result of the subsequent restoration of the nave and aisles, the clean, bright steel of the new organ pipes accords with the clean, bright stonework.

Six of the stained-glass windows had been removed to safety and have since been replaced. They are all that remain of a magnificent ensemble. They have the rich colouring and the effective use of brown and gold typical of the École de Beauvais. The one in the chapel near the Tanners' pillar – also devoted to St Claude – can be dated to 1526 and attributed to the glazier Engrand Leprince.

Trie-Château, east of Gisors, was another centre of defence against the Normans, but the château itself, rebuilt in the seventeenth century by the Bourbon-Conti family, has preserved only one tower from the original eleventh-century building. It was here that Rousseau, granted protection by Conti, was able to finish his *Confessions*.

The house is not open to the public. If the château has little to tell us about the defence of this part of Vexin, the **Hôtel de Ville** is a reminder that, in times of peace, progress in civic administration was already being made. Built in 1160, this is the oldest Town Hall in the Ile de France.

Another manifestation of the arts of peace is in the elaborate decoration of the Romanesque **Church of Ste Marie-Madeleine.** Basically it is a twelfth-century nave with a thirteenth-century choir with a flat east end. But it is the portal which is the most impressive feature of Ste Marie-Madeleine. Fortunately or unfortunately it was restored by Viollet-le-Duc during the nineteenth century: fortunately, in that there was thereby preserved some superb twelfth-century carving; *un*fortunately in that we cannot be quite sure how true to the original it was kept.

Higher up the valley of the Troesne, at **Chaumont-en-Vexin**, the church of St Jean-Baptiste rises beautifully against the richly wooded hillside. It was built in the early sixteenth century in a late Flamboyant Gothic with the beginnings of Renaissance ornament. From the town it is approached up a flight of steps towards which it presents a noble apse with exceptionally tall windows set between buttresses and ringed round at the top by an elegant, open-work balustrade.

The west front, which may be approached down another steep flight of steps, is clearly unfinished. There are remains of an interesting Renaissance doorway under a sort of penthouse roof. The main entrance, however, is by way of the north transept where there is a truly magnificent Flamboyant porch. The statues with their plinths and canopies which fill the deep groove of the archivolt are of exquisitely fine carving. They frame a tall tympanum, more or less the shape of a mitre, which is decorated with Renaissance motifs, again of an astonishing delicacy of execution.

The interior creates that satisfying impression of unity and purity that comes when a building results from one single campaign of construction. We are seeing what the architect himself conceived and realized.

It has all the virtues of its style: a wide-openness which derives from the broad arches and narrow columns, and an almost austere economy of detail. Prodigal in their ornamentation of the façades, the architects of the Flamboyant era often confined themselves to an extreme simplicity within. The little sculptured chaplets which do duty for capitals and a few well-disposed niches and statues are the only purely decorative features. The columns have been pared down to a minimum; the shallow embrasures of the windows suggest that the walls are no thicker than they need to be; as so often at this time the triforium is omitted.

A happy result of this open-work architecture is that it provides an admirable show case for the beautiful stained glass, of which there is a nearly complete array. The windows are for the most part Renaissance in their upper lights with nineteenth-century replacements in the lower parts, but these harmonize well in colour if not in style and from the body of the church this restoration is not apparent.

Some fifteen kilometres south-west of Chaumont is **Monjavoult**, which occupies the highest ground in the area and commands a panoramic view over most of Vexin. It is claimed that on a clear day the Eiffel Tower can be seen from the belfry of the church.

The **Church of St Martin** dates from the late fifteenth century and the mid-sixteenth. Its most important feature is the portal, built about 1560 and often attributed to Jean Grappin of Gisors. The deeply recessed archway is an interesting treatment of the old Gothic theme and far more clear and clean-cut than that at Gisors. It is beautifully framed between two tall Corinthian columns.

North-west of Montjavoult is **Boury-en-Vexin**. The château, built by Guillaume Aubourg, marquis de Boury in 1688, was one of the few provincial houses built by Jules-Hardouin Mansart, the architect of Versailles. As might be expected, the façades have a lofty elegance which is only slightly impaired by the loss of the original glazing bars in the windows of the centre section. But the total effect is somewhat marred by the disproportionately tall mansard roof pierced by rather ignominious little dormers.

After belonging to the La Ferronays in the nineteenth century, Boury came back into the possession of the Aubourg family, who still own it today.

At **Parnes** there is a Romanesque church with nave and aisles which were rebuilt in the fifteenth century. There is a lovely Flamboyant porch with a typical tall tympanum framed in an elaborate series of archivolts not unlike that of Chaumont-en-Vexin. Like Chaumont it was designed to receive a Renaissance decoration in the tympanum which appears to be unfinished. To right and left of the double doors are figures of St James and St John which show clear signs of their original polychroming.

The interior is not at first remarkable. As was common in the fifteenth century the nave and aisles are of the same height, an arrangement which provides ample illumination to the nave by means of the large side windows. But the first object to attract the attention is the magnificent baldachino over the font – a ring of eight columns supporting an entablature and corona, surmounted by a ball and cross. The old box pews, with their slender balustrading, are interesting also. Those in the choir aisles are at least older than 1756, when Charles Lesueur carved his name on one of them.

The floor is also remarkable for the preservation of the original tiles. It is seen at its original level in the apse, but it was relaid just over one metre higher in the rest of the church.

South of Parnes is the **Château d'Ambleville**, obligingly situated at the side of the road, its façade being a continuation of that of the parish church. It has been recently and accurately restored by the marquis de Villefranche who has, among other things, replaced the tall pointed *poivrières* with the Renaissance cupolas which originally surmounted the turrets.

303

Villarceaux, to the south, offers the somewhat rare attraction of two châteaux within the same lay-out. There is the old **manoir** of the fifteenth and sixteenth century in which château and farm buildings formed a single ensemble. The sixteenth century was the golden age of the *Gentilhomme Campagnard*, when the lord lived close to his land and his house was built, as Charles Estienne advised, 'where we are more to regard profit, joined by a mean and moderate beauty, than any unnecessary sumptuousness'.

The manoir de Villarceaux was just such a house. It was part and parcel of the countryside, its brown roofs and plaster walls conferring upon it a sort of physical beauty which is more easily identified than described. But the new **château**, built in 1755, is the exact opposite. The comte de Ganay describes it as having '*l'apparence d'une belle maison de ville, hôtel particulier d'allure seigneuriale*'. The château of the classical age seldom has the appearance of belonging to the countryside, from which, on the contrary, it had to be insulated by acres of formal garden. In this case it is also a building of great beauty, but it is a beauty which springs from Art, not chance.

The old manor has obviously suffered modification in the course of time. There are abundant signs in its masonry of a former and apparently more interesting architecture. What have survived largely intact are the gardens – known as '*le jardin François I*' and certainly Italian in inspiration. But time has done for the gardens what the age of the Renaissance could never have done; the atmosphere of trim formality has been replaced by one of rather shabby grandeur; 'laughing Ceres' has to some extent re-assumed the land and it has the peace of a forgotten backwater.

The place belonged, in the seventeenth century, to one of the Don Juans of the epoch, Louis de Mornay, marquis de Villarceaux, who held the office of *Grand Louvetier* – Master of the Wolf Hounds – to the King. It must be remembered that as late as 1595 wolves were recorded in the streets of Paris. Louis de Mornay was a fine figure of a man – '*des plus magnifiques*' according to Mme de Maintenon. Mornay said of her: 'I would sooner make an indecent proposal to the Queen than to that woman'. He had, however, a painting done of her in the nude which had to be delicately extracted from his possession when she became the wife of Louis XIV.

The most famous of Louis de Mornay's amours was with the celebrated beauty and wit Ninon de Lenclos, whom he kept here at Villarceaux in the pretty little painted parlours of the tower which stands out from the façade, originally to protect it but incidentally obtaining the most panoramic view of the water garden. 'St Evre-

The Monks' Refectory, Abbaye de Royaumont

Château de Chantilly:
interior of the
stables

The entrance court,
Château de Raray

monde wants to send some Knight Errants to carry you off from your old castle,' wrote Mme de Maintenon; 'come back my pretty Ninon and bring Grace and Pleasure along with you.'

In 1737 Villarceaux passed to Charles du Tillet, marquis de la Bussière, and in 1755 he built the new château, from the designs of Jean Courtonne – architect also of the Hôtel de Matignon. The new château was built on an eminence which commands a series of terraces down to the lake which forms the common factor between these gardens and those of the old manoir.

The new château is a pure and perfect example of the *style Louis XV* – simplicity which is saved from monotony by a minute attention to detail. The windows of the ground floor are slightly arched; those of the floor above rectangular. The windows of the central pavilion are accentuated by delicately carved keystones; the others are plain. Wrought-iron balconies of the lightest fancy add a touch of ornament to an almost unadorned façade.

It is worth following the road round the park to see the entrance front as well, set back behind a deep forecourt with a very beautiful little chapel and Pavillon de Garde, framed by high clipped hedges through which a number of alleys are pierced.

Inside, Villarceaux was one of the most perfectly preserved period pieces. Until the recent sale, most of the furniture could be identified in the inventory of 1797. The beautiful transparent colours of *vernis Martin* still glowed from the panelling, and the profusion of bibelots and objets d'art recalled in detail the age of elegance associated with Madame de Pompadour.

In spite of their taste for exquisite living, the Tillet family were good landlords and were left unmolested by the Revolution. Their house is unfortunately not now open to the public.

The Epte Valley and Lower Seine

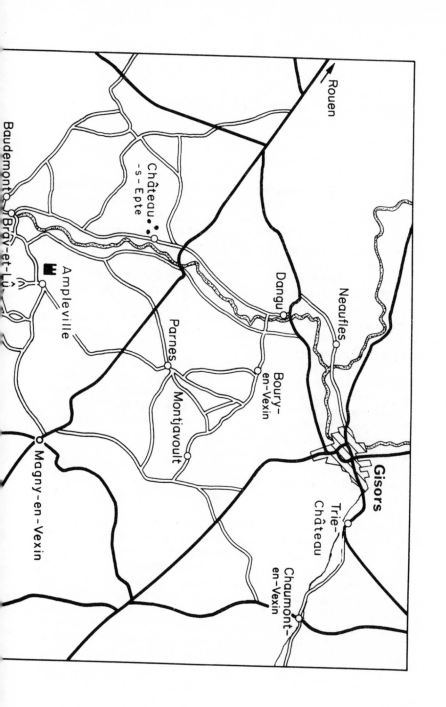

Rouen

Baudemont

Bray-et-Lû

Château-s-Epte

Ampleville

Dangu

Neaufles

Parnes

Montjavoult

Boury-en-Vexin

Magny-en-Vexin

Gisors

Trie-Château

Chaumont-en-Vexin

CHAPTER TWENTY-EIGHT

The Lower Seine

To lovers of the Impressionist School, the church of **Vétheuil** is well known from the paintings of Monet, who lived here for several years and made it the subject of many of his pictures. Perched high above its village and overlooking one of the wide meanders of the river Seine, it fits beautifully into the landscape, its long brown roof harmonizing with those of the houses grouped beneath it. There is structural evidence that its tower once carried a stone spire which would have eliminated its one discordant feature – the slate pavilion roof with which it is at present crowned. From the outside the tower marks the division between two completely different styles – the choir and apse of the late twelfth century and the nave and aisles of the early sixteenth century.

The apse is one of the most original and striking in the whole of the Ile de France. The great buttresses, stepped out five times as they descend from the cornice to the ground, have lost all perpendicularity and lean heavily against the wall they were built to support. In the spaces between them are lancet windows, each surmounted by a deep-set oculus. This deep recessment conveys an immediate sense of the strength and thickness of the apse wall.

The east end sets a high standard which has been admirably matched in the west end by an architect of the Renaissance – possibly Jean Grappin to whom we owe the central portion of the west front at Gisors.

He has focused his whole attention upon the nave façade leaving the two wings blank; only the elaborate, open-work parapet links these blind walls with the rich decoration of the central façade. The balance of this has been upset by the removal of the statues, which a drawing by Israel Sylvestre shows adorning all the niches. The meaningless lacuna beneath each of the richly carved canopies destroy the unity of the design. We may obtain some idea of the missing statues – which represented the Virtues – by the figure of Charity, placed between the twin doors, and by that of Prudence, placed against the westernmost pillar of the north arcade of the nave. She is holding a sphere which enabled her, by the study of the stars, to predict the future – thus exemplifying the original meaning of prudence or providence – the ability to foresee.

The interior, which may be visited only after previous application to the curé, is somewhat disappointing. The nave is unexpectedly narrow and derives its character mostly from the statues which adorn the pillars of the arcade. But the choir is a building of great beauty. The magnificent 'spider vault' of the apse articulates with its broad, flat ribs, the seven bays which contain the lancet windows, and their 'portholes'. Some modern glass, pleasing and appropriate, adds a necessary complement of colours to the scene.

The south front is essentially Flamboyant. It has the same parapet as the west front, above which peep three gables which mark the side chapels of the aisle. In the centre is another fine Renaissance porch which is recessed into the façade and in fact takes the place of one of the chapels. The doors, similar to those of the west front, have some lively carvings.

Between Vétheuil and La Roche-Guyon is **Haute-Isle**, one of the oldest inhabited areas in the region, for it certainly dates from the Merovingian epoch. Until the eighteenth century there were no houses here above ground; they were all hollowed out of the cliff like the troglodyte dwellings of Touraine.

The **Church of the Annunciation** was no exception to this rule. It was built – if built is the word – by Boileau's nephew Dongois in 1670. It is entirely a work of excavation, even the pulpit being carved out of the chalky rock. From here it is no distance at all to **La Roche-Guyon**.

It is a little unexpected to find a ducal residence in so restricted a site, with no park, no parterres and practically no gardens. The **Château** of la Roche-Guyon is closely confined between the river Seine and the high chalk cliffs which border its valley. The reason for accepting this limitation was doubtless the clinging to feudal precedent so dear to the French aristocracy.

At the end of the twelfth century a round keep was built here high up on the cliffs, with two concentric curtain walls to guard it. It communicated by means of a passage cut into the chalk with a rather more residential building at the foot of the slope.

In 1474 this castle passed by marriage from the family of Guy de la Roche to that of Silly. In 1621 the estate was raised to a dukedom in favour of François de Silly, who thus became first duc de la Roche-Guyon. From him it passed to the family of la Rochefoucauld, and it was here that that arch-cynic of the seventeenth century, the duc de la Rochefoucauld, wrote some of his famous *Maximes*.

The building today has a certain magnificence without possessing any architectural coherence. Begun in the thirteenth century, from which it preserves a battlemented tower or two, it has been added to and altered throughout the centuries, but chiefly during the Renaissance and the eighteenth century. The Duke Alexander was exiled from Versailles by Louis XV and took up permanent residence here, building on the two requisites for noble living – a capacious library and extensive stables. These latter are the buildings nearest the road and on the left as one looks at the main façade.

In 1819 the château passed to Louis-François-Auguste de Chabot, duc de Rohan. A devoted churchman, he became one of the few dukes to take Holy Orders. L'Abbé duc de Rohan, however, was fairly soon preferred and became Archbishop of Besançon. He died in 1833 at the age of forty-five of an infection caught when ministering to the sick.

During his fourteen years as châtelain of La Roche-Guyon he formed a deep attachment to Lamartine, who was frequently his guest, and it was here that a specially selected retreat was arranged which bore fruit in the poem 'La Semaine Sainte à la Roche-Guyon'. Maurice Levaillant has described in his biography this week of Christian fervour in the church and of exalted friendship in the château.

In March 1944, Rommel established his headquarters here. He is remembered for his modesty and for being a very bad shot. Admiral Ruge tells how, whenever Hitler telephoned him, he passed the second receiver to his Chief of Staff in order to have a witness. It was the time of the heavy bombardments on Meulan and Mantes and the château received several hits. On 17 July, as he was returning to La Roche-Guyon, his car was machine-gunned from the air and his driver killed. As the result of his own injuries he was taken to hospital at Bernay. It was this circumstance which enabled Hitler to have him arrested for complicity in the Generals' Conspiracy.

From La Roche-Guyon there is a pretty route along the south side of the Seine, giving an attractive view of Vétheuil again, leading on to the high ground known as **la Corniche de Rolleboise**. A little further upstream is the **Château de Rosny**. This was the paternal home of Maximilen de Béthune, better known as duc de Sully, the great Minister of Henri IV.

In 1595 the old château was totally demolished and a new building begun. Fifteen years later, when Henri IV was assassinated, the work was still in progress. The two wings which broke forward from the entrance front to frame the forecourt had not been completed and Sully 'wished to show proof of his grief at the death of the King, his benefactor, in leaving the wings unfinished, as they were at the moment of that sad event'.

It was not until 1826 that they were made habitable by the duchesse de Berry. The job was done so badly that fourteen years later they had to be pulled down by the new owner, the comte de Marois. He built instead a single-storey projection across the entrance front, which may have increased the comfort of his abode but certainly constitutes a blemish to the architecture of the forecourt. It is therefore only the garden front which remains as Sully built it.

Inside, Rosny contains but one room which dates from the time of the great Minister – his own bedroom with one of the best examples of the painted beam ceiling typical of the epoch.

The house is chiefly famous for its tapestries, of which one set – *les Aventures de Psyché* – at least was ordered for a daughter of Sully. The best known are *les Chasses de Louis XV* after cartoons by Oudry.

For most of the eighteenth century the château belonged to the Senozan family, from whom it passed to that of Talleyrand-Périgord. It was probably under the latter that the Salon which overlooks the Seine received the five overdoors by Hubert Robert. The room is very much as the duchesse de Berry knew it.

Caroline of Naples, duchesse de Berry, was the wife of the younger son of Charles X; but since the elder son, the duc d'Angoulême, was childless, the duc de Berry was heir apparent. In 1820, two years after his marriage, he was assassinated in the Opera House, leaving Caroline a widow, but pregnant. She duly produced a son – *'l'enfant du miracle'* – who was first known as duc de Bordeaux and later as comte de Chambord. In 1871 he might have become King of France as Henri V, but he insisted that he would only accept the throne if he was allowed to reinstate the white flag of the Bourbons. The condition was refused and he returned to exile. When he died in 1883 the direct line of the Bourbons became extinct.

Caroline withdrew to Rosny. In order to keep her widowhood unblemished, Charles X forbade her any male society. His misgivings were not unfounded, for not long after his own departure into exile she bore a child to the Count Luchessi Palli, to the great scandal of pious royalists. She had already caused twitterings in the Court by bringing in the fashion for short skirts – that is to say skirts which ended five centimetres above the ground – and for her habit of bathing at Dieppe attended by her fully dressed *Grand Chambellan*.

Her taste for bathing is enshrined in another delightful building in the park, the **Pavillon des Bains**. It is a charming mid-eighteenth-century building, exquisite in its simplicity, which bears a strong resemblance to the Pavillon du Butard, built by Gabriel at Vaucresson, near Versailles, as a hunting lodge for Louis XV. Cleanliness is said to lie next to godliness, and under the comte de Marois this pavilion was converted into a chapel.

Mantes-la-Jolie, a name which was once justified by the frequent inspiration which it afforded to Corot, is a town which suffered badly during the last war. It has been rebuilt well, the design making good use of the amphitheatre shape of the Old Town, and it is fortunate in preserving intact its magnificent church.

Notre Dame de Mantes owes its magnificence, in part at least, to the remorse of William the Conqueror. In 1087 he claimed the whole of Vexin Français from Philippe I, who not unnaturally refused, qualifying his refusal with an uncomplimentary reference to William's belly, famous for its dimensions. William retaliated by laying waste the town of Mantes, including its church. It was when riding round its smoking ruins that he was thrown from his horse and received the injury from which he died, but not before he had made up for his act of desecration by bequeathing a large sum for the reconstruction of the church of Notre Dame. It was, however, many years before his money was thus spent; Mantes is a Gothic building contemporary with Notre Dame de Paris.

The oldest part of the church is the east end which was started in 1170. One is immediately struck by the extreme simplicity of the original style; the broad pointed arches of the clerestory windows and the large roundels which give light to the tribunes are barely decorated with a single row of dog-tooth moulding. Beneath them, the little apsidal chapels, in Geometric or Decorated style, form a happy contrast to the rude simplicity overhead.

The apsidal chapels are part of a second campaign of building which lasted from 1285 to 1325. The effects of this are even more evident on the west front. Here the balance of the triple portal has been completely upset by the emphasis placed on the doorway in the south tower, which was, in the year 1300, framed and encased in a Flamboyant screen, which covered the buttresses with blind tracery and raised a high, open-work gable over the point of the arch. The whole is clearly inspired by the Portail de la Calende at the Cathedral of Rouen, and one can only suppose that it was intended to treat the whole of the south front in the same style. This, however, was never accomplished.

The rest of the portal is in a sadly mutilated condition, most of the statues having been decapitated. The carvings are in a somewhat stiff style, their lines not following the parabola of the archivolts.

The upper storeys of the west front owe their present appearance to a major work of restoration undertaken in 1844 by the architect Alphonse Durand. It was he who gave the towers their perfect symmetry and extended the open gallery, originally confined to the south tower, so as to embrace the whole façade.

On the south front, next to the tower, can be seen one of the original circular windows to the tribune which formed, as at Notre Dame de Paris, the original design.

But it is the interior of Notre Dame de Mantes which is the most impressive aspect. The first impact comes from the great height of the vaulting – thirty metres to the keystone – a height which is emphasized by the uninterrupted vertical lines of the colonettes which support the transverse ribs. The slight elevation of the arches communicates a particularly graceful line to the vaulting.

Another attractive feature is the tribune which forms a large open gallery with a triple arcade to each bay upheld by remarkably slender columns and underlined by an open-work balustrade.

There is one rather peculiar effect in the apse, where each of the five openings of the tribune forms a separate chamber with a barrel vault and a round window at the end. The sides of these chambers are seen in different perspectives according to one's standpoint in the nave or choir, so that often only one of the windows can be seen in its entirety.

Notre Dame was built at a time when architecture and stained glass were regarded as equal partners and although very little of the original glass survives – the western rose window is not the most distinguished product of its era – the modern age has come to the rescue. It must be admitted that the new glass by Gruber makes most of the older work look simply ugly by comparison. His set of lights in the apsidal chapels is one of the most distinguished achievements in the whole church. That of the Lady Chapel is outstandingly beautiful in its subtle mixture of bright and dull colours.

In the south choir aisle is the Chapelle de Navarre, so called because the kings of Navarre were counts of Mantes. It is a lovely piece of mid-fourteenth-century architecture with elegant Geometric windows, many of which have been further enhanced by Gruber's glass. The chapel is divided into two aisles of very unequal width so

313

that the vaulting forms a somewhat irregular canopy overhead. It used to be separated from the church by a stone screen which was destroyed in the Revolution. There survive from it four statuettes of ladies who were either princesses of Navarre who became queens of France or princesses of France who became queens of Navarre.

Just uphill of the church, on the south side, are some fine buildings of the seventeenth and eighteenth centuries incorporating the **Hôtel Dieu**, with an impressive figure of God the Father, arms open wide to receive the sick and the suffering, set in a fine façade with a Corinthian order. The crown and the interlaced L's remind us that Mantes was a royal town and that the church was set within the precincts of a royal château. The château had its last moment of glory when Henri IV used it – appropriately, for he was King of Navarre. He used to say 'Mantes was once my Paris, this Château my Louvre and this garden my Tuileries'.

The upper part of the town is dominated by the ruined tower of **St Maclou,** a Renaissance church demolished during the Revolution. Notice the little canopies, like classical pagodas, over the niches. From the tower we can follow the rue d'Alsace through into the rue de Gassicourt, at the end of which is the **Church of Ste Anne de Gassicourt.**

Considering that the church was badly damaged by the bombardment of 1940 it has managed, thanks to sensitive restoration, to remain a remarkably interesting and attractive building, and it has some of the most beautiful thirteenth-century glass in the whole of France.

It is essentially a Romanesque structure with thirteenth-century continuations in the choir and transepts. The façades have great strength and simplicity, which sets off admirably the elaborate carving of the west door and the cornice of the tower. The main motif is a continuous arcade supported at the spring of every arch by a head, human or animal.

The interior is most impressive, the effect being obtained from the contrast between the very rough stonework of the walls and the clean-cut masonry of the capitals in the nave and the colonettes which support the ribbed vaulting in the sanctuary and transepts. There is a further contrast offered between the austerity of the nave and the richer treatment of the east end, culminating in the brilliantly coloured windows already mentioned. Those to the north of the sanctuary seem to have been placed inside out, for the writing is back to front.

Of the antique furniture of the church there survive the fifteenth-century choir stalls with an interesting set of misericords, the six-teenth-century choir screen and one or two carved wooden figures: a majestic thirteenth-century Virgin and two little groups from the former retable, the Descent from the Cross and Joseph of Arimathea.

Gassicourt was badly bombed in 1944, but the church has been excellently restored and imaginatively refurnished and lit. If all the churches in the area were as well maintained and cared for a tour of the Ile de France would be an even more enjoyable experience.

Appendix:
Opening Times of Museums, Châteaux, etc.

ANET
château:
1 Mar–31 Oct: Wed, Thurs, Sun & hols, 10–11.30, 14.30–18.30; rest of year: Sun & hols, 10–11.30, 14–17
chapel of Diane de Poitiers
closed Tuesdays; 1 Mar–31 Oct: 9.30–11.30, 14.30–18.30; rest of year: 9–11.30, 14–17

BLANDY-LES-TOURS
château:
9–11.30, 14–18

BRETEUIL
château:
Sun & hols: 11–12.30, 14–18.30 (17.30 in winter); other days: 14–18 (17 in winter)

CHAÂLIS
former abbey:
1st Sun in Mar–All Saints: Sun, Mon, Wed, Sat & hols: 14–17.30
gardens:
May–Nov: open every day except Tues

CHAMPLIEU
Roman ruins:
1 Apr–30 Oct: 10–12, 14–18; rest of year: 14–16

CHAMPS
château:
closed Tues and when owners are in residence; other days: 10–12, 13.30–18 in summer (earlier in winter)
park:
closed Tues; other days: 9.30–20 in summer (earlier in winter)

CHANTILLY
museum and park:
1 Mar–14 Nov: closed Tues; other days: 10.30–17.30; rest of year: Sat, Sun & hols: 10.30–17.30
stables:
Easter Sun–1 Nov: Sat, Sun & hols except racing days: 14–18

CHARTRES
cathedral towers:
Apr–Sep: 9.30–12, 14–18; Oct–Mar: 10–12, 14–17
crypt:
tours at 10.30, 11.30, 14.30, 15.30, 16.30 (in summer also 17.30)
museum:
closed Tues; other days: 10–12, 14–18 (17 in winter)

CHEVREUSE
Château de la Madeleine:
1 Mar–31 Oct: Sun, hols: 10–12, 14–18; Mon, Wed, Sat: 14–18

COMPIÈGNE
Armistice clearing – Marshal Foch's carriage:
1 Mar–11 Nov: 8–12, 13.30–18.30; rest of year: closed Tues; other days: 9–12, 14–17.30
Musée de la Figurine historique:
9–12, 14–18
Musée Vivenel:
closed Tues and main hols; 9–12, 14–18
Palace and Musée de la Voiture:
closed Tues; other days: 9.45–12, 13.30–17.30 (16.30 in winter)
park:
dawn to dusk

COURANCES
park only:
1st Sun in Apr–2 Nov: Sat, Sun & hols: 14–18

CRÉPY-EN-VALOIS
Archery museum in Old Château:
15 Mar–15 Nov: closed Tues; other days: 10–12, 14–18 (19 on Sun & hols)

DAMPIERRE
château:
1 Apr–15 Oct: closed Tues; other days: tours 14–18

DOURDAN
castle:
Wed, Sat & Sun: 14–18

ERMENONVILLE
park:
9–19 (17 in winter)

ESCLIMONT
park only:
Palm Sun–1 Nov: 14–18

FONTAINEBLEAU
palace:
closed Tues; other days: 10–12, 14–18 (17 in winter)

GROS BOIS
château:
Sat, Sun & hols: tours, 14–17.30; 1 May–31 Aug also Thurs, 14–17.30

GUERMANTES
château:
15 Mar–15 Nov: Sat, Sun & hols: tours 14–17.45

GUIRY
Archaeological Museum:
Sun & hols: 10–12, 14–19 (18 in winter); Sat 14–19 (18 in winter)

JOUARRE
former abbey and crypt:
closed Tues; weekdays 9–11.30, 14–18.30; Sun & hols: 10.30–12; 14–18.30

LONGPONT
abbey ruins:
1 Mar–1 Nov: closed Thurs; tours 10–12, 14–18; rest of year: Sat, Sun & hols

MAINTENON
château:
15 Apr–15 Oct: closed Tues; Sun & hols: 11–12.30, 14–18.30; weekdays 14–18.30; rest of year: Sat, Sun & hols: 14–17.30

MAISONS-LAFITTE
château:
Wed, Sat & Sun: tours 15.30

MALMAISON
château, carriage museum, Pavillon Osiris and Bois-Préau:
closed Tues; Easter–15 Oct: 10–12, 14–17; rest of year: 10.30–12, 14–16.30

LE MARAIS
museum and park:
1 Mar–All Saints: Sun & hols: 14–18

MEAUX
Episcopal Palace:
closed Tues; other days: 14–17

MEUDON
museum:
Sun & hols: 14–18
Musée Rodin:
18 Apr–30 Sep: Sun, 13–18
Musée de l'Air:
weekdays; 9–16.45; Sat, Sun & hol: 10–12, 14–18

MONCEL
former abbey:
closed Aug; Sun & hols: 10–12, 13–18 (16 in winter)

MONTCEAUX
château ruins:
closed Tues; 10–12, 14–17

MONTFORT-L'AMAURY
Ravel Museum:
Mon, Wed & Thurs: 14.30–18; Sat, Sun & hols: 9–11.30, 14.30–18

MONTMORENCY
Rousseau Museum:
1 Apr–31 Oct: closed Tues, 1 May & 14 Jul; 14–18 (17 in Oct)

MORET
keep:
15 Mar–15 Nov: Sat, Sun & hols: 10.30–12, 14–19; Jul & Aug also other days: 14.30–18.30; rest of year: Sun 14–17

ORMESSON
grounds only:
open on application to comte d'Ormesson

PIERREFONDS
château:
closed Tues; 10–11.45, 14–18.30 (16.30 in winter)

PONTOISE
Musée Tavet-Delacour:
closed Tues & main hols; 10–12, 14–18

PORT ROYAL
abbey ruins:
closed Fri morning & Tues; 15 Apr–15 Oct: 10–12, 14–18; rest of year:
Sun & hols: 10–12, 14–17; other days: 14–17
museum:
closed Mon, Tues and all Sundays except holidays; 10–11.30, 14–17.30
(17 in winter)

PROVINS
Porte St Jean, Grange aux Dîmes, Tour de César:
1 Apr–30 Sep: 10–12, 14–17; rest of year: 14–16.30
Hotel Dieu:
Mar–Nov

RAMBOUILLET
château:
closed when President is in residence, and Tues; 10–12, 14–18 (17 in
winter)
Bergerie:
Sun & hols: 14.30–17.30
Laiterie:
closed Tues; 10–12, 14–18 (16 in winter)

RARAY
château (exterior only):
15 Mar–15 Nov: Sun & hols: 13–19

ROSNY
château:
closed Tues; 20 Jul–30 Aug: 14–18

APPENDIX

ROYAUMONT
former abbey:
15 Mar–11 Nov: closed Tues; tours 10–11.30, 14–17.30; rest of year:
Sat, Sun & hols: 10–11.30, 14–17

ST GERMAIN
château and Musée des Antiquités nationales:
closed Tues; 9.45–12, 13.30–17.15
Sainte Chapelle:
apply to custodian
roof:
summer: Sun from 15.00

SCEAUX
Musée de l'Ile de France:
closed Tues; open 14–18

SENLIS
Musée du Haubergier, Musée de la Vénerie and château:
closed Wed morning, Tues, 15 Dec & 1 Jan; 10–12, 14–18 (17 in winter)

SÈVRES
Manufacture de Sèvres:
closed Tues; open 10–17

VAUX-LE-VICOMTE
château and gardens:
1 Mar–31 Oct: Sun & hols: 10–18; other days: 10–12, 14–18; rest of year:
gardens only, 10–17

VERSAILLES
state apartments of the palace:
closed Mon; 10–17.30 (17 in winter)
museum: room 144, 1792 room and Galerie des Batailles:
closed Mon; 10–17
museum: other rooms
closed Mon; open in rotation 14–17
Grand Trianon, Petit Trianon and Musée des Voitures:
closed Mon; 14–17.30 (17 in winter)
gardens and park:
every day from dawn to dusk
Musée Lambinet:
closed hols; Tues, Thurs, Sat & Sun: 14–18

VEZ
château:
15 Sep–15 Jun: Sun: 10–12, 14–18

VIGNY
park only:
15 Mar–15 Nov: Sat, Sun, Mon & hols; also every day in April

VILLARCEAUX
old manor:
Thurs, Sat & Sun: 14–dusk

VILLECONIN
château:
1 Aug–10 Sep: 11–19

VILLERS-COTTERÊTS
château:
8.30–10.30, 14–17
Dumas Museum:
closed Tues & 4th Sun in every month; Sun: 9–12, 14–17; weekdays
14–17

Bibliography

❧

As I have done all my researches for this book in France my bibliography is almost entirely concerned with French books.

GENERAL

Merveilles des Châteaux de l'Ile de France, Réalités Hachette, 1963, looks like a 'coffee table book' but contains, as well as its excellent illustrations, fascinating little articles on the châteaux.

Comte de Ganay, *Châteaux et Manoirs de l'Ile de France*, 1938, is more scholarly, more about the architecture and less anecdotal.

Georges Poisson, *Moyen Age en Ile de France*, 1965. A succinct introduction to the ecclesiastical and military architecture by the foremost living authority on the area.

Georges Pillement, *Les Environs de Paris Inconnus*, 1961. The word 'inconnus' can hardly be applied to a list which includes Chantilly, Vaux-le-Vicomte and Chartres, but his two volumes give the most exhaustive coverage to the area available.

Comte de Cossé Brissac, *Châteaux de France Disparus*, 1947. Short and well-illustrated articles invaluable for one who shares my love of vanished glories.

Dictionnaire des Églises de France, vol. 4, Editions Laffont, 1968. A severely factual and well-illustrated catalogue.

SPECIAL SUBJECTS

Ian Dunlop, *Versailles*, 2nd edition, 1970. My full treatment (in English) of the subject of chapters 2 & 3.

Roger Berthon, *Saint Germain en Laye*, 1966. Full of historical anecdotes.

Jean Villette, *Chartres and its Cathedral*, 1975. A good historical introduction giving a guided tour of the cathedral and town. Well translated from the French.

Emile Mâle, *Notre-Dame de Chartres*, 1948. A concise and beautifully illustrated work by a great scholar.

Felix Herbert, *Le Château de Fontainebleau*, 1937. A difficult book to use with no index and no list of contents, but the only magnum opus on the subject.

Louis Dimier, *Le château de Fontainebleau*, 1930. A history of the Court in its architectural setting.

Marquise de Maillé, *Provins: les monuments religieux*, 1939. A detailed work by the foremost authority on the subject.

Prince Raoul de Broglie, *Chantilly*, 1964. An appreciation of the château and its collections written after ten years as assistant curator.

Index

❧

Donnemarie-en-Montois, 176
Dorbay, François, 28
Doudeauville, duc de, 111
Dourdan, 131
Dreux, Pierre comte de, 118, 120
  Robert comte de, 192
Duban, Félix, 78
Du Barry, comtesse, 21, 64
Dubois, Ambroise, 143
Dubreuil, Toussaint, 143
Duchesne, André, 100
Dumas, Alexandre, 225, 226
Du Prat, Antoine, 208
Durand, Alphonse, 313

Écouen, château, 209, 279
Edmund of Lancaster, 167
Edward VIII, 80
Enghien, duc d', 271
Ermenonville, château, 262ff
Esclimont, château, 110
Este, Hippolyte d', 265
Estouteville, Guillaume d', 289
Estrées, Gabrielle d', 146
Estrées, Raoul d', 234
Étampes, duchesse d', 144
Eugénie, Empress, 59, 138, 152, 153, 245ff

Fabing, Abbé, 194
Feuillet, Octave, 152
Fleury-en-Bière, château, 158
Foch, Marshal, 185
Fontaine, Pierre, 58
Fontainebleau, 134ff
Fontenay-Trésigny, church, 185
Foucauld, Anne de, 233
Foucques, Claude de, 98
Fouquet, Jean, 273
Fouquet, Nicolas, 25, 162, 179, 187
Francini, François, 141
François I, 67ff, 134ff, 225, 255
Fréminet, Martin, 143

Fulbert, Bishop of Chartres, 112, 114

Gabriel, Anges-Jacques, 34, 35, 44, 45, 71, 149, 240
Gadancourt, 293
Gaillon, château, 289, 293
Gallardon, church, 109
Ganay, comte Ernest de, 111, 157, 304
Gassicourt, church, 314, 315
Genlis, Mme de, 284
Gesvres-le-Duc, château, 219
Girardin, marquis de, 262
Girardon, François, 40, 181
Gisors, 298ff
Glaignes, 227
Goujon, Jean, 98, 280
Grappin, Jean, 292, 300, 303, 308
Grappin, Robert, 300
Grisy-Suisnes, church, 194
Gros Bois, château, 190ff
Groslay, church, 283
Grouchy, Sophie de, 295
Guérin, Gilles, 40
Guermantes, château, 198ff
Guiry, 292, 293

Halatte, forest, 255ff
Hamon, Jean, 82
Haute-Isle, 309
Hautils, Hauteurs d', 295
Helen of Mecklenburg-Schwerin, 149
Héloise, 170
Henri II, 68, 95, 137, 139
Henri IV, 139, 141, 146, 183, 253, 310, 314
Henri le Libéral, comte de Champagne, 164, 169, 173, 209
Henry I, 298
Henry II, 299
Henry VIII, 143
Herces, château, 95
Hézècques, comte d', 31, 47

Orléans, Louis duc d' [cont'd]
 duchesse d' (daughter-in-law of
  Louis-Philippe), 150
Orme, Philibert de l', 68, 96, 97, 137,
 139, 140
Ormesson, château, 187
 comte d', 187
Othis, church, 264

Pages at Versailles, 48, 49
Parnes, church, 303
Pascal, Blaise, 75
Patel, Pierre, 26
Penthièvre, duc de, 20, 89, 99
Percier, Charles, 58
Perrault, Charles, 20
Philippe IV (le Bel), 132, 162, 167,
 205, 257
Philippe V, 132
Philippe-Auguste, 131, 253, 299
Pierrefonds, château, 221, 235
Pinaigrier, Robert, 125
Pius VII, Pope, 134, 150
Poisson, Georges, 22, 53, 185
Poisson de Beauvalais, Georges, 196
Poitiers, Diane de, 95ff, 140, 279
Polignac, duchesse de, 36, 100
Pompadour, marquise de, 21, 34,
 44, 147, 197, 284
Pont Sainte-Maxence, 256
Pontchartrain, château, 83ff
Pontoise, 288ff
Pontpoint, church, 257
Port Royal, 75
Praslin, duc de, 181, 182
Primaticcio, Francesco (Le Prim-
 atice), 52, 138, 141, 142, 144,
 145, 158, 215
Prondre, Paulin, 199, 200
Provence, comte de, see Louis
 XVIII
 comtesse de, 51
Provins, 164ff
Pujol, Abel de, 144

Racine, Jean, 27, 66, 75, 81, 82, 107,
 222
Rambouillet, château, 20, 88ff
 marquise de, 88
Rameau, Louis-Jean-Jacques du, 38
Rampillon, church, 175
Raray, château, 258, 259
Ravel, Maurice, 87
Redouté, Henri-Joseph, 57
Regnaudin, Thomas, 40
Renard, Charles, 54
Rhuis, church, 257
Richard, Claude, 45
Richebourg, church, 94
Richelieu, Cardinal, 56
 Maréchal de, 21
Riesner, Jean-Henri, 34, 148
Robert, Hubert, 40
Rohan-Chabot, duc de, 310
Rolleboise, Corniche de, 310
Rommel, Field-Marshal, 310
Rosny, château, 310, 311
Rosso, Gian Battista, 142ff
Rousseau, Antoine, 37
Rousseau, Jacques, 66
Rousseau, Jean-Antoine, 148
Rousseau, Jean-Jacques, 262ff, 281,
 301
Rousseau, Théodore 'Doua nier'
 159
Royaumont, abbey, 275
Rueil, church, 55, 56

St Arnoult-en-Yvelines, 132
St Blaise des Simples, 155
St Cloud, château, 54, 55
St Cyr-sous-Dourdan, 131
St Denis, abbey, 112
Saint Germain, château, 26, 67ff
 château de la Muette, 71
 château du Val, 70
 church, 70
St Jean-au-Bois, 248
St Loup-du-Naud, church, 169, 173